The Writer and His Craft

The WRITER *and his* CRAFT

being the Hopwood Lectures, 1932-1952

ROBERT MORSS LOVETT · MAX EAST-
MAN · ZONA GALE · HENRY HAZLITT ·
CHRISTOPHER MORLEY · WALTER
PRICHARD EATON · CARL VAN
DOREN · HENRY SEIDEL CANBY ·
EDWARD WEEKS · JOHN CROWE
RANSOM · MARY M. COLUM ·
LOUISE BOGAN · STRUTHERS BURT ·
HARLAN HATCHER · ROBERT PENN
WARREN · J. DONALD ADAMS ·
F. O. MATTHIESSEN · NORMAN COUSINS ·
MARK VAN DOREN · HORACE GREGORY ·
Foreword by ROY W. COWDEN

Ann Arbor · The University of Michigan Press

1954

The use of quotations from the following works is gratefully acknowledged:

Complete Poems of Robert Frost. Copyright, 1930, 1949, by Henry Holt and Company, Inc. Copyright, 1936, 1942, 1945, by Robert Frost. Used by permission of the publishers.

Gone with the Wind, by Margaret Mitchell. Copyright, 1936, by The Macmillan Company. Used by permission of the publishers.

The Collected Poems of Thomas Hardy. Copyright, 1925, by The Macmillan Company. Used by permission of the publishers.

"Ash Wednesday" and "Little Gidding," by T. S. Eliot. From *The Complete Poems and Plays* of T. S. Eliot. Copyright, 1930, 1939, 1943, 1950, by T. S. Eliot. Copyright, 1934, 1935, 1936, 1952, by Harcourt, Brace and Company, Inc.

The Collected Poems of Rupert Brooke. Copyright, 1915, by Dodd, Mead and Company, Inc. Reprinted by permission of Dodd, Mead and Company.

"Arms and the Boy," from *Poems,* by Wilfred Owen. New Directions, 1949.

The Grapes of Wrath, by John Steinbeck. Copyright, 1939, by John Steinbeck; published by The Viking Press.

Finnegans Wake, by James Joyce. Copyright, 1939, by The Viking Press.

Ulysses, by James Joyce. Copyright, 1934, by Random House.

"Jasmine's Beautiful Thoughts underneath the Willow," from *Harmonium,* by Wallace Stevens. Copyright, 1923, 1931, by Alfred A. Knopf, Inc.

"Sad Strains of a Gay Waltz," from *Ideas of Order,* by Wallace Stevens. Copyright, 1935, 1936, by Wallace Stevens; published by Alfred A. Knopf, Inc.

Archy and Mehitabel, by Don Marquis. Copyright, 1927, 1930, by Doubleday and Company, Inc.

The Almost Perfect State, by Don Marquis. Copyright, 1927, by Doubleday and Company, Inc.

The Life and Opinions of Walter Richard Sickert, by Robert Emmons. Copyright, 1941, by Faber and Faber, Ltd.

Sketches in Criticism, by Van Wyck Brooks. Copyright, 1932, by E. P. Dutton and Company, Inc.

"In Defense of a Writing Career," by Norman Cousins, appeared as an editorial in the *Saturday Review of Literature,* June 17, 1950.

FOREWORD

THE AVERY HOPWOOD AND JULE HOPWOOD AWARDS FOR THE BEST creative work in the fields of dramatic writing, fiction, poetry, and the essay were established at the University of Michigan under the terms of the will of the dramatist Avery Hopwood (class of 1905). In 1930, when the Hopwood Committee first began to make plans for the annual awarding of these substantial prizes, it was suggested that the presentations be public and, furthermore, that they be celebrated by a talk delivered by some well-known writer. The first twenty of these talks, which have been given every year since 1932, with the one exception of 1936, are brought together here in book form.

The speakers have all been craftsmen who have shown an interest in young writers, and their choice of subjects indicates what they themselves have thought might be useful to the apprentice. In these talks will be found critical opinion as broad and varied as our American culture. Here also is a revelation of the ways of the writer as writers understand them.

ROY W. COWDEN

June, 1952

v

TABLE OF CONTENTS

Literature and Animal Faith

by ROBERT MORSS LOVETT

THE HOPWOOD FOUNDATION IS THE LARGEST AND MOST AMBITIOUS attempt to invigorate and sustain literature from without, through such aid, material and intellectual, as even a mechanized society can offer to its artists. Its establishment was a profession of faith in the importance of literature to the society from which this aid was derived. In associating the foundation with a university, the official guardian of inherited wisdom and of the aesthetic values which have arisen from the experience of mankind, the seat of scientific research and social criticism, the donor implied a belief that literature is not an esoteric and exotic product, an expression of the writer's emotion for his own release or healing, but a public enterprise, a part of the effort of humanity to live adequately, even richly and nobly, by employing all the resources of its environment; an effort which it is the object of the university to promote, and which is symbolized in its name. It is therefore not inappropriate on this occasion, when the fruits of Mr. Hopwood's beneficence are awarded, to devote some minutes to a reconsideration of literature as a contribution to society. This reconsideration has been suggested to me by reading the essays submitted in the contest, many of them sharing a certain distrust of material, a present tendency of literature to shrink away from reality into itself, which it is the purpose of my remarks to deplore. It is the more pertinent to press such an inquiry at the present time when it is beginning to be understood that humanity is in danger, when skepticism prevails concerning the structural strength of western civilization to support its own weight, when defeatism is ringing changes on the decline of the West.

Can art help a sorry world? The arts-and-craftsmen of the late nineteenth century had no doubt of the answer, and in the early twentieth we have had the affirmation of philosophers to whom I shall refer later. If the question be asked today, it is to literature that we turn most expectantly for answer. Of all the fine arts, literature is the most democratic, the least self-conscious, the least removed from popular understanding by an exacting technique, the best fitted to serve toward the appreciation of the other fine arts and as the introduction to them. Our culture is largely literary. Hence the question is asked more urgently of literature than of music or sculpture: Can it in a social sense help to save the world? But another question must be asked preliminary to this: Can such salvation become a source of aesthetic values? For unless this be answered in the affirmative, the literature of salvation will cease to be literature, and will become propaganda in the form of books, magazines, newspapers, moving pictures, or radio eloquence, which apparently it was not the purpose of Mr. Hopwood to subsidize.

Mr. Lewis Mumford remarked in a recent review of Mr. Max Eastman's book, *The Literary Mind,* "Any sensible pronouncement on the function of literature must be based upon a first hand study of the way it acts and works, not upon the way other critics may imagine it acts and works." Taking this pragmatic principle as a starting point, we may begin with the commonplace that of all the fine arts literature is most definitely based upon content. Great periods of literature have depended upon a body of material which invited the imagination of poets and prose men, and with which they could freely and confidently deal. Such material naturally resulted from man's sense of knowing, of conduct, of beauty; it included values drawn from all three, and represented, sometimes naïvely, sometimes with conscious striving, a unity among them. It is necessary only to mention as examples the age of the Greek epic and of Greek tragedy, the Augustan age of Rome, the Middle Ages, the Renaissance, the Age of Enlightenment. The existence of material endowed with a sort of prescriptive authority was clearly a boon to the writer. It determined the original intention whether of Homer or Aeschylus, of Virgil or Dante or Shakespeare.

The less illustrious nineteenth century differs markedly from these periods in possessing no material of authoritative prescription. It is true, it owed to Romanticism the discovery of one great source of original material in nature; but with this exception we find a growing uncertainty as to subject matter—a novel form of self-consciousness in literature. Matthew Arnold expressed it most definitely in the preface to his *Poems* of 1852, concluding that the poet must seek his subject in excellent actions "which most powerfully appeal to the great primary human affections," such material to be found chiefly in the heroic past. Other poets also felt the search for themes a hampering necessity before which inspiration wavered, and which Browning and Whitman alone seem to have escaped entirely. The past offered the common refuge. History was the chief subject of intellectual inquiry for the early Victorian Age, providing themes for works of first magnitude to Carlyle, Macaulay, Grote, and Buckle. Novelists wrote or conceived their masterpieces against the historical background, and the revival of the literary drama was based on historical characters. But equally characteristic of the age was a growing preoccupation with the present as the problems of man's life in society became more pressing and more menacing. The Victorian Age is a long descent from Parnassus. Almost every one of its great figures in literature emerged, under the compulsion of social necessity, from the romantic isolation of an art founded on the past. Carlyle, beginning his career as a critic of literature, became a master of applied history. Tennyson deserted the "Palace of Art" and converted the epic of the Round Table into a social allegory. Mrs. Browning passed through a series of transmigrations to confess at last—

> I do distrust the poet who discerns
> No character or glory in his times
> And trundles back his soul five hundred years
> Past moat and drawbridge, into a castle court.

Matthew Arnold turned from poetry to criticism and from criticism of poetry to criticism of life. Morris exchanged *The Earthly Paradise* for *News from Nowhere*.

It is a commonplace to assert that one reason for the uncertainty of the nineteenth century about the content of literature was the triumphant advance of science. The upholders of traditional culture found themselves, like the defenders of the Roman Empire, threatened by barbarian hordes pressing upon the frontiers. And, as in that historical parallel, they were afflicted by divided counsels. On the one hand they saw the values of authority, of "the best that had been thought and said in the world on matters that most concern us" reduced to mythology and allegory by a new body of factual truth. On the other hand, in recognizing the advent of new and vital knowledge which, according to precedent, should have furnished the inspiration and content of a new art, they were disconcerted by its recalcitrance to absorption in literature. It is rather cruel to recall today the cordial words with which Wordsworth in his Preface to *Lyrical Ballads* welcomed the science which was to destroy his God.

If the labors of men of science [he wrote] should ever create any material revolution, direct or indirect, in our condition, and in the impressions which we habitually receive, the Poet will sleep then no more than at present, but he will be ready to follow the steps of the man of science, not only in those general indirect effects, but he will be at his side, carrying sensation into the midst of the object of the science itself. The remotest discoveries of the Chemist, the Botanist, or Mineralogist, will be as proper objects of the Poet's art as any upon which it can be employed, if the time should ever come when these things shall be familiar to us, and the relations under which they are contemplated by the followers of these respective sciences shall be manifestly and palpably material to us as enjoying and suffering beings. If the time should ever come when what is now called science, thus familiarised to men, shall be ready to put on, as it were, a form of flesh and blood, the Poet will lend his divine spirit to aid the transfiguration, and will welcome the Being thus produced, as a dear and genuine inmate of the household of man.

The reasons for the failure of science and poetry to lie down together are two. In the first place, the "discoveries of the Chemist, the Botanist, or Mineralogist," while they have created a "material revolution in our condition," have never in the sense Wordsworth envisaged—that is, a complete, satisfying, and fruitful reorientation—become "manifestly and palpably material to us as enjoying and suffering beings." On the contrary, the relations under which the discoveries of science are contemplated reveal a cosmos indifferent and even hostile to man in his higher life of sensibility and aspiration. In the second place, these discoveries are tentative, depending on hypothesis, and liable to repudiation. Science refuses to speak with the assurance of revelation; it refuses to give the artist the certainties upon which his imagination has heretofore been able to build. The attitude of the scientist is indeed the opposite to that of the artist, or poet. According to Huxley, "The improver of natural knowledge absolutely refuses to acknowledge authority as such. For him, skepticism is the highest of duties; blind faith, the one unpardonable sin."

While science did not directly supply content to art, however, it provided an intellectual background and suggested a method. Realism or naturalism in art is the concomitant of science in nature. As science undertakes to give a complete account of the universe in terms of mathematical-mechanical relationships, so realism in its confident youth undertook to describe completely the phenomena which fall under our observation. Both scientist and realist, relying on the evidence of the senses, accept the objective world in the spirit of animal faith. Indeed no scientist could make a more robust confession of this faith than Chekhov when he declared that "outside matter there is neither knowledge nor experience, and consequently there is no truth." With Zola we find the novelist boldly taking his place beside the physicist and physiologist, and in his well-known manifesto announcing his graduation from the preparatory school of art into the university of science, indeed claiming the highest rank in that institution: "The novelist . . . gives facts or observes them and, through experiments, shows that their succession will be such as determinism exacts . . . . We continue by our observations and our experiments the work of the physiologist, who continues that of the physicist and chemist."

The sublime and arrogant audacity of that pronouncement testifies to the confidence which for a brief period the example of science gave to literature, and which accounts for the speed and scope of the conquest which realism achieved in Europe at the close of the nineteenth century, approximating the domination of the romantic mood at its beginning.

The collapse of naturalism at the end of the nineteenth century resulted in part from those reasons to which I have ascribed the failure of scientific knowledge to impart substance and vitality to art. More and more it became evident that the cosmos of mathematical-mechanical relationships did not supply a sanction for the things in which alone consciousness has found significance. Hence the decline of literary values—not only those of sin, repentance, renunciation, but also of tragedy and romantic love, the passing of which Mr. Krutch chronicles poignantly in *The Modern Temper*. Science, after stimulating realism to emulation of its methods, revealed a *reductio ad absurdum*: if man is essentially meaningless in any terms with which his mind can deal, a negligible accident in the cosmos, what justification has the realist for conscientiously recording the phenomena of his existence?

In addition to this revelation of an unfathomable crevasse between the essential purposes of art and science, there has been the circumstance that science itself has, as it were, lost its way. Not only is man without meaning, but nature also. An article by Professor P. W. Bridgman a year or two ago included a statement of the so-called bankruptcy of science which contrasts sharply with Zola's optimistic declaration: "The physicist thus finds himself in a world from which the bottom has dropped clean out . . . he must give up his most cherished convictions and faith. The world is not a world of reason, understandable by the intellect of man, but as we penetrate ever deeper the very law of cause and effect, which we had thought to be a formula to which we could force God Himself to subscribe, ceases to have meaning."

This pessimism, based on complete loss of orientation, is first of all an affair between the scientist and his God; but it challenges also the poet, and indeed every thinking inhabitant of the world which science describes. Long before it emerged, however, to convict realism, in addition to all else, of being unscientific, the psychological inadequacy of realism had become evident. Almost spontaneously, symbolism came to supplement and modify the method of the realist. For the human mind, in addition to demanding an inner reality behind the visible, has the quality of endowing realistic detail with extra-realistic significance; so that, automatically, the higher examples of realism took on a symbolical aspect. Ibsen, in his later prose dramas, turned naturally to symbolism; he was succeeded as the all-European dramatist by Maeterlinck, who stated as the third requirement of high poetry "the idea which the poet has of the unknown, in which float the beings and things he evokes, of the mystery which dominates them and judges them and presides at their destinies."

Symbolism is necessarily dependent on the intuition of a single mind; it lacks the authority of knowledge controlled by experience of external facts. Fascinating as guesswork, it is without any check upon the validity of the guess. Moreover, symbolism led to a technique in which substance and meaning suffered further attenuation in the interest of the artist's mood. As realism, in despair before its task of recording all the visible and all the audible, found relief in impressionism, the limitation of approach to a single point of view and concentration upon salient detail, so symbolism found its correlative method in expressionism, which deals with the external world, not directly, but through the state of emotion which it arouses in the consciousness of the artist. Again, the fascination of experimental technique led to increasing concern with the methods of art and emphasized the slogan of the nineties, "Art for art's sake."

Even for writers who continued to deal with the problems of man in his world, the emphasis shifted under the influence of Ibsen and Butler to an individualistic point of view. The novel became iconoclastic in its attack on social institutions, marriage, the family, the church, the state. But the individual himself under intense scrutiny revealed contradictions hitherto unsuspected. Human character was increasingly pictured as a chaos of incongruities, the normal man evolving into a mass of pathological potentialities. Among the literary values more and more subject to depreciation was the self. "Be yourself," was Ibsen's message. "Well," replies Mr. Aldous Huxley, "I try to be sincerely myself, that is to say, I try to be sincerely all the numerous people who live inside my skin and take their turn in being master of my fate."

This development was immensely forwarded by psychological research, emphasizing in human character the place of the unconscious, defined by Lawrence as "that essential unique nature of every individual creature which is by its very nature unanalyzable, indefinable, inconceivable. It cannot be conceived; it can only be experienced in every single instance." The effort of fiction to deal with experience in a detail which eludes classification is indicated by Mr. H. S. Peterson in his account of Mr. Conrad Aiken's novel *Blue Voyage* as "not so much a unitary work of art as a melancholy *cauchemar* of ghosts and voices, a phantasmagoric world of disordered sounds and colors, a world without design or purpose, and perceptible only in terms of the prolix and the fragmentary."

These are, of course, merely instances of a tendency which is obvious. Fiction has become increasingly introvert and disconnected from the flow of general life. The natural sciences in so far as they have conditioned contemporary writing have reënforced this separation. The author, returning to the ivory tower, shares the tendency of his material, which more and more has become autobiographical, developing methods dependent upon private association and eccentric reaction. The result is evident in techniques which impose upon the reader an effort unprecedented in fiction—the work of James Joyce in England and William Faulkner in America are examples of the necessity laid upon the reader to grapple first with the author's medium before coming to grips with his import.

The willingness to be incomprehensible has been even more clearly manifest in poetry than in prose. Mr. Max Eastman in his book, *The Literary Mind,* scathingly likens exponents of what he calls the "cult of unintelligibility" to children soliloquizing in public, in a jargon no one else can understand. M. Lanson less violently observes: "The laws which preside over the relation of words have had as their end, up to now, the intelligible; the new schools have wished that they should have as their end the emotional. To group words not according to logic, to realize a sense perceptible to all, but according to sensation, to manifest an impression perceived for the poet alone, has been the end more or less consciously pursued."

So far as the mere facts are concerned, such criticism is valid. Even discounting the accelerating response of the public to new techniques, which makes the incomprehensible of one generation easily understood by the next, there is no doubt that communication between reader and writer is at low ebb in the writing labeled "modernist." The tendency is but a natural symptom of a psychological state induced by acute consciousness of frustration and bewilderment in a world where man is no longer at home.

This attitude of literature, its repudiation of material which connects the individual with the outside world, its attenuation of meaning, its indifference to communication, above all its preoccupation with itself, is a phenomenon parallel to that skepticism in philosophy which since the Renaissance has not ceased its disintegrating criticism of knowledge. Both are expressions of the same discouragement, rendered acute by disappointment with the results of science, the inadequacy of instruments to conquer the unknown, the lack of any positive relation between man's consciousness and the cosmic process which includes it.

Obviously one reaction to the unknowable is to ignore its existence; one reaction to an unmeaning universe is to mean as little as possible in dealing with it. Much modern poetry has direct affinity with the solipsism of the romantic philosopher cherishing his solitary dream of the world. But in any situation there are three ways of meeting the issue: to evade, to stand pat, or to attack. Already philosophy, schooled by the physical sciences, is preparing to enter the field: it is abandoning infinite assumptions, discarding absolute goals, and extending the experimental method to all human interests. "The function of perception and natural science," says Dr. Santayana in *Scepticism and Animal Faith,* from which I have borrowed my title this afternoon, "is not to flatter the sense of omniscience in an absolute mind, but to dignify animal life by harmonizing it in action and thought with its conditions. . . . What matters is that science should be integrated with art, and that the arts should substitute the dominion of man over circumstances . . . for the dominion of chance."

Such contemporary writers as Mr. Aldous Huxley and Mr. T. S. Eliot can by no means be convicted of failing to integrate science with art, though not to the end indicated by Dr. Santayana. Their integration of the two has only tended to confirm the tendency to helpless withdrawal. Mr. Eastman's reiterated complaint that the modern writer ignores science must be amended: he has heeded scientific data and been overwhelmed by them. Even for purposes of art the defeatism represented by the typical science-conscious writers of today offers resources that must soon be exhausted. In the realm of actual experience their point of view is yet more sterile. What is needed is not further study of scientific fact, but an emulation of the intrepidity with which the scientist meets the crumbling of the foundations on which the structure of his belief has been reared. The pendulum seems to have swung as far as possible toward the inaction of despair; the only direction left would appear to be a return toward something more constructive, whether the pragmatic acceptance urged by Professor John Dewey, or such a mellow stoicism as seems to be foreshadowed in the poetry of Mr. George Dillon. Either course indicates that it will be possible for man to accept the implications of science without renouncing the demands of his own nature for affirmation and action.

This is the consummation toward which Dr. Santayana looks in the passage quoted. The basis upon which it is to be achieved is the quality which he distinguishes from philosophic skepticism by the term "animal faith," which he defines as "the faith I live by day by day." This faith is part of human nature, depending on the fact that "man is an animal in a material and social world." He continues to expound this faith. "In regard to the original articles of the animal creed—that there is a world, that there is a future, that things sought can be found, and things seen can be eaten—no guarantee can possibly be offered. . . . But while life lasts, in one form or another this faith must endure." "All the animals trust their senses and live: philosophy would persuade man alone not to trust them, and if he was consistent, to stop living."

I trust that the application which I have in mind of this doctrine to the arts, and especially literature, will be clear without long exposition. It is, in brief, that there is a definite body of material prescribed to literature today. That material is the experience of man in the world. It is true that human experience has been the subject matter of literature in the past, but usually of minor forms and subsidiary to so-called higher interests. Today this subject matter, properly recognized as knowledge, is invested with a new and compelling importance. If theology and science alike have failed to sustain man in his sense of unique significance in the scheme of things, he has only his own experience as a body of material upon which his consciousness can work to elicit values of living. This pursuit of significance had taken place in the past in a world outside of experience, a world which no longer exists. Within experience itself must in future take place those activities which will give to man's career on earth the enrichment and dignity that justify it to finite ends. "By experience," says Dr. Santayana, "I understand a fund of wisdom gathered by living. . . . I think it mere mockery to use the word experience for what is not learning or gathering knowledge of facts. . . . Experience presupposes intent and intelligence, and it also implies . . . a natural world in which it is possible to learn to live better by practising the arts."

In this falling back of humanity upon animal faith, upon experience and its lessons, it is clear that literature has a function which cannot be fulfilled by abolishing substance, by repudiating meaning and avoiding communication, by dealing with experience at one remove or treating the individual as if he alone experienced in an isolated world. The contemplation of art in its relation to life leads directly to a contemplation of life in the living. If experience is to be the substance of art, then experience itself must be enriched; if experience is trusted to furnish meanings, then primary experience itself must be improved; and if the most imperative extension of experience, in the event that civilization shall be saved, is social integration, then experience must be communicated.

Enrichment of man's experience is a function of the fine arts. There is no doubt that the resources of mankind in this direction are, if not infinite, at least immeasurable. As I have said, our common culture is largely literary. The very obvious growth of appreciation of music, painting, sculpture, indicates that these other arts will share to a far greater extent in the culture of the future than in that of the past. Literature is peculiarly fitted to act as mediator between the other arts and man's apprehension of them, to introduce them more widely into his experience. For literature remains the art most immediate to his rational faculty: man is a thinking animal, and it is part of human nature to demand meaning.

It is not the mission of literature to impose its special form of intellectual imagination on the other fine arts—we have had too much literary painting, sculpture, and music. The literary imagination differs essentially from the pictorial, the sculptural, the musical imagination. To these latter, material is valuable in proportion as it lends itself to translation into the language peculiar to each. While it is certain that literature will constantly gain aesthetic values through its penetration by the other fine arts, examples of which come to mind in recent poetry and fiction, this is far from saying that literature, in subordinating its material to a technique borrowed from another art, can find justification in limiting itself to plastic values, or sound, or color—in seeking to become music or painting.

Enrichment of experience by art may take place in a declining civilization, in a dying world. The colors of autumn are more brilliant than those of spring; there is a fascination in decay. But such enrichment is temporary and individual, for it is in contradiction to one of the most masterful impulses of animal faith, that of survival. Experience for most men can never be satisfying except as it moves toward the realm of further experience, through more harmonious relations with environment. This again is the function of art, the organization of experience toward the improvement of man's lot on earth. Throughout the quotations which I have drawn so copiously from Dr. Santayana, you may have noticed the undercurrent of belief in improvement. He speaks of "the waxing faith of an animal living in a world which he can observe and *sometimes remodel*." Particularly does he speak of living better by practicing the arts, and of using the arts "to substitute the dominion of man over circumstances for the dominion of chance." This is strikingly similar doctrine to that of certain philosophers with whom Dr. Santayana finds himself frequently in disagreement—the Pragmatists. "All art," says Professor Dewey, "is a process of making the world a different place in which to live." "The history of human experience is a history of the development of the arts." And again, "Art is the sole alternative to luck."

Mr. Havelock Ellis is more specific in attributing social force to the aesthetic impulse. Not only is art in his conception "the sum of the active energies of mankind," "the moulding force of every culture that man has produced"—more than this, art sharpens experience by bringing us into contact with "the reality of things behind the veil of convention which is the result of simplification and classification for intellectual purposes." And what is greatly to the purpose of the world today, it trains the aesthetic instinct to counteract the possessive, for the aesthetic instinct gives us "the power of enjoying things without being reduced to the need of possessing them."

In promoting this social function of art, literature again has a primary responsibility. Indeed Ruskin when he began to teach art at Oxford found it his first work to set about the creation of a society in which a worthy art was possible, and his tool was literature. Nor can it be doubted that literature will profit by contribution to the value of life through social integration. If experience is the proper subject of literature, the enrichment and improvement of experience will be of direct benefit to literature, which will move to its own fulfillment as activity by bringing along with itself a release of further activities.

I am not speaking especially of the literature directed primarily to social criticism, though I am far from admitting such direction as a shortcoming and a reproach. In the late nineteenth century that impulse was one of the strongest motives behind the literature characteristic of the period represented by Carlyle and Mill, by Ruskin and Matthew Arnold, by Disraeli, Dickens, Kingsley, and Mrs. Gaskell among the novelists, by Mrs. Browning, Swinburne, and Morris among the poets. It is the notable distinction of the Edwardians, of Mr. Wells, Mr. Galsworthy, Mr. Shaw, to have revived that tradition. I do not feel that literature has in the long run lost literary values by the effort, consciously put forward, to spread a sense of these values and of other values of living more widely among men. I believe on the contrary that it has gained in robustness and energy by the possession of purpose. I think it a hopeful sign for literature and for society on which literature depends that the younger literary people in the United States are becoming a social force.

As the line is drawn more sharply between the writers who have a social point of view and those who aspire to a purity of aesthetic which excludes not only purpose but meaning, I am forced to ask myself whether, in event of the social changes which it is granted on all sides are imminent and necessary, the future historian of literature will not consider the former group of more importance than the latter. I am speaking, however, not specifically of novels of purpose or poems of social protest, but of literature in general, which accepts the reality of the world of human beings and experience and knowledge. To literature in this sense the primary function will be communication. And "communication" as Professor Dewey reminds us, "is an immediate enhancement of life enjoyed for its own sake"; and again, "shared experience is the greatest of human goods."

That communication is fundamental in the enjoyment and improvement of our lot in this world, which we perceive and live in by virtue of our common animal faith, who will deny?

At present for most of us the faculty of communication does not extend even to our fellow men beyond the bounds of our race, our nationality, especially our class. Disraeli, in his famous and terrible arraignment of class division, points out that the two nations over which Queen Victoria ruled, the rich and the poor, are as ignorant of each other's habits, thoughts, and feelings as if they were inhabitants of different planets; that there is no intercourse between them, and hence, no sympathy or understanding. Class separation is the wound in the side of civilization from which the lifeblood of humanity is ebbing. Readers of Tolstoi's *What to Do?* will recall his statement of the difficulty he found in meeting men of another class than his own, how "on looking at our lives, or at the lives of rich people, from without, I saw that all that is considered as the *summum bonum* of these lives consists in being separated as much as possible from the poor, or is in some way or other connected with this desired separation."

That art may be one of the forces which keep classes apart is unhappily true. As Morris declares in one of his lectures: "Until something or other is done to give all men some pleasure for the eyes and rest for the mind in the aspect of their own and their neighbors' houses, until the contrast is less disgraceful between the fields where beasts live and the streets where men live, I suppose that the practice of the arts must be mainly kept in the hands of a few highly cultivated men, who can go often to beautiful places, whose education enables them, in the contemplation of the past glories of the world, to shut out from their view the everyday squalors that the most of men move in."

But that art may be the means of bridging the gap between classes, nations, and even races, is the revelation of the period after the World War. In Russia, Germany, Austria, Great Britain, there is today a proletarian art which shows its potency in the breaking down of class barriers, in bringing people of different backgrounds to speak the same language, to share experience on a common basis. One of the most notable examples of a shared experience and a common understanding among nations is seen in the literature of the war. From every country there comes the same cry of disgust and horror, from Barbusse, Rolland, Latzko, Remarque, Arnold Zweig, Markowitz, Montague, Mary Lee, and many more. The Honorable Frank Kellogg has not outlawed war; it may be that literature has done it. Again, in such progress as we have made toward bringing together two races in this country, it is not the material advance of the colored that has counted most, but their art. I am not prepared to defend Tolstoi's definition of art, with all its rigorous exclusions; but I submit that in the present crisis of humanity his emphasis is right when he says: "Art is not, as the metaphysicians say, the manifestation of some mysterious Idea of beauty, or God; it is not, as the aesthetical physiologists say, a game in which man lets off his excess of stored-up energy; it is not the expression of man's emotions by external signs; it is not the production of pleasing objects; and above all, it is not pleasure; but it is a means of union among men, joining them together in the same feelings, and indispensable for the life and progress toward well-being of individuals and of humanity."

The material of literature is derived from humanity and human experience. It returns, revitalized and reinterpreted, to be received again by human beings and to become once more a part of their experience. In this process the artist is mediator and agent. Surely neither artist nor art can profit by being divorced from the great community which is for both, and in a double sense, the source of life.

Literature in an Age of Science

by MAX EASTMAN

I THINK I WOULD BETTER BEGIN THIS SPEECH BY TELLING YOU THAT I won't keep you waiting long. I know how you feel. There are probably several dozen of you poets counting on these prizes to enable you to pay your bills and get out of town. That was how I managed to leave college. Moreover, one of the prizes that I was particularly counting on, and that I won, and that belonged to me in all right and justice, fell into the hands of some warped and prejudiced and crooked-minded judges, congenitally incapable of delivering a just and honest decision about anything, and instead of giving me the prize, they divided it between me and another man who had no right to it whatever, except that he worked harder than I did, and hadn't run up any bills, and didn't need it, and moreover wouldn't even lend me his half after he got it. That mistake of those judges gave me a bad start in life financially that I've never got over. And so when a majority of you poets go out of here, as you are inevitably bound to do, saying that I have no taste whatever in poetry and am constitutionally blind, deaf, dumb, dishonest, and reactionary, please remember that I agree with you. I think all prize judges are like that. And I realize now that if I had any sense I would never have come up here after judging your poetry, and submitted my own feeble oratory to your withering criticisms. It was, to tell you the truth, an act of weakness. I could not resist the temptation of the peculiar opportunity afforded by this occasion for making a few timely and appropriate remarks about my own books.

My latest book is called *The Literary Mind: Its Place in an Age of Science*. And it starts off by drawing a few teeth out of the ogre that is called up in the minds of a good many people by that word "science." If you have a brain and a certain amount of energy and make a systematic effort to find out what is the cause of any event, or what are the properties of any object, and your effort is successful, why that is science. It does not matter whether you are moved by pure curiosity or by some purposive interest. It does not matter how important or how trivial the problem is in which you are interested. If you sincerely want to know, and go at it persistently and systematically, and with the only means available—observation, study, reasoning, and above all experiment—that is science. Science is merely the mature and disciplined use of the mind and the stores of human knowledge about any problem.

This first chapter about science is very important. Very important that it should stand first. If you carry into my book any of those old-fashioned, credulous, fairy-story views of what science is that were so popular with people who thought they were hardheaded thirty or forty years ago, you will go utterly astray on my argument. That is what a lot of my extremely learned critics have done—they have read only the title of this first chapter, "The March of Science." "Oh, yes, the 'march of science,' " they have said—"he belongs to the period of Spencer, Huxley, Haeckel. He still believes that the world is a machine, that all knowledge is quantitative, and that an absolute determinism prevails throughout nature which makes human choice a delusion. He is doubtless also a Behaviorist." If these extremely learned critics had happened to read my chapter on the march of science they would have found all those opinions listed as credulous metaphysical fabrications which science has left behind on its march. They would have found Behaviorism listed there. These views are not scientific findings but wild jumps at emotional conclusions. And jumping at conclusions—whether you take science for your springboard or whether you take religion or poetry—is not science. It is the opposite thing. Science consists only one half in knowing what is known: the other half is never pretending to know what is not.

Now this attitude of skeptical and disciplined experimental inquiry, born, you might say, about the middle of the sixteenth century, has for four hundred years been steadily advancing into one department of human experience after another. In the sixteenth century, astronomy and geography and physiology; in the seven-

teenth, physics and chemistry, optics and mechanics; in the eighteenth, economics and political science; in the nineteenth, biology and
sociology; in the twentieth, psychology. This is a mere rough suggestion of the general course of development. But you see how this
organized and mature technique for getting reliable knowledge has
very gradually spread over the whole field previously occupied by
emotional guesswork and literary eloquence. And the process is only
just now, in our own days, complete. I do not mean that scientific
knowledge is complete, but only that scientific knowledge exists,
and is distinguishable from amateur opinion in every field. You
may say that with the development of a psychology and sociology of
religion this four-hundred-year triumphant march of science came
to an end. Science has now pitched its camp in every field in which
men have opinions.

I will not try to convince you that this is the most momentous
change that is to be found in the whole history of human culture,
although I think it is. I only ask you to believe that this steady, relentless, step-by-step invasion by verified knowledge of all the fields
heretofore occupied by literary eloquence is the most momentous
thing that has happened or could possibly happen in the history of
literature. The whole literature of our modern epoch ought to be
read and studied primarily, although not of course exclusively, in the
light of its relation to this change. Particularly the literature of these
recent years, when, with the development of psychology and sociology,
science has overthrown the last bulwark and invested the last field
that was still held sacred to the poet and critic—the field which used
to be described as "humane letters" or "the humanities."

In the next section of my book, therefore, I take up one or two
of the outstanding literary schools or tendencies of our day and I
show that in their main outlines they are either defense reactions, or
reactions of retreat before this invasion by verified knowledge of the
fields which used to be occupied by literary eloquence.

The efforts of T. S. Eliot and his very British and very priggish
friends, for instance, to revive a regime of what they call "intellect"
in literary criticism—their attempt to go back, as they say, to seven-
teenth- and eighteenth-century tradition—is a mere maneuver in
the defensive warfare of literary truth against science. It may seem
strange to you that people should be resisting science in the name of

intellect, but that is because you belong to an age which has so completely embraced the viewpoint of science as to have forgotten the meaning of the word "intellect," or come to look upon intellect as a slightly comic affliction. On the lips of Emerson and Matthew Arnold the word "intellect" was consciously opposed to the exercise of the mind in experiment and investigation. It meant literary as opposed to scientific thinking. T. S. Eliot is trying to head off the advancing prestige of science by making literary truth look very cool and rational and unemotional and extremely scholarly and high-brow. He is yearning back to the seventeenth and eighteenth centuries, in which literary intellectuals still had a social prestige higher than men of science.

The New Humanists, on the other hand, are trying to head off the march of science with a moralistic propaganda. At least they were a year or so ago. They seem to have given up the sponge for the time being. It is a notable and surprising fact, at least, that their central fortress and arsenal and mighty organ of propaganda, the *Bookman,* has never yet printed a word of reply to the attack on them contained in my book. Of course these literary battles are not carried out under the Marquis of Queensberry rules, but I have already counted nine issues of the *Bookman* since I landed my blow, and I maintain that if I count ten it is a knockout.

Here, at any rate, is what I said: I said that with all the expert writers writing about it, and the expert teachers teaching it, it remained an insoluble riddle and mystery just what the New Humanism really is. The New Humanists believe in some eighteen different principles or points of view, all held together by the fact that the New Humanists believe them, but not in any other way that anybody has ever been able to discover. I asserted that I had discovered what it was that held these eighteen heterogeneous things together, and that I could prove it. Every single one of them was either a direct defense of literary eloquence as against scientific knowledge, or else a strategic position which enabled them to direct some sort of cross-fire on the advance of scientific method into the field heretofore dominated by literary eloquence.

The humanists pretend, for example, to be very much interested in something which they call the "inner life." In the name of the "inner life" they attack psychology, which is a serious attempt to find out about the inner life. In the name of Socrates, who adopted for his own the motto written over the temple of the Oracle at Delphi, "Know thyself," they attack Sigmund Freud, who—with all his mythological propensities—has perhaps contributed more than any one man since Aristotle to the knowledge of the self. And this "inner life" about which our humanists make such a fuss that you might think they would be ready to abandon father and mother and go sell all they have and give to the poor, and turn their backs on all the advantages of place and position and property in this exterior world, in order to achieve it—this "inner life" turns out to be nothing more illuminating and, for that matter, nothing more "inner" than decorum, or the art of behaving like a gentleman or a lady with a proper amount of money in the bank. Those humanists are not interested in morals, and they are not interested in the inner life—not any more than the rest of us. What they are interested in, like so many of the human beings around them, is their own profession. They are defending the right of literary critics and essay writers to talk loosely and yet be taken seriously in a scientific age. They are defending the profession of humane or polite letters against the inexorable advance of a more scientific study of man.

After discussing these critics and professors of literature who are fighting science in the name of "intellect" and "morals," I take up those poets and creative writers whom we group under the general term "modernist." Their literary character also is fundamentally determined by this advance of scientific knowledge. But instead of a defense reaction, theirs is an attitude of retreat. Instead of opposing the advance of science into the field of literary truth, they have abandoned the field. They have ceased even to pretend to make any serious comment upon life, or give us any important thought, counsel, or direction as to its conduct. They have taken refuge in what I call a "cult of unintelligibility" on the one hand, and in a tendency toward "pure poetry" on the other. Under these two chapter headings, "The Cult of Unintelligibility" and the "Tendency toward Pure Poetry," I have summarized the outstanding features of those modern kinds of writing which are to be found so often upon people's drawing-room tables, but so rarely in anybody's hand when he reads.

If you pick up a book by Wallace Stevens, or E. E. Cummings, or Hart Crane, or James Joyce, or Gertrude Stein, or Edith Sitwell, or T. S. Eliot as a poet, and read a page innocently, the first feeling you will have is that the author isn't telling you anything. It may seem that he isn't telling you anything because he doesn't know anything. Or it may seem that he knows something, but he won't tell. In any case he is uncommunicative. He is unfriendly. He seems to be playing by himself, and offering you, somewhat incidentally, the opportunity to look on.

Here for instance is a book of poems by Wallace Stevens. Let us open it at random and read a poem. I am not really opening this book at random—I have it trained so it will open where I want it to. I have read this poem aloud forty-four times, and no one has ever been able to tell me what it is, or what it has to do with. Let's see if you can do any better.

JASMINE'S BEAUTIFUL THOUGHTS
UNDERNEATH THE WILLOW

My titillations have no foot-notes
And their memorials are the phrases
Of idiosyncratic music.

The love that will not be transported
In an old, frizzled, flambeaued manner,
But muses on its eccentricity,

Is like a vivid apprehension
Of bliss beyond the mutes of plaster,
Or paper souvenirs of rapture,

Of bliss submerged beneath appearance,
In an interior ocean's rocking
Of long, capricious fugues and chorals.

Did you get it? It's a simple poem, you see, and from a distance beautiful, but if you come up close and try to make friends, it won't confide in you. It won't tell you candidly and exactly what it's thinking about. I have read Wallace Stevens' book through, and with the exception of one or two brief moments I do not feel that I have ever been in communication with him.

And that is typical. I think you might say that the dominant tendency of the advanced schools of poetry—and of art in general—for the last twenty years has been to decrease the range, the volume, and the definiteness of communication. I should put that simple statement, which has the advantage of really meaning something, in place of about one half the misty "literarious" talk of the poets and poet-critics of the modern movement. They are not abandoning romanticism, or going back to an eighteenth- or seventeenth-century tradition. If the words "romantic" and "classic" mean anything at all, which is subject to question, then the height of the romantic movement is the idea of these modernist poets that they are classical.

Let me read you something from T. S. Eliot's famous poem *Ash Wednesday*. This is said to be a religious poem, and it was first published in a tiny, thin volume containing only nineteen pages of ten-point Caslon type, and which nevertheless sold for five dollars— a point relevant to my argument that this modern poetry is distinguished by a decrease not only in the volume and definiteness, but also in the range, of communication. Let me give you a small sample of this expensive religion—about sixty-five cents' worth, as I figure it. And do not forget that T. S. Eliot considers himself a neoclassical poet. He thinks that he represents a return to the manners in poetry established by John Dryden, who said "The first object of a writer is to be understood."

> If the lost word is lost, if the spent word is spent
> If the unheard, unspoken
> Word is unspoken, unheard;
> Still is the unspoken word, the Word unheard,
> The Word without a word, the Word within
> The world and for the world;
> And the light shone in darkness and
> Against the Word the unstilled world still whirled
> About the centre of the silent Word.
>   O my people, what have I done unto thee.

Now I don't say that that is weak, unctuous, and invertebrate poetry, a mere oily puddle of emotional noises, although that is what I think about it. I merely say that anything farther away from John Dryden, or what is generally called classical in poetry, or the kind of poetry that prevailed in the later seventeenth and eighteenth centuries, would be impossible to find. And I say that the number of people to whom Eliot is going to communicate this religion at five dollars a shot is very small. These poets are not returning to an eighteenth-century tradition. They are not returning to any tradition at all. They are not going anywhere. They are withdrawing into themselves. They are communicating with fewer readers; they are communicating less; and what they communicate is less definitely determined.

The cult of unintelligibility might be described as a tendency toward privacy in an art condemned by its very nature to employ as materials the means of social communion. However, this cult of unintelligibility is only a part, and probably a transient part, of the modern tendency in general. Indeed, some people tell me it has all but gone out of fashion. It might be described in medical terms as an "exaggerated reaction" to the march of science. "All right, if you won't let us be fountains of truth any longer"—the poets say—"why, we won't communicate at all. We'll have nothing to do with you. To hell with the reader." And so they have climbed way upstairs and are sitting there in the middle of the nursery floor playing with words and ideas all by themselves, with an egotistical pout on their lips. The cult of unintelligibility is a sulk on the part of poetry brought on by the greater attention which is being paid to science in these modern days.

The other aspect of the modern tendency is more serious, more long-lasting, a more adult and inevitable reaction to the march of science. That is the tendency toward pure poetry. By pure poetry I do not mean anything mystical or queer. I merely mean poetry that is free from the motive to persuade, or educate, or give advice, or point a moral, or convey knowledge, or "criticize life," poetry which is solely concerned, as music generally is, to communicate an experience. The most important thing in my book is an essay right in the heart of it entitled "What Poetry Is." In that essay I show that poetry differs from prosaic language in that it dwells upon the qualities of the things it mentions more than is necessary for practical understanding. And pure poetry is poetry that mentions things solely in order to convey qualities, and not in order to interpret them or tell you anything *about* them.

I have explained this in that chapter in a psychological manner. In another I have approached it historically, and I want to repeat my historical outline—to make you realize what poetry is in its own nature by imagining it originating, as it doubtless most often

did, in the incantations of medicine men and magicians. Names are
supposed by all primitive people to have an occult power over the
thing named. They have the power of evoking the being of that
thing and compelling its obedience. But in order to do that they
have to be just the right names. And the medicine man or shaman or
poet-magician would get the idea spread abroad that he knew the
right names of things. He could bring rain, for instance, by standing
out under the sky and saying the right words. That is a very wonderful and exciting way to use words, you see, and yet totally unrelated to science or everyday practical communication. The ordinary
way to use words when the garden gets dry is to say, "Well, don't
you think we'd better find the old sprinkling pot?" And the scientific
way is only a little more elaborate: "Let's build a dam and dig ditches
and irrigate the whole valley." But the sorcerer, the poet, this wonderful and deep-eyed man who is in touch with the heart of reality
through language, gets out there in the middle of the valley, and
spreads out his hands, and says words which do not mean a thing.
And then the rain falls. Or else it doesn't! In any case it ought to.
And among all primitive peoples, all human tribes who have not
yet passed under the affliction of statistics, the opinion is that if the
poet has got the right words, the rain does actually fall.

That was undoubtedly the principal mother lode from which
poetry arose. But that is not what poetry is. In the mind of that won-
derful-tongued magician, naming the raindrops out of the sky, there
was an actual vision of the drops he named. His words did have the
power to evoke the being of things—in his imagination. For him,
moreover, the line between imagination and sense was not too clearly
drawn. He was not entirely a sorcerer, but something also of a child.
And he had an *interest* in raindrops, an absurd and altogether important interest in raindrops, which had nothing whatever to do
with agriculture or the problem of watering the soil. He had a like
interest in the sky. It is not too much to say, in view of what we know
about his successors, that he sometimes loved the sky, in a mournful
way, even when it failed to rain. He loved, whether with joy or
sorrow, the whole business of "being" in this world. And, like all
people who love a thing, he enjoyed calling it pet names. Set free
by his profession from any other very steady occupation, he developed a great habit of sitting around thinking up pet names for

things—the names that would most exactly and vividly evoke them into his imagination. That was how he kept awake when he was not working. And that was pure poetry.

It is to this original and pure form of poetry that the modernists, with all their sophistication and their city things, are tending back. They are abandoning practical meanings, themes, preachments, all that stuff of education and edification that led Wordsworth to describe poetry as "the breath and finer spirit of all knowledge," and Matthew Arnold actually to define it as a "criticism of life." In place of a criticism, these poets offer us in each poem a moment of life, a rare, perfect, beautiful, ugly, grotesque, or intense moment, and nothing more. They offer us awakening—they even offer to keep us awake for the few moments while we are reading their poem— and that seems to them enough. Poetry is a thing like music or the morning, which stands in no need of ulterior justification for those who are sensitive enough to perceive it.

And the reason why they are doing this is that their former function, the function of interpreting things and criticizing life, has been taken away from them by the advance of scientific knowledge. To put it crudely, the reason the poets don't teach us anything is that they have become aware of the fact that *as poets* they don't know anything. The business of knowing things has become a highly specialized technical function in the hands of scientific experts. Where our fathers consulted Browning and Tennyson for actual guidance in the moral and social crises of their lives, we consult the psychoanalyst or the expert in home economics or the theory of business cycles or the class struggle for the seizure of power. That is what is happening. Just as in the seventeenth century Galileo and Isaac Newton and Robert Boyle were driving poetry out of the books which interpret physical and chemical experience and show us how to deal with external nature, so in our day the physiological psychologists, and the Freuds and the Marxian Lenins—to mention only a few—are driving poetry out of the books which interpret mental and social phenomena, and show us how to deal with man.

I think it is very important that this fact should be clearly faced, and that is why I express it in these crude terms. Poets *as poets* don't know anything. Men of letters *as men of letters* are not to be looked to any longer for reliable knowledge in any field. Such statements as this which I am going to read from John Masefield, the poet laureate of England, are the feebly extravagant gestures of a dying belief: "There is another way to truth: by the minute examination of facts. That is the way of the scientist: a hard and noble and thankless way. It is not the way of a great poet, the rare unreasonable, who comes once in ten generations. He apprehends truth by power: the truth which he apprehends cannot be denied save by greater power, and there is no greater power."

And such statements as this from Archibald MacLeish—politically backward enough to be our own poet laureate!—are equally moribund to any man of clear intelligence with the courage to face facts: "The contemporary critic who sees nothing significant in a poem unless it uses the word dynamo, waves a submachine gun and draws its symbols from New York morning papers of even date will eventually die—as the esthetical critics and the moral critics died before him. And his grandchildren will find in 'Anabase,' with its biblical and Asian images, and in 'The Waste Land,' with its Eastern references and its Elizabethan phrase, the understandable answer to questions neither Mr. Keynes nor Major Douglas nor the whole literature of Marxism will be able to resolve."

That is not the way to defend poetry, or assert its future possibilities or independent rights. That is the way to destroy everybody's respect for it. *The Waste Land* does not give an understandable answer to any question, and every man of clear sense knows it, and will know it from now on. There is no use trying to defend poetry with this old, elevated jabber about truth come at by Power with a capital P any longer. There is no use. The facts to the contrary are too obvious.

I am as much concerned to defend poetry, and assert its independent rights and future possibilities, as these poets are. For that very reason I insist that poetry—whatever it may at times be used for—be defined as a communication of experience, and that we fearlessly acknowledge that the progress of intellectual culture has demanded a steadily growing separation of the function of communicating experience from that of communicating knowledge about experience. The limit to which this separation will go is defined only by the limit to which exact and reliable knowledge will go. And the fundamental way to defend poetry, even in the face of an infinite progress of science, is to point out that in devoting yourself to the cultivation and communication of knowledge *about* life, you fail to cultivate and communicate life. The scientist is as much lamed and crippled by the division as the poet. Poetry is not knowledge—no, but it is life. Is it so small a thing to live? And to live vividly? And to live *together?* That is what poetry is—living vividly and living together.

This point of view always makes my Marxian friends a little angry. They think I am deserting the banner because I do not affirm that all literature and all art is a mere reflection of that economic evolution which lies at the basis of social life, and point out that this tendency toward pure poetry and this cult of unintelligibility that I have been discussing are reflections of the approaching break-down of the bourgeois-capitalistic regime. I cannot repeat these dogmas of the philosophy of dialectic materialism, because I know that they are not true. I have explained at length, in a book which you never heard of, that Marx confuses the conditions which make a thing possible with the causes which determine its nature. He does this because, being a German romantic philosopher, he thinks he has to prove communism is historically inevitable, and not merely that it is possible—which is all that any scientific revolutionist needs to know. It is true that we could not have had the literature we have if there had not been a certain development of the technique of industry. But that is not saying that the developing technique of industry determines what kind of literature we have.

However, I am not going into that philosophical question just now. Suffice it to say that I have taken upon myself the task of keeping the philosophy of dialectic materialism out of America while helping to bring the Marxian contribution to science in. This subject of the relation of art and literature to social movements in general, and more particularly to the Communist dictatorship in Russia, will be treated in my next two books.

Meanwhile, I will say only this—that it is just as true in the sphere of social engineering as it is anywhere else that science, or the communication of knowledge about experience—knowledge of its relations—is separating itself from poetry or the communication of experience itself. And it is because their philosophy does not recognize this fundamental and inevitable division of labor that the

Bolsheviks under Stalin have found it so easy, and made it appear so noble, to strangle poetic literature in Russian.

When this fundamental division *is* recognized—when poetry, I mean, is defined as a communication of experience and it is recognized that with the advance of human culture this function becomes increasingly set apart from science, or the communication of knowledge about experience—then, of course, you have to make some qualifying statements. And here my friend Professor Boynton, of the University of Chicago—and your friend, too, undoubtedly—who is one of my most kindly and understanding critics, succeeds in poking a little fun at me. He calls me the "Angel with the Flaming Sword," and says that after I have driven the poets and literary professors out of the Paradise of truth-seeking with what seems a terrible wrath and ruthlessness, I relent in a most gentle manner—in fact in the manner of an anticlimax—and let them back in on certain conditions. And that is quite true, and I am very proud of it. There is in fact only one virtue, only one genuine old-fashioned virtue, that I have ever laid claim to, and that is that I am really interested in finding out and stating what I believe to be true, and I am more interested in that than I am in building up an imposing argument.

I could have made quite a sensation, perhaps, if I had concluded this book by saying that everything except pure poetry is now dead, and the professors of literature can go and shoot themselves. Instead of that I turned round and pointed out some obvious facts which qualify the increasing separation of poetry from science, and make the future of poetic literature and of teaching literature a gorgeously exciting prospect.

One of these obvious facts is that the same single individual, if he is big enough, can be both scientific and poetic. That is, he can learn the scientific point of view, understand the validity of science, lay up a certain store of information, and so, without ceasing to be a poet, win back, or retain, his old place in the forefront of human culture. For that purpose, however, he will have to be very big.

Another of these obvious facts is that in certain fields in which scientific knowledge is not very specialized or mathematical, truths *ascertained* by the methods of science can be *expressed* in poetic language. I cannot go into all the ways in which this can be worked out, but for one thing a general statement can often be conveyed to your mind—and conveyed with weight and living warmth of color and convincingness—by a particular instance or concrete example. That is the most simple and natural reunion of poetry with science, and probably the most simple instance of that is the significant story. Telling tales that teach or convey an attitude of wisdom essentially based upon science—tales of which Goethe's *Faust* is an example— will, I think, be one of the prevailing forms in which *Dichtung* and *Wahrheit* will be united in the future.

Another of these obvious facts is that verified knowledge, although it now exists in every field, is nevertheless extremely limited in content. There is still a vast kingdom of ignorance in which the man of letters has as good a right to make imposing guesses as the man of science. Indeed he has a better right, for he will not be misusing the authority of science, which derives from an opposite procedure, in order to give more weight than they deserve to emotional guesses. Moreover, these literary guesses stand a chance of planting some seed of a new hypothesis, which will be nourished by men of science and bear fruit of verified knowledge.

In short, the division of labor I am talking about can never be absolute, either among people—as to say, these men are wholly poets, these wholly scientists—or among books—these books are poetic literature and contain no knowledge about experience, these are science and contain no communication of experience to the imagination. But nevertheless it is a fact that these two *functions* are separating, and their separation is an inevitable accompaniment of the progress of civilized culture. It inheres in the very nature of experience and of our knowledge about it. The important thing is to recognize the fact. Literature, and also the teaching of literature, have a great future. But the great future of literature is in the hands of those who understand what has happened and accept it, not of those whose writings are a blind reaction to it, whether of resistance or of flight.

Writing as Design

by Zona Gale

WHEN WE USE THE WORD "FICTION" HERE WE ARE CONSIDERING fiction as a mode of transposition between living material and a fresh participation in that material by the reader. The reader is helpless. He will receive that material sentimentalized or boiled very hard, scaled down to be less than it is or left as a flat record of fact. Or he will receive it as that which celebrates and transfigures, points his understanding through and beyond, offers glimpses of some farther fields for us—and thus for fiction. We may not yet enter upon those fields, but art can do so. Fiction can do so, and can do so through the only materials with which it has to work—human appearance and relationship.

At Zion National Park, one of the most beautiful of the parks of the United States, the lodge is set between the canyon walls, sheer rises of rock of a thousand feet and more, before and at the rear of the buildings. There the waitresses, the bellboys, the drivers are college men and women, earning for next year's schooling. We sat in the lodge lounge after dinner, when we heard an excited voice crying: "Come out here! Everybody, out!" Everyone went to the doors and out onto the stone terrace. What was happening? No violence, no sudden claim to difference, no action among creatures. No—but over Lady Mountain, a thousand feet high, the full moon was rising. Pine boughs of the summit were cut black and slim on the gold. There was the impulse to fiction in the call of the bus boy or the bellhop who experienced the moment and let us know: *The moon was rising.*

Out on the oval of lawn before the lodge a man and a woman were walking—a husband and wife, for certain. In the pouring silver of that night she was moon-struck, without a question. "Let's stay out here for hours," she said. "Let's walk and walk. I never saw moonlight red on rock walls. Look at those peaks. We mustn't miss it!" But he said, "Margaret, I've looked at peaks since breakfast. I'm dead tired. My legs won't walk." She was making the transposition of material from its appearance as flat fact to its inner energy and intensity. He was no fiction writer.

There was a poet so glamoured by such values that once he sent a telegram to a beloved woman. Name. Address. "The moon is rising." No signature.

A young girl on a western train, going home from college. What college did she attend? "B. Y. C.," she said. What was B. Y. C.? As she answered there was a certain upward look of the shy, the one aware of her difference, or of the one forced to speak against her will. She was saying, "Brigham Young College," and one unfriendly to her religion might have fancied that there, in her look, he caught the future of a whole system of thinking. One either experienced this with her—or one merely took her reply and passed by on the other side. The first way exercises the impulse to fiction. The second exercises the receiving apparatus for fact.

Years ago I saw a tiny clearing on the desert, a little adobe house, a few willows, a few geraniums, some pans turned to dry. No sign of creatures about. But in the yard, a child's painted wagon. A child's wagon. The race safe in the commonplace cradle of routine, of the human program, so long as a child's wagon was to be seen, made, hammered, painted, used. Lately, on a desert train, I wondered: Was that sense of safety warranted? For some said (I thought) that the program and the race were now whole points off-center, were a compass crazed by too much electricity. Dramatically, on the moment, the train passed a mean settlement, a handful of unpainted houses. And in one yard lay a small, dusty, blue toy automobile and its truck. Frame and motor replaced adobe and wagon, and the race still seemed safe—not perhaps cradled in its routine, but safe on some new tangent of direction, ambiguous and beautiful.

All through the West lie the camps of the Civil Works Administration—or its substitutes—temporarily abandoned in the summer while the men go to the higher altitudes, where they could not work in winter. One catches the comments: "Foolishness. Unnecessary work. Why don't they do something that *is* something? Who's paying them?—You and I, out of our own pockets. The taxes are going to wreck us." And so on. But now and again one who says: "It is tomorrow. Men and women giving service as a matter of course to the government—for one year, two years—not for war and destruction but for social construction, before they go to their own personal constructing and earning jobs." And one remembered: "Professor Charles Zueblin used to say that every man and woman before he entered upon his profession or trade should be conscripted to give a year's work to the state—for forestation, for municipal building and design, for irrigation, for that which he himself could best do. Not, then, artist set to road work or skilled salesman to digging— as was inevitable in the rush and skelter of our present need—but men and women, serving the state according to their gifts and equipment, for one year or two, for a stipend, before beginning to work for livelihood and for possible accumulation." In the first comments there was apprehension of flat fact; in the others, creative comprehension.

Riverside, California, is a city which lies as a jewel among cities. The great asset of the town is a mountain, high and rocky, planted by the people with thousands of trees and shrubs, watered, set with bronze tablets to men who have loved it; and one there to Jacob Riis, who suggested the Easter sunrise service which yearly sends twenty thousand people to the summit for a chorus of trombones and music, and for prayer. The town has a great community hall, with an exquisite sunken garden and waterfall. Its Shanty-town has been demolished, and bears green and flowers and fountains to greet its guests—welcomed, too, on the motor road, by a vast curved bridge over the Santa Ana River and a shrine to St. Francis of Assisi, patron saint of its unique and magic Mission Inn. Dedicated to Fra Junípero Serra, this is the inn, host to presidents, where art galleries and organ music, and a chapel set with a priceless shrine and vestments from a Mexican palace, are marvels even in a state of marvels—the inn which caused Mr. Archer Huntington to say that an occupation with an historical significance and a religious background could never die. And now the town moves towards a civic center—with municipal and federal buildings, churches, Y.W.C.A., and the inn to be set about a stately court, lighted by the double cross, with mission bells, knit by the unique pergola which covers with beauty miles of foot pavement of the streets.

One man, Frank A. Miller, has stimulated it all—from developed mountain to civic center. And he says with a smile, "Moses said that godliness is profitable. I say that *Beauty pays.*" The essence of modernity—*Beauty pays.* Not the modernity of those sad library posters which proclaim, "Learn more, earn more." But the modernity which knows that beauty and order, in a business or in conduct, are the rule. That you recognize evil—as Baudelaire did in fiction and as the Continental and English and American moderns do—as quite gorgeous local color, as a contribution, but that order and beauty and delicacy and sensitiveness are the rule. And against such there is no law, and to such the order of the stars and time and electricity and crystals and human fate witness abundantly. You look at a town creatively, or you look at it as a cart driver sees it, his profile, blank and oblivious, etched on the gold California sky.

I think of the cry of a farm woman: "The grain burned up, the clover didn't catch, the corn hung small in the ear." Hebraic that, biblical in its bitter cry against her lot—Greek, rather, in her woe before fate. I think of the Winnebago Indian woman who, at fifty-odd, had a wish to live in a house. She, who had never lived save in a wigwam, had a wish to raise her standard of living, to have a sewing machine and curtains. Once one gave her a yellow rose, and she threw back her head and said in the Winnebago tongue and with half-closed eyes: "Last night I dreamed of flowers." Material for fiction—but not more truly so than when this Indian woman asked a neighbor to telephone to a friend: "We don't want my son-in-law here no more. If you would please take him away." In any of these multiple incidents it is not—and here lies the magic—it is not the incident itself which is the material for fiction; no one could make a *tale* of any of these. But it is that which lies within, and it is the complementing power to be mazed and bemused by them, to be thrown into a mood and then to induce a mood in others—in a current of emotion.

Never think that a tale has been told if it has not moved the beholder to that moment of emotion. That emotion—the catharsis—is the power to experience creatively that which is occurring. Perception is the tale's conception, action is its body, style is its garment, emotion is its soul. Emotion—as the power to experience creatively that which is happening to another. The sensibility to experience it as if it were happening to one's self.

How shall one deepen that sensibility which gives one this self-identification with others—for the purposes, shall we say, of fiction writing or of fiction reading?

A distinguished Japanese, a professor of Oriental literature at an American university, said recently that one of the exercises of students in Japan is sometimes to try to catch one another's meaning swiftly. To know at once what another is trying to say, either about some abstraction or about some sensitively perceived concrete fact. Not to be left staring at another to see if one *can* have caught that which he is trying to impart, but to catch it, like a flash! Also to experiment in saying those things which are truth, which delight or which wound, so that the other may recognize in himself why he is wounded or why delighted, and in himself can resolve both reactions to their due proportions. Exercises in heightening perception—why not? As one sharpens one's musical ear or sensitizes one's piano or harp touch. Exercises in raising to the nth power one's sensibility, one's awareness. Awareness—there is the key. Matching the integrated jewels of experience, for fiction. Or, to change the figure, playing on all the moments of human relationship so that one may be aware of their constant orchestration—of the dissonance or the resonance of our momentary performances.

But *do* we thus sharpen our sensibilities, through the day? No—for all the way from the heightened delicacies of which the Japanese professor reminds us to our simplest instances, as of that moment at breakfast when one of the family ventures a little joke and looks about the table, bright-eyed and expectant, to one and another and another, hoping for an answering spark, and everyone goes right on eating oatmeal and no one smiles; and from school to business, when one utterly fails to sense another's situation or need or human fineness or weakness—all the way, we miss our opportunities to sharpen our tools or preparation for the writing, or for the reading, of fiction. We can multiply these remembered instances, simple or intricate, in which we have failed to exercise the fiction writer's craft, in which we have missed the content of a given moment.

Now if one is exercising any human relationship whatever it is important to catch these implications. But if one is writing about human relationship, one *must* catch them, for otherwise one will have a flat, dead, two-dimensional fiction—a fiction with a form perhaps, perhaps even with a style, but a fiction lacking the beauty not only of its integrated ornamentation but of its potential pattern. Lacking not only that which Edgar Saltus called, in architecture, "excesses of grace," but lacking the full energy of *design*. Design, which is the secret synthesis of art—as of life.

Design, in fiction, is theme treated with heightened awareness. And design, as such, has no dependence and indeed no dealing with plot. Foreordained plot is that mechanism which twists to its own uses the lovely materials of design, often indeed giving to design one arm and one wing, one foot and one wheel, and instead of a spirit, a motor. Almost as much as to unawareness, it is such plot to which fiction has fallen victim, as if the sky were to be platted by visible boundaries. Fiction, winged by theme, powered by design, is often chained and tortured by plot.

Fiction at its best, then, is the fruit of perfect self-identification of the writer with his materials—with beings, with situations, with objects, with time and place. It is the application to life of a heightened perception which experiences people and all things as if the writer *were* those people, those things. For the fiction writer "There, but for the grace of God, go I" is heightened to "There go I," is heightened to "While there is a poorer class, I belong to it, while there is a criminal class, I am of it, while there is a soul in jail, I am not free." It is the literal self-identification "with every fault, frailty and futility," and also with every magnification and enhancement of the human being. It is to see within, it is to see through, it is to see all material, as it were, as intimate and as *warm* as one's self. These walls, this separation of being which we set up and imagine, are specious. The appearance—and this is what the realist deals with— is separative; but the consciousness, which the creative writer deals with, is one.

The creative writer must pass at will not only into the awareness of another being, but he must see objects and settings and scenes with a like intensity. There was the thorn tree in May Sinclair's "The Three Sisters." The girl crossed the lawn and saw a thorn tree. There it was, abruptly alive—bursting with its whole inner power, doing its utmost, poignant, wrapped in light. Not a bush, but a burning bush. Not a cup, but the Grail. That is the process of Art.

The process of art was to be observed of late in a great factory. Attached to the floors of roaring machines were long sheds where cotton had been stored against the needs of the years. Looking down those dim stretching aisles of bales a visitor observed: "This is like having money in the bank." But the great manufacturer saw the bales differently, saw them transfigured: "Bent backs," he said.—Bent backs of those who picked the cotton, of those who should spin it into yarn and weave it into fabric. That observation employed the process of creative art.

Consider the objects in a cabinet. To one observing, there may be a vase, a figurine, a cruet, a luster pitcher. But to the owner these leap with life, life of the dead lady who gave the vase to his mother in 1863; of the figurine, brought to him when he was eight; of the great artist who left the cruet with him until he should come west again; of the luster pitcher, coming to him from the daughter of the friend of his mother's girlhood. It is to uncover, like that, but in a flash and in emotion, the meaning of all persons, all things, that the artist strives. So that objects and events and situations, like beings, shall be transfigured into their real meaning, that at last they may find their common denominator—their unity.

In a recent address in Ohio, Superintendent Wirt, of the Gary schools, put this simply and impressively in its application to social living. He said: "There is a key, a factor which we all seek, which shall work upon living the true transformation of art. This key, this unknown factor, will shape life into new meaning, even as the artist's vision re-shapes and re-assesses and transfigures his material. The magic touch is possible to the life of men as it is possible to the material of art. Only the artist has found his key. We have not yet found ours."

This is more than Dreiser's need for "self-identification with every fault, frailty and futility." More even than a need for self-identification with great experience. It is the significance of the theory of *revelation* as applied to living. It is the true Design for Living—and Writing.

A psychologist defines the artist as "the seer who does pioneer work in perceptual understanding, in finding the hidden possibilities in our perceptual world." And Bernard Shaw's definition runs:

"The great artist is one who adds a fresh extension of sense to the heritage of the race."

What, then, shall be said of the fiction which finds its area of expression exclusively among the gangster, the parasite, the dissolute, and those who regard the patterns of most law and all convention merely as inhibitions? Those novels which confuse with a strong style the frequent use of certain words which heretofore have not been considered permissible in fiction? Those novels which deal with the primitive still among us, richly aware of the rich reactions of the body, but yet unaware of its extensions, more exquisite.

But these novels need not trouble anybody. Indeed, these, as they disappear, and they will disappear, may leave major contributions to fiction—even as futurism and cubism, as they disappear, are leaving important contributions to pictorial art. For because of futurism and cubism and realism and naturalism we extend our materials, and any extension of materials often results in abuses, in overemphasis, in crudity, in extremes. But once we are accustomed to our new, and really valuable, mediums, we shall begin to treat these too with the process of art—to mellow, to subdue, to transpose, to integrate, to transfigure.

The one who writes at his best, like the one who lives at his best, must achieve this new attitude towards his materials and therefore towards life. He may write about gangsters and the dissolute, but in that case he will write of them as Tolstoi or Hugo or Balzac wrote— not as a smirking schoolboy might write.

Too often this social experience of achieving a new attitude towards life has been confined to religion. People have had a great experience of increased awareness of themselves, of their neighbor, and of God—and they have called it being saved. "Brother, are you saved?" That is, have *you* had this intense experience of entering into a sense of God, of life, of one another? Salvation, the West calls it. Illumination, the East says. As awareness, the creative writer knows it. As penetrating through appearance, as experiencing all aspects of life *anew,* as coming into a special grace of seeing, of under-standing. The religious would say, "The practice of the presence of God." The creative writer would say, "The practice of the signifi-cance of life." (And how do these differ?) All the time, the artist has been having the revelation alone as he worked. *If he was an artist.* Otherwise he was a transferrer, as the old priests copied out, transcribed beautifully, illumined. Priests of the closet, realists. But the creative writer was the priest of the altar. No copyist he. For he must work a kind of transfiguration of human beings, of experiences and of objects, resolve them into their essential meaning, hidden until he touched it.

Art and science grope for the look within. And today we are thinking of art, and specifically of literature, as the power to interpret and to communicate values which, without due process of art, are incommunicable. That there are these values no one can doubt. We live on the edge of intelligence, and the powers and perceptions of tomorrow are veiled from us by our own limitations. But art and science are two peepholes into man's future. There are others. Love is one. Conduct is one. In the power to enter upon fuller living which both bring, they are in themselves keys to the more abundant life which all the world is seeking. Indeed love and conduct are the chief means of apprehending life which the majority of the race possesses or ever has possessed in the past. Art and science but carry farther the inner perception of life, whose common language is love and conduct—love and conduct raised to their high powers. There are those who do not divine enough in the wonders of art and science and who refuse to enter upon their own heritage of love and conduct, who will not love highly and will not make conduct yield its treasure. But the universe of those who accept these wonders, who do love highly, do behave exquisitely, or do touch reality in science or art—their universe is our universe, yielding wonders of which we have but dim glimpses. Love was man's first gesture towards wonder, conduct or religion was his second. Art is another means of apprehension, permitting man to peer farther within. This is the soul of design, that it is a way of extension of apprehension.

This, then, we may demand of fiction—that it present to us our material not scaled down to be less than it is or left as a flat record of fact, but that it transfigure its material, that it let us look through and beyond. We have need to sift and winnow that which comes from the presses as fiction and to demand of it that it tell the truth about the world of men, women, and events—tell it "for all there is in it," so that it shall hold for us the glimmer of some farther field than we yet know.

Literature versus Opinion

by HENRY HAZLITT

THE WILL OF THE LATE AVERY HOPWOOD EXPRESSED THE DESIRE THAT the literary prizes for which he so generously provided should be especially used to encourage "the new, the unusual, and the radical." It is interesting to recall that the will was made in 1922. It was about that time that those whom we now think of as the older generation in American literature, symbolized by such figures as Theodore Dreiser and H. L. Mencken, emerged into real prominence. Just before that period the waters of literary discussion had been relatively stagnant. Mencken and his disciples, deserting the genteel tradition, began calling their opponents harsh and extraordinary names, and the attention of youth was arrested. A fight is always exciting: moreover, if literature was something worth fighting over, it might be worth looking into.

That particular battle has not continued, but a series of battles have followed each other with only the briefest intermission. Meanwhile the issues have altered and even the sides have changed, so that many of those who were previously on the left now somehow find themselves on the right. The battle lines, moreover, have become so widely extended that it is no longer clearly possible to tell the literary front from the political front. Whatever one may say of the present era, it is not stagnant. One result, at least, is that "the new, the unusual, and the radical" are today much more certain of a hearing than they were thirteen years ago. But another result, less happy, is that the growing bitterness of the battle, and the extent and depth of the issues involved, have placed the most serious obstacles in the way of a sober objective evaluation of the current literary product, whether new, unusual, radical, or otherwise.

39

The tone of political discussion in the last few years has been increasingly acrimonious. It is not merely that arguments have been growing more passionate and less reasonable; the extremists on both sides have been losing faith in the efficacy of reason itself. One should not attempt to persuade one's opponent; one should suppress or imprison or execute him. This is the philosophy of the rulers of Germany and of Russia; it is shared only to a lesser degree by other rulers who have not yet consolidated their power, and it has influenced the tone of political discussion even in the great democracies. It has spread to the field of letters, and it emerges there as the theory that no such thing as an objective judgment of literary work is possible: there are only proletarian, bourgeois, or Fascist judgments; and writers are praised or denounced in accordance with their political or economic sympathies and doctrines.

Now I cannot believe that this attitude is either a salutary or a lasting one. It is, of course, the most natural thing in the world to praise those who are on our side of any question and to denounce those who are against us. Some of the so-called Marxist critics have built up elaborate rationalizations of the process. But the critic of literature who yields to this temptation, whatever good he thinks he may thereby be doing for his particular "cause," betrays his function as a literary critic.

The great critics of the past have always recognized this fact, and have been great critics partly through that very recognition. One of the most interesting examples is William Hazlitt. Now few writers have ever had more violent and uncompromising political opinions than he had. He was an ardent and tireless defender of the French Revolution; the uncompromising vehemence of his Jacobinism, indeed, led him into constant quarrels with most of his friends. But these differences of opinion, or even violent personal antagonisms, seldom perverted his literary judgments. No better illustration of his sanity and insight in this respect appears than in his numerous discussions of Edmund Burke. Here was a writer who had thrown the whole weight of his eloquence and passion against that French Revolution which to Hazlitt was one of the great historic landmarks in the eternal struggle for human liberty. Yet Hazlitt almost never wrote of Burke except in terms of the most ungrudging praise. In an essay devoted to him in 1807, Hazlitt tells us that Burke "enriched every subject to which he applied himself"; that "he was the most eloquent man of his time, and his wisdom was greater than his eloquence." "It has always been with me," he added, "a test of the sense and candor of any one belonging to the opposite party, whether he allowed Burke to be a great man." Hazlitt apparently had never met more than one or two political opponents who would make this concession; and he set their reluctance down either to the fact that party feelings ran too high to admit of any real candor, or to "an essential vulgarity in their habits of thinking."

Hazlitt's praise seems to have been misunderstood. In a later printing of his "Character of Mr. Burke" he inserted the following explanatory footnote: "This character was written in a fit of extravagant candor, at a time when I thought I could do justice, or more than justice, to an enemy, without betraying a cause." But the truth was that Hazlitt was always subject to such "fits of extravagant candor," and seldom had fits of any other kind. In his essay "On Reading Old Books," he tells us that when he first encountered Burke's writings he exclaimed to himself: "This is true eloquence: this is a man pouring out his mind on paper." "The most perfect prose style, the most powerful, the most dazzling, the most daring . . . was Burke's." It was "forked and playful as the lightning, crested like the serpent." And here Hazlitt wrote the sentences that may serve as a sort of text for the present lecture: "I did not care for his doctrines. I was then, and am still, proof against their contagion; but I admired the author, and was considered as not a very staunch partisan of the opposite side, though I thought myself that an abstract proposition was one thing a masterly transition, a brilliant metaphor, another. I conceived too that he might be wrong in his main argument, and yet deliver fifty truths in arriving at a false conclusion."

Let us look at some of the implications of this attitude, and see to what extent we can apply them to the literary controversies of our own day. One of the favorite slogans of the Marxist critics is that "art is a weapon." We need not ask, at the moment, in what sense or to what extent this is true. But I should like to point out that even if art *is* a weapon, and even if we grant also that we must all line up on one of two sides in wielding it, it is still possible for us to judge it objectively. Machine guns are certainly weapons, and we should prefer to have them all on our side, but a sensible man's preferences have nothing to do with his realistic observation. Allied military commentators during the World War were able to say quite objectively whether the Germans had better or worse rifles, artillery, airplanes, or gases than they had, or whether they made more or less effective use of them. An objectivity that is possible in a war of bullets ought surely to be possible in a war of pamphlets. A Communist critic ought to be able to discuss the ability of a bourgeois or a Fascist writer with the same cool detachment with which the high command in a war must estimate the ability of the opposing leadership. Wars are not won by dismissing all the enemy's generals as scoundrels and fools.

Here, then, is one form of critical objectivity of which even the most embittered class-conscious critics should recognize the need. We must correctly estimate the skill and ability of our opponents. This correct estimate is one of the primary functions of literary criticism. The important question for such criticism is not which side a writer is on, but how able he is in the service of that side. For estimating him it is not the bald conclusion at which he arrives that counts, but the mental process by which he arrives at it. It is not what he nakedly contends; it is the persuasiveness with which he states it. There are dull minds on both sides of every great controversy—minds that deal only in stereotypes and clichés, minds that can only repeat, parrot-like, the phrases the leaders have coined. But there are also brilliant minds on both sides of every great controversy; it is these that develop the new arguments and put them forward with the greatest force. The cardinal business of literary criticism in such a situation is not to declare that side A is right and side B wrong; it is to distinguish, on whichever side, the brilliant and original writers from the empty ones.

In brief, it is the paradoxical function of the literary critic, *as* critic, to detach himself as completely as possible from the actual merits of the controversies of his own time. In appraising the comparative qualities of individual writers, he must judge not the controversies but the controversialists. He will sometimes be obliged to say, at least to himself: "What A writes is perfectly sound, and I agree with it passionately; but I am obliged to add that it will be completely forgotten ten years from now." At other times he will have to say: "This man B is utterly wrong; his perversity sometimes infuriates me; but, damn it all, there is some quality in what he says that leads me to fear that a century from now it will still be quoted." Few people could be more thoroughly wrongheaded, according to most of our current standards, than Dr. Johnson, but his aphorisms live because they have this quality. As for the philosopher, there is almost as much disagreement today as in his own lifetime whether Berkeley, or Kant, or Hegel was right or wrong. It is not being right or wrong that counts: it is having an interesting and original and powerful mind.

But this brings us to a further question. There is a certain ambiguity about the phrase "being right." For there are several kinds of truth, and the truth of literature is not necessarily the truth of science. We recognize this as soon as we come to deal, in fiction, with the differences between realism and romanticism, naturalism and fantasy. *Gulliver's Travels* is a true book; but it is not true that there are midgets of six inches, or giants seventy feet high, or nations of horses. The truth of *Alice in Wonderland* is not the truth of Main Street. The truth of poetry is not the truth of prose. Departures from fact, even when not purposely made for a certain effect, must be judged by different standards, depending on where they occur. The recognition of this principle is as old as Aristotle. When an error has been made in poetry, he remarks, it is important to ask whether it is a matter directly or only accidentally connected with the poetic art. For example, he tells us, it is a lesser error in an artist not to know that the hind has no horns, than to produce an unrecognizable picture of one. To speak of stout Cortez and all his men, silent, upon a peak in Darien, may be bad history but excellent poetry.

What all this comes down to is that we cannot apply ordinary fact-standards or opinion-standards in any crude or direct way to the judgment of literature. We have first of all to recognize that the elements of literature are so various and complex, as Lytton Strachey once reminded us, that no writer can be damned on a mere enumeration of faults, because he may always possess merits which make up for everything. If this is true, as I believe it is, then it is surely still more absurd either to dismiss a writer, or to regard him as important, merely because he holds or rejects some specific doctrine.

I am afraid that most Marxist critics would disagree with this. They might say that this would doubtless be so if the doctrine were one of secondary importance, but that the question of the class struggle happens to be paramount and central. A writer must align himself either with the proletariat or with the bourgeoisie, either with the forces of light, or with the forces of darkness. In the first case, the effect of his work will be beneficent; in the second it must be pernicious. They might go even further, and hold that the abler a bourgeois or capitalistic writer is, the more harmful the effect of his writing will be.

Now when we examine this reasoning it begins to strike us as strangely familiar. The class struggle is not the first so-called paramount or central question to divide mankind. Historically there has always been some issue that partisans have declared to be the central one, and historically it is always a different issue. For centuries writers have been damned for not holding the correct religious or theological beliefs, or for not belonging to the right political party, or for not having the correct attitude toward sex. In the Victorian period, and during the 1920's, we were accustomed to having novels judged by so-called moral standards, which usually referred to sexual morality. The Victorians condemned their predecessors, from Rabelais and Boccaccio to Wycherly and Congreve, for their indecency, and disapproved of the Voltaires and Swifts for their cynicism. Our critics of the twenties dismissed the Victorians for their prudery and puritanism, and derided them also because they were sentimental, and not, as they should have been, cynical. Our new Communist critics now dismiss contemporary writers who have only a "sterile cynicism" in place of a fighting faith.

There are two ways of dealing with Marxist criticism. One may begin by questioning its premises. Is it true that there is an inevitable class struggle? Is it true that social and economic classes divide themselves basically into just two? Is it true that this social cleavage is more important than any other? Even before we begin any close scrutiny of the matter we are entitled, certainly, to our suspicions. For it would be astonishing if the objective facts were to fit in so neatly with the requirements of drama. Immemorially playwrights have recognized that audiences want to see a clash of just two great contending forces. If the contending forces are three, four, five, or twenty, the audience is distracted and confused. Its attention is scattered, its sympathies dispersed. To economize attention and sympathy, it is necessary that there be essentially just two contending forces, and that the audience should wish to see one triumphant and the other crushed. The theory of the class struggle conforms providentially to this law of the theater. It is obliging enough to conform also to the requirements of Hegelian logic. This second conformity is perhaps not so surprising, because the Hegelian logic, by which Marx was so deeply influenced, was itself unconsciously created by Hegel to accord with the rules of dramatic appeal. Marx acquired from him the habit of looking in the actual world for the embodiment of logical categories, with sharp boundaries, clearly opposed to each other.

So we have presented to us in the Marxist drama a world consisting essentially of just two classes engaged in a death struggle: on the one side the capitalists and their hirelings; on the other the onmarching proletariat. When we look at the world, however, unencumbered by this rigid theory, we see that the border line between economic classes, particularly in America, is vague and shifting. We see that the president of a great steel corporation, working on salary and holding little or no stock in his company, is technically an employee, while the owner of a fruit stand with one assistant is technically a capitalist and an employer. More importantly, we know that, for all the appalling contrasts in wealth and income at the two extremes, income classes in the United States shade gradually into each other. The National Bureau of Economic Research, a statistical organization of the highest standing, for example, recently divided the country, not into two, but into seventy-four separate "income classes."

Space will hardly permit an extensive examination of the postulates of Communism, and fortunately such an examination is not necessary. Let us for the moment, instead, accept some of the premises of Marxist literary criticism. Let us accept the premises that there are essentially just two economic classes, that the division between them is real and sharp, and that membership in one of these classes affects our whole point of view. Even if we cannot believe that our opinions are mere rationalizations of our class status, let us grant at least the large element of truth in the contention that our class

status influences the opinions of nearly all of us in various unconscious
and subtle ways—and sometimes even in pretty obvious ways.

The question we must then ask ourselves is this: Is it impossible
for the exceptional writer to surmount these limitations? Is it impossible for him, once he has been brought to recognize this bias, to
guard against it as he tries to guard against other forms of bias?
For the limitations and biases that may affect the human mind are
almost innumerable. There is the limitation imposed by a man's
language and nationality. What can Thomas Mann and Spengler,
and Proust and Gide, and Pareto and Knut Hamsun, and Dostoevski
and Tolstoi, have to say that could interest Americans with their so
different experience? Yet somehow they seem to have a great deal to
say to us. There are Americans who feel that they get more of value
from some of these foreigners than from any of their own writers.
Anatole France once regretted that we could not, like Tiresias, be men
and remember having been women, that we are shut up in our
personality as in a perpetual prison. But his own works, and the
works of hundreds of other writers in all ages, of Shakespeare, of
Flaubert, of Hardy, of Dreiser, prove otherwise. The great male
writer, by the power of his imagination, can portray the soul of a
woman more fully and truthfully, even in the opinion of women,
than the overwhelming majority of women writers can. And the
great woman novelist can tell us more of what goes on in the mind
of a man than most men can.

To take but one more example, there is the limitation imposed
upon a writer by the historic era in which he lives. If any limitation
seems absolutely insuperable, this one does. How can Karl Marx,
who died fifty years ago, who knew nothing of the immense social,
political, scientific, and technological changes that have taken place
in the half century since then, how can Marx possibly have anything
to tell us that is still of value? How can Shakespeare and Montaigne,
in their graves three centuries and more, possibly have written words
that we can still cherish for their wisdom or beauty, that may even
come to us with a shock of delight? What could be more absurd
than to suppose that Aristotle and Plato and Homer, who knew
nothing at all of the knowledge and experience that a hundred
generations of mankind have garnered in the years since they passed
on, what could be more absurd than to suppose that any of them

could have written works that can still give us intense pleasure, or a sense of encountering flashes of penetrating wisdom for the first time? Yet this miracle is achieved.

In brief, the great writer, with supreme imaginative gifts, can universalize himself. He can vault over the apparently insuperable barriers of race, sex, and time. And yet there is a new school of critics who tell us, in effect, that he cannot vault over the barrier of his class. This contention is an astonishing one. For while no writer can, in any literal or physical sense, change his race, his sex, or his historic era, the one thing he can and frequently does change is precisely his economic status. He can have the experience of being poor, as well as of being "comfortably off," not merely in imagination, but in actuality. Economic class boundaries are so uncertain, indeed, that even Marxists have difficulty in deciding upon which side of "the coming struggle for power" certain great groups will be aligned, or which "ideology" controls them.

We are obliged to conclude, then, that it is surely no more difficult for the great writer, in a functional sense, to transcend the barriers of class than to transcend those of nationality, sex, and time. And we are also entitled to conclude that the great upper- or middle-class writers of the past, or even of the present, have as much to say to the intelligent proletarian as they have to the intelligent bourgeois. We may acknowledge that class bias sometimes enters into what these writers have written. Where it does, it is the duty of the critic to point to the extent and nature of the bias. The positive contribution of the literary Marxists is that they have sharpened our eyes in this respect. But it is not the duty of the critic to declare a priori that this class bias necessarily affects and invalidates everything that a middle-class writer has written; or to point to this bias to the exclusion of all others; or to make it the central theme of all his criticism. Such criticism merely rests on the ancient fallacy of the *argumentum ad hominem*—of trying to discredit an argument or an attitude (and thus to seem to prove the opposite) by abusing the one who advances the argument or who holds the attitude. Such criticism, moreover, must miss all the infinitely rich and subtle values that literature has to offer. It must end by being dreadfully monotonous and tiresome.

Now I must confess that some of the views I have been discussing up to now are extreme. They are by no means held by all critics who call themselves Marxists. For the more intelligent Marxists have been uneasily aware of the narrow and absurd judgments into which this type of reasoning must lead them. So they have sought to rescue themselves from their dilemma by making a distinction. They have, in fact, sawn literature itself into two sharply contrasted aspects, as they have sawn society into two sharply contrasted classes. This might almost be called the official cleavage. The resolution on literature, for example, adopted by the Political Bureau of the Communist Party of the Soviet Union in 1924, begins by declaring that "such a thing as neutral art in a class society does not and cannot exist." It then divides literary works, however, into their "social-political contents" on the one hand, and their "form and style" on the other. On all questions of "content," it holds, the Party must take a firm and positive stand; but on questions of "form and style" it may permit considerable freedom. A similar division is made by a number of American Marxist writers when they distinguish between the "social significance" or the "ideas" of a literary work, and its "craftsmanship." Something of the same sort seems also to be in the mind of the English Marxist, Mr. John Strachey, in his somewhat confused volume called "Literature and Dialectical Materialism." After praising Mr. Granville Hicks, for example, as "the foremost Marxist literary critic of America," he adds that Mr. Hicks "hardly seems to pay enough attention to the merits of writers as writers."

This whole attempt to split literature into its "ideas" or "social significance" on the one hand, and its "form and style" or "craftsmanship" on the other, seems to me mistaken. Literature will simply not submit to such a violent bifurcation. "Style" and "form" are not separate qualities that can be thrown over "content" like a raincoat: they are determined by content. A work of literature is an organic whole. It is true that, for convenience of discussion, either "craftsmanship" or "social significance" can be discussed as if it existed in isolation—provided the critic always remembers that it does nothing of the kind. What is even more important for us to keep in mind, in relation to the present point, is that after we have discussed the "social-political contents" of a literary work on the one hand, and its "craftsmanship" on the other, we may still have left out what is chiefly important about the work—unless, of course, we happen to have stretched one or the other of these two terms far beyond its legitimate meaning.

Let us see what would happen if we applied these standards, for example, to *Hamlet*. I am afraid that on the question of social-political content a Marxist critic would give that play a very low rating. For in the usual sense of the phrase, it seems simply to have no social-political content. It aims at no reform; it does not imply the need of any change in social-political institutions. It takes for granted the institution of monarchy, and the class relationships and moral code of Shakespeare's time.

Ah, says the sophisticated Marxist critic, but the value of Hamlet lies in its "craftsmanship," in its "style and form." Now, certainly, part of its value does reside in these qualities. To take but one example, in the way in which he leads us up to the scene in which Hamlet first sees his father's ghost Shakespeare reveals a masterly technical adroitness. But if the reputation of *Hamlet* rested wholly on its "craftsmanship," as that word is ordinarily used, it would not be higher than that of hundreds of other plays. For it is full of what today would be thought of as technical crudities. It is a sprawling drama of five acts and twenty scenes, overloaded with improbable accidents and coincidences. Any second-rater today could probably do a neater job of mere carpentry.

In what, then, does the greatness of *Hamlet* consist? We might, if we wished, here begin to introduce further criteria. We might speak of "character delineation," which is not "social-political content" and which is surely something broader than mere "form and style." We might talk of the magnificent poetic imagery, which may mean "style," but which implies a good deal more than that. We might talk of the truth or wisdom of the ideas in the famous soliloquy, or in the advice of Polonius. But whatever our detailed analysis, we should be obliged to say, finally, that what made *Hamlet* great was the whole range and texture and quality of its creator's mind.

This is what counts, in the end, in literature—the quality and nobility of the author's mind—and not either mere technical excellence, or the author's social and political sympathies. If we were to judge authors by our agreement or disagreement with their leading doctrines, a very strange sort of criticism would result. But in recognizing this, as the more intelligent Marxist critics do as well as the rest of us, it is unnecessary to fall back upon so narrow a standard as "craftsmanship." We can, instead, recognize more completely than before the wisdom of William Hazlitt's criticism of Burke. "Burke must be allowed to have wanted judgment," he wrote, "by all those who think that he was wrong in his conclusion. . . . But if in arriving at one error he discovered a hundred truths, I should consider myself a hundred times more indebted to him than if, stumbling on what I consider as the right side of the question, he had committed a hundred absurdities in striving to establish his point."

So far we have been discussing the duty of the critic in the present situation. What shall we say of the duty of the creative writer? Supposing his sympathies to be radical, shall he devote himself to writing propagandistic novels, propagandistic plays, propagandistic poetry? Shall he plunge into the center of the fight, or shall he stand "above the battle"?

These questions are by no means easy to answer. There is, to begin with, the difficulty of determining exactly what "propaganda" is. There is a sense in which all art is propagandistic because it reflects and propagates some vision of the world. Propaganda, it has been argued, does not need to be conscious; it may express itself through the unconscious acceptance of existing values and institutions that have been taken for granted. And it is on this basis that Marxists hold that all "bourgeois art" is propaganda for capitalism.

Now while there is perhaps an element of truth in this contention, it seems to me that it does make a difference whether propaganda is conscious or unconscious. To say this, however, does not solve the problem, for it is sometimes difficult to say to what extent propaganda is conscious. Perhaps we can get at the question best by looking first at propaganda in the strict sense, then at the examples of literature which are difficult to classify in this respect, and finally at literature which can be called propagandistic only by the greatest possible extension of the term.

Strictly propagandistic art may be provisionally defined as art which is not regarded by its creator as a sufficient end in itself, but merely as a means of achieving some further end which its creator considers more important. It aims usually at some specific social or political reform: the abolition of capital punishment or of vivisection, a revision of the divorce laws or of sexual mores, the need for revolutionary action. Thus *Uncle Tom's Cabin* is clearly a propagandistic novel, as are most of the novels of Upton Sinclair and the later plays of Elmer Rice.

But now we begin to move into more doubtful territory. As the implied reform becomes broader and vaguer, as the implication itself becomes less definite, the propagandistic nature of a work of literary art becomes more doubtful. The mere fact of whether the work under consideration is good or bad does not always help us in deciding upon its propagandistic nature. Horatio Alger's novels seem propagandistic enough, for they very clearly imply the importance for material success of the virtues of ambition, pluck, hard work, and thrift. But there is a question even here. Alger was certainly not, in the ordinary sense, *advocating* material success; it was a value that he took for granted and assumed that his readers took for granted. Further, the question may be raised whether he was deliberately advocating these means toward material success, or was again merely utilizing the values he assumed his readers already to believe in, in order to secure the undivided sympathy for his heroes and the undivided hatred for his villains deemed essential to create interest and suspense.

Most of the plays of Shaw are propagandistic, as are many of the dramas of Ibsen; *Pillars of Society, A Doll's House, An Enemy of the People, The Wild Duck,* all imply a definite social philosophy, and the need of some sort of social renovation. But clearly we have begun here to move toward works that it is getting to be more difficult to classify. This doubtful field is a very broad one. It includes many of the novels of Dickens, which helped in the movement toward prison reform and the alteration of the debtor laws; it includes Hugo's *Les Miserables,* which affected the French attitude toward criminals. And almost too propagandistic to be doubtful are the novels and plays of Dumas *fils,* which inculcate such morals as the duty of a seducer to marry the woman he has seduced, or the right of a husband to take the law into his own hands and kill the wife who has been unfaithful and worthless. The propaganda in a novel need not necessarily take the form of solemn advocacy of a given attitude: it may consist merely in derision of its opposite. Thus Voltaire's *Candide* is a clear piece of propaganda against the philosophy of optimism.

We come at length to those works of literature which are as free from propaganda as it is possible to imagine. They include some of the greatest works in the language and some of the worst. It would be a rash critic indeed who would venture to say that there is much propaganda in the poetry of Keats, or who could find much more than a shade of it in the plays of Shakespeare. Shakespeare, it is true, sometimes reveals a social attitude; he had, for example, a hardly disguised contempt for the mob. But for the most part his work merely reflects an acceptance of, or an indifference to, the dominant social values and institutions of his time; he portrays no interest in changing them. The average detective story of our own day is just as non-propagandistic.

What conclusions can we draw from this casual survey? We are entitled to conclude, I think, that no clear-cut division can be made between propagandistic and nonpropagandistic work. But this absence of a clear boundary line does not mean that the distinction is unimportant. On the spectrum it is impossible to tell at precisely what point blue becomes green or green becomes yellow, but this does not mean that there is no difference between blue and yellow. And it is pointless in view of this survey to continue to argue that *all* literary work is basically propagandistic, whether definitely or vaguely, consciously or unconsciously, aggressively or passively, because even if we were to grant this it would still be necessary, for purposes of intelligible discussion, to distinguish between definitely, consciously, and aggressively propagandistic work and vaguely, passively, and unconsciously propagandistic work. It saves time to call the first propagandistic and the second nonpropagandistic.

Making this distinction, then, what can we say about the duty of the writer? Shall he write propaganda or unflinchingly eschew it? I think we are obliged to say, after our perfunctory glance over the field, that it is folly to lay down any general rule. We can merely point to some of the possibilities and dangers of the alternative courses. The dangers of writing propaganda are almost too numerous to mention. At its lowest level the propagandistic novel or play is too unreal and mechanical to be convincing or even interesting: the sheep are all on one side and the goats on the other—the characters are either white or black. Close to this is the danger of falling into a shopworn formula: there is a picture of the oppression of the working class in the first two acts, for example, with a triumphant revolution or strike or a sudden outburst of proletarian consciousness in the third act. Even the best writer runs the danger of subordinating his characters to his thesis: instead of being interesting for their own sakes, instead of impressing you as living, breathing people that act on their own account, they then become obvious marionettes built to fit the plot and to prove the equation; and one is always conscious of the author pulling the strings. For all his cleverness, most of Bernard Shaw's plays suffer from this defect.

"I hate poetry," said Keats, "that has a palpable design upon me." That line points to the central difficulty of propaganda in all art. It has a design upon you, and the task of the writer is to prevent it from becoming a palpable one. It requires the highest skill to succeed in that task. It would be unfair to condemn all propagandistic work merely by pointing to the innumerable examples of bad propagandistic works, but they must forever stand as awful warnings to the new aspirant. He must never forget that he always has the direct pamphlet in which to agitate specific reforms, and that it is possible to keep them out of his art.

There are, on the other hand, especially in an eruptive period like the present, also dangers in avoiding propaganda. The artist has every right, if he wishes, to ignore the social and political upheavals of his time, and if he is a great artist, he may increase his chances for immortality by doing so. "The world," as Joseph Wood Krutch has eloquently reminded us, "has always been unjust as well as uncertain. . . . It is too bad that men had to be hungry and women had to be dying at the very moment when Newton was inventing the method of fluxions or Gibbon was composing the history of the downfall of Rome. It is too bad that these things had to be done then; but it was far better that they should have been done then than that they should never have been done at all."

There is only one rule: the writer should write about what most interests him, and in the way that he prefers to do it. Good literature is any literature that intensely interests his fellow man; and that is likely to mean, whatever most intensely interests the writer himself. A more narrowly propagandistic literature may interest more men now and fewer men later. A literature with broader aims, without conscious propaganda, on some theme that has little to do with economics or politics, may be neglected today but widely read by the next generation. But what in any case will finally save a work of literature, and make it worth reading, is not the specific doctrines held by its author, but the whole quality and texture of the thought and imagination that go into it.

A Successor to Mark Twain

by Christopher Morley

IF I WERE TO SPEAK OF AN AMERICAN WRITER WHO WAS RAISED IN A
village near the Big River, who had relatively little formal education,
worked in a country printing shop, drifted from city to city as a
newspaper reporter, wrote his first book in rustic Middle West dialect
about an ignorant foundling boy who ran away and went trouping
with patent-medicine doctors and county-fair showmen, you would
know to whom I refer.

Suppose I were to add that this writer, whose faculty of self-
criticism is only vestigial, by some sure instinct reached his best vein
in dealing with outcasts, freaks, ham actors, dogs, boys, kings and
queens, newspaper men, drunkards, and Shakespeare—in fact anyone on the losing side of society but still alert to the bewildering
absurdity of life. That he was always infatuated with theology, and
profoundly reverent in spirit, but united with this so potent a vein
of mother-of-pearl blasphemy and—shall we say—verbal froward-
ness, that his private correspondence will remain mostly unquoted. In
his own person a creature of such high and simple charm that it
would be no exaggeration to call him, in his own circle, the best-loved
man of his time. If I add further, though trying to remain this side
unseasonable intimacies, a man afflicted in private by tragedy's most
savage strokes, you would certainly recognize him. A writer who
fulfills with singular exactness the most vital native tradition of
American letters; whose grotesque and ironic humor was often put
in parables too blunt for intellectuals to perceive; a man whose work
bears on almost every page the stigmata of its origin, conceived under

This essay is from *Letters of Askance* by Christopher Morley, copyright, 1939, by
Christopher Morley, published by J. B. Lippincott Company.

compulsion, blotted before the ink was dry. Of course, you would say, Mark Twain.

But he is not Mark Twain.

The most precious capacity of criticism is the intuition of excellence near at hand, while it still lives and hopes and hungers. It is easy to praise established renown; perhaps a little too much of our academic energy is devoted to that. Do you remember Stephen Leacock's delightful passage where he says that the classics are only primitive literature, and there is no reason why we should revere primitive literature more than primitive machinery or primitive plumbing. But, he says, wrap that message round a stone and throw it through the window of the nearest university, and watch the professors buzz. It is commendable to say, for instance, that La Rochefoucauld was a great master of moral maxims, but that knowledge should also fit us to recognize a man writing with the edge of La Rochefoucauld in the afternoon newspaper. It is often by their living analogues that we get our keenest relish of the great minds of the past. I remember that once when I wrote something in praise of the verse of a contemporary poet, I had a letter from a friend. He wrote: "I'm glad you said what you did about Bill, while he's alive and can enjoy it. I don't think anything is ever quite the same to us after we're dead."

I had intended to withhold a little longer the name of my hero, but since I find myself quoting him already, I'll tell you now. I am talking about Don Marquis. I will try to speak as simply and judiciously as possible. There cannot be time, on such an occasion, to trace in full detail my thesis that he is our closest spiritual descendant of Mark Twain. (The Old Soak would say, descended off of Mark Twain.) That will remain to some extent implicit in these remarks. I suggest the idea to anyone who desiderates a rewarding study in literary ramification. I attempt here only to give something of the psychic background for such an essay.

I had a queer dream about Don once. In that dream he and I were riding in a taxi-cab, furiously driven along Wabash Avenue, Chicago, in a roaring hurry of traffic under the dingy L trestles of the Loop. We were escaping, or trying to escape, from some vast calamity that pressed close behind. What, I don't exactly know—whether fire, flood, storm, earthquake, or, perhaps more likely in Chicago, what insurance policies call "civil commotion." At any rate we were fleeing desperately, looking over our shoulders through the back window of the cab to see whether the terror was gaining on us. And I vividly remember Don saying, "If we can get out to the Dunes it'll be all right." He meant, of course, the famous sand hills of Indiana, along the shore of the Lake.

In our obsession of horror they symbolized a clean escape into sunlight and open spaces and peace. How often I have said to myself: "Dear old boy, he never got out to the dunes." Few of us ever do. Every imaginer dreams of that perfect equilibrium, where pure sensibility of reception is balanced by the joyful pulse of accomplishment. (The physics department would have a less pedantic phrase for it. They would probably say, where stress divided by strain is constant.) There is always one more bit of hackwork to be ground out before we can get at the great masterpiece. More ironical still, when we deliberately sit down to tackle the annunciated masterpiece, how often it goes wooden in our hands. The journeyman job we drudged at day by day, and grimly estimated as potboiling, perhaps was the big thing after all. I'm sure dear old Dr. Johnson, as he ground away at his *Lives of the Poets,* cursed them as hackwork; yet in every paragraph they show the volume and pressure of that leviathan intelligence, breaching in the white foam of humor.

So it was with Don Marquis. In the recurrent hodiernity of the Sun Dial, from 1913 to 1922 in the New York *Evening Sun,* six days a week, bedevilled by a million interruptions and beclamored by all the agreeable rattles, the social riveters who gang round a man trying to work, Marquis created something utterly his own. It was as racy of our day as Addison and Steele's *Spectator* of theirs. I have said before, the American press has much to apologize for—more all the time with its increasing elements of what Lewis Carroll called Uglification, Distraction, and Derision—but much can also be forgiven when you think of the newspapers, the *Sun* and the New York *Tribune,* that saw Don's quality and gave him free hand.

I speak feelingly, for when I came to work in New York in 1913 as a boy fresh from Oxford—how fresh, you would have to have been a pre-War boy to realize—the Sun Dial, then less than a year old, was the first journalistic specialty I noticed. Its freakish pungency, offhand gusto, bewildering alternation of seriousness and buffoonery, of delicate lyric and prattfall slapstick, how different from the prim journalism I had been trained to esteem. Contagion was immediate. I had lately passed through the fevers of an early Stevensonian influenza, and was ripe for new inoculations. Literary beginnings are always imitative. At once I wanted, if not necessarily to write like Mr. Marquis, at least to get a chance to try to run a column of that kind. Eventually I did, and if anyone were to embarrass me by studying the matter they would see how admiringly I followed Don's technique. I don't think anyone noticed it, because I started in a Philadelphia paper, the most perfect form of secrecy.

I must have absorbed the Marquisian style fairly well, because some years later he and I planned to do a novel in collaboration. We mapped out the story in alternate sections to be told by two narrators: he to impersonate one and I the other. Then Don was prevented by illness from doing his share, so I wrote the whole thing; but the portions that had been allotted to him I tried to write as I thought he would have done. The book was published over both our names, and almost every reviewer remarked how easy it was to tell where Morley stopped and Marquis began. That book gave me one of my few opportunities to break even with Don for many practical japes; I sent him a copy inscribed "With regards from the author."

Don's own literary beginnings were dangerously close to mimicry. His first book, *Danny's Own Story,* published in 1912, is much too obviously Mark Twain material. It is written with savor and charm, but the memory of Huck Finn and Tom Sawyer keeps blurring the reader's focus. And there's another interesting influence to be noted. Marquis worked as a young man in close association with one of America's very greatest geniuses, Joel Chandler Harris. In his late years Harris conducted *Uncle Remus's Magazine,* of which Marquis became assistant editor. If you take a man who has the natural bent of Mark Twain, and then have him trained by Uncle Remus, you needn't be surprised if the result is remarkable (it's rather astonishing that he can write conventional English at all). Also, Marquis's formative years as a short-story writer were during the meteor passage of O. Henry. All these three can be divined in some of his work. But, as I say, almost every writer begins on borrowed capital. The important thing is to be able to pay it back, in due course, with earnings of your own.

I suppose we should have some biographical data. It is always disconcerting to realize how little we know, even in our intimate friends, of the factors that have been really operative. In the case of one who becomes to any degree a public figure, legend quickly coalesces; and sometimes the legend is truer than the fact. A good many years ago (in 1916) Don wrote out at my request a sketch of his life up to that time. It is obviously jocular, but the jocularities are sincere and reveal more of the man than you might suppose:

Born July 29, 1878, at Walnut, Bureau Co., Ill., a member of the Republican party.

My father was a physician, and I had all the diseases of the time and place free of charge.

Nothing further happened to me until, in the summer of 1896, I left the Republican party to follow the Peerless Leader to defeat.

In 1900 I returned to the Republican party to accept a position in the Census Bureau, at Washington, D.C. This position I filled for some months in a way highly satisfactory to the Government in power. It is particularly gratifying to me to remember that one evening, after I had worked unusually hard at the Census Office, the late President McKinley himself nodded and smiled to me as I passed through the White House grounds on my way home from toil. He had heard of my work that day, I had no doubt, and this was his way of showing me how greatly he appreciated it.

Nevertheless, shortly after President McKinley paid this public tribute to the honesty, efficiency, and importance of my work in the Census Office, I left the Republican party again and accepted a position as reporter on a Washington paper.

Upon entering the newspaper business all the troubles of my earlier years disappeared as if by magic, and I have lived the contented, peaceful, unworried life of the average newspaper man ever since.

There is little more to tell. In 1916 I again returned to the Republican party. This time it was for the express purpose of voting against Mr. Wilson. Then Mr. Hughes was nominated, and I left the Republican party again.

This is the outline of my life in its relation to the times in which I live. For the benefit of those whose curiosity extends to more particular details, I add a careful pen picture of myself.

It seems more modest, somehow, to put it in the third person:

Height, 5 feet 10½ inches; hair, dove-colored; scar on little finger of left hand; has assured carriage, walking boldly into good hotels and mixing with patrons on terms of equality; weight, 200 pounds; face slightly asymmetrical but not definitely criminal in type; loathes Japanese art, but likes beefsteak and onions; wears No. 8 shoe; fond of Francis Thompson's poems; inside seam of trousers, 32 inches; imitates cats, dogs, and barnyard animals for the amusement of young children; eyetooth in right side of upper jaw missing; has always been careful to keep thumb-prints from possession of police; chest measurement, 42 inches, varying with respiration; sometimes wears glasses, but usually operates undis-guised; dislikes the works of Rabindranath Tagore; corn on little toe of right foot; superstitious, especially with regard to psychic phenomena; eyes blue; does not use drugs nor read his verses to women's clubs; ruddy complexion; no photograph in possession of police; garrulous and argu-mentative; prominent cheekbones; avoids Bohemian society, so called, and has never been in a thieves' kitchen, a broker's office, nor a class of short-story writing; wears 17-inch collar; waist measurement none of your business; favorite disease, hypochondria; prefers the society of painters, actors, writers, architects, preachers, sculptors, publishers, edi-tors, musicians, among whom he often succeeds in insinuating himself, avoiding association with crooks and reformers as much as possible; walks with rapid gait; mark of old fracture on right shin; cuffs on trousers, and coat cut loose, with plenty of room under the armpits; two hip pockets; dislikes Roquefort cheese, "Tom Jones," Wordsworth's poetry, absinthe cocktails, most musical comedy, public banquets, physical exercise, Billy Sunday, steam heat, toy dogs, poets who wear their souls outside, or-ganized charity, magazine covers, and the gas company; prominent calluses on two fingers of right hand prevent him being expert pistol shot; belt straps on trousers; long upper lip; clean shaven; shaggy eye-brows; affects soft hats; smile, one-sided; no gold fillings in teeth; has served six years of indeterminate sentence in Brooklyn, with no attempt to escape, but is reported to have friends outside; voice, husky; scar above the forehead concealed by hair; commonly wears plain gold ring on little finger of left hand; dislikes prunes, tramp poets, and imitations of Kipling; trousers cut loose over hips and seat; would likely come along quietly if arrested.

There was always a sort of pleasing astonishment to me in the name of Don's birthplace: the village of Walnut, in Bureau County. It will take some searching before you find it on the map (even in the latest census the population was only 833). Don once described it as one of those towns that prop two cornfields apart. It's in northwestern Illinois, about on a line with Rock Island and only some thirty miles

from the nearest bend of the Mississippi. I've always wanted to make
a pilgrimage to Walnut, which would excite me every bit as much
as my boyhood excursion on a bicycle to Stratford on Avon. I've
never even seen photographs of the place, because all the Marquis
family souvenirs were destroyed by fire a good many years ago.
It must have been a very Tom Sawyerish boyhood. What I would
particularly like to see is if there isn't a big swamp somewhere near
by, so many of Don's stories deal with queer people and happenings
in a sort of wild morass on the outskirts of town. I was thrilled a
couple of years ago to find myself on a Rock Island train going
through that part of the country, but Walnut itself is not on a main
line and I missed it. I remember sitting in a swaying club car writing
a poem to Don about it; he complained afterward that the hand-
writing was so bad he never could read it. As a matter of fact the
train rolled and pitched so that we were across the Big River before I could get my rhymes firm on their feet, so for my refrain I
used Iowa instead of Illinois. The last stanza went like this—

> O plant the flat feet, porter,
>   As firmly as you may;
> O sleeper, cleave to mattress,
>   O waiter, clutch your tray.
> Past Mark Twain's Mississippi
>   That flows dark brown with clay
> We're swinging, clinging, singing
>   Our Middle-West hurray:
> We ride the old Rock Island
> That goes to Denver's highland,
> The rockety Rock Island
> That rolls through Ioway!

I mentioned this doggerel only as an incentive to Middle Western
patriotism, for Marquis remains the greatest writer of that origin
who has not really been discovered by his own country.

In later years Don used to insist on a family tradition that he was
born during a total eclipse of the sun. Considerable stress was to be
laid on this in a book he and I sometimes meditated, which was to
be ostensibly a life of Shakespeare but actually a sort of double
autobiography of ourselves. We were struck, as everyone must have
been, by the extraordinary number of our own intimate thoughts that

Shakespeare had expressed—often rather better than we could. He must have been somehow spying on us; and the idea was to see what episodes in our own experience might account for or confirm what Shakespeare had written. To avoid any possible embarrassment we would each attribute to the other any behavior that might seem discreditable; or if necessary ascribe it to Shakespeare. We had heard rumors that there was doubt among scholars as to Shakespeare's identity, or even whether there ever was any such person; we felt that if he had used so much of our own private circumstance we had as good a right to him as anyone else. We were astonished and grieved when we learned presently that Mark Twain had done something along this line, though certainly not so carefully thought out. I think it was called *Is Shakespeare Dead?* So the "Life of Shakespeare–Marquis–Morley" was abandoned, but it started Don thinking about an "egobiography" of his own. He made a good many starts at it, and the later versions I never saw, but I have here the very first, Codex A. I think I must share a little of it:

Dear Kit:

I am engaged upon writing a Biography of Don Marquis, which will (or may if I don't get tired of it) some day appear as if it had been written by Perry Gordon. The first few pages I have just written in the last few minutes. It will be the literal truth about my life, but it will always have the double feeling, Well, believe it or not! Many won't. That's where the joke will come in. I'm going to put into it a lot of letters which Mr. Marquis wrote to various people; some of which he just wrote as he wrote the book. I enclose a sample of it; there will be a number of these letters to you, and if the point ever comes up—I don't see how it could— you must swear I wrote them to you.

Yours as per eternally,
Don

THE BIOGRAPHY OF DON MARQUIS

by

Perry Gordon

Chapter One

Any biographer of Don Marquis is assailed at once by the initial difficulty that Mr. Marquis has always taken a perverse delight in mystifying people with regard to himself. Christopher Morley charged him with it, ten or twelve years ago, when Mr. Morley was preparing a biographical essay concerning him, and Marquis wrote in reply:

> It is quite true that I have invented for myself a good many experiences which I never really had. But they were all experiences which belonged to me by right of temperament and character. I should have had them, if I had but had my rights. I was despoiled of them by the rough tyranny of Circumstance. On the other hand, I have suppressed a number of incidents which actually happened, because I did not, upon mature reflection, find them in consonance with my nature as I like to think it is—they were lies that were told about me by the slinking facts of life. Evangelists of various descriptions assure us that we can make the future what we will, if we can but attain a sufficient degree of spirituality. It has been my endeavor to attain such a degree of spirituality that I may be able to influence the past as well as the future. You may think the aspiration is a trifle too optimistic, but you can scarcely deny that it is a worthy aspiration. I should not care to have any notes written about my life at all, unless they were notes that had a tendency to redress these balances. If there are numbers of people, sufficient to justify a biographical paper, who wish to know the truth about me, I must insist that it is the truth which they get, and not merely a series of dislocated facts—facts which, but too frequently, have no logical relation to my character as I know it to be. And who should know it better than myself?

There is always the doubt as to whether a man is the best judge of himself. And it is almost certain that he will not show the figure to the world that he sees in his bright moments of self-appreciation—and Marquis is a queer mixture of flamboyant self-appreciation and really humble self-depreciation. I never knew a man who devoted more time to thinking about himself; I never knew a man who thought of himself more variously, or who was less capable of a steady clarity in looking at himself. So I have made it my business to investigate every incident recorded in this book, wherever possible; and sometimes with surprising results.

The difficulties go as far back as the date of the man's birth, and even include his proper name.

"I was born (Mr. Marquis habitually told this to his friends for many years; he put it in print several times, and he wrote it in a number of letters to friends which I have seen)—I was born during a total eclipse of the sun, at 3 o'clock in the afternoon of July 29th, 1878."

The fact is, that Mr. Marquis does not know whether he was born during the eclipse, or merely on the same day. There is no doubt of the day and year, but there is no one now living who can testify to the exact hour. Not that it makes any great difference; but it shows the character of the difficulties which confront a biographer; difficulties which Mr. Marquis, as often as not, refuses to take seriously—although he can usually be made to confirm the literal fact in the end if it is presented to him and enough insistence made. I wrote him, asking him how he knew he was born during the eclipse itself, for I had received a hint from other quarters to the effect that he did not know, and was romancing. I quote from the reply which I received:

> Don't take that eclipse from me! I have always loved that eclipse. It makes me seem more remarkable to myself. I've told about it and written about it so often that it would make me look like a liar if it should not turn out to be literally true; and while I don't mind lying now and then I always hate to look like a liar. How do you know it isn't true? How do I know it isn't true? The fact is, I was born on July 29th, 1878, and there was an eclipse that day—you can go and look that up, if you don't believe it—and it may very well be that I was born just at the time the eclipse was going on. Poems have been written about it; and anything that a poem has been written about becomes true at once, if it is a good poem. Look at the siege of Troy! How much truer that story is because we do not know the literal truth of those skirmishes which Homer sang into immortality. I do not want my life related with a dribble of cold facts; I want it sung, as Homer would sing it. I insist on the eclipse. To me it has always seemed a portent from the gods. I would like you to say: "The sun retired, brooded apart, thought, shadowing his forehead in his hands; and then, his mind made up, tossed Marquis upon the surface of this planet." This is the thought at the center of my life which has enabled me to survive many discouragements and traverse many vales of vicissitude; this thought that, after all, I was *intended* by the sun himself. Do not take it from me. How do I know that it was not literally true? Even in the face of a definite literal record (which does not exist) I should continue to believe it. I must. It is a necessity of my nature to connect myself with the core of the universe by every possible strand. I am either a child of the gods, or I am nothing at all. I believe in gods, and I love gods; an honest god is the noblest work of man. "I will have my eclipse!"

The definite literal record does not exist; this is the one definite literal fact which we get from Mr. Marquis's rhodomontade. And the present biographer has had no end of trouble winnowing such small facts from such overflowing measures of chaff.

That subtle psychological observation that the things that actually happen to us are often wretchedly unrepresentative of our true selves is one to which Marquis often recurs. But I want to make plain that I think the twelve years of column writing in New York, theoretically the worst possible vehicle for a finely imaginative talent, were in fact magnificent. There, with increasing power, his essential originality came through. From those newspaper files most of his best books have been scissored out—or, to be exact, photostatted. As a note for bibliographers, I suppose Marquis is one of the few authors whose original book manuscripts exist chiefly in the form of tall albums of newspaper columns photographed from the Public Library. I remember one time he came out to our house for dinner, and as he entered the door took out a narrow roll of newsprint from his pocket, trailing it behind him. He crossed all the rooms on the ground floor, emitting this ribbon of paper, and then, as it was still uncoiling, started upstairs. Finally of course came the question he was playing for: "What do you think you are, a spider?" "It's the manuscript of my new play," he said. It had been running in his column, at irregular intervals, for months. He had cut out all the sections, and pasted them together endways.

From the files of the column came his book of *Prefaces;* then that notable series of philosophic ruminations called *The Almost Perfect State;* the volumes of verse; the soliloquies of the Old Soak; and the adventures of archy and mehitabel. These things were born in the rough and tumble of a newspaper office: I remember that in the early days of the Sun Dial when the paper moved from Park Row to Nassau Street, Don's typewriter desk got lost in the skirmish; so for some years he rattled out his daily stint with his machine perched on an upended packing case. This box had stenciled on it the statement I GROSS TOM CAT, which meant Tomato Catsup, but became by legend the first suggestion of mehitabel.

In a daily column, necessarily a great deal of matter is of ephemeral reference. Much of Marquis's most brilliant work in those years was in the form of oblique comment on public affairs; it requires the current event to make it understandable, and has not come through into book publication. But with sufficient lapse of time it becomes again important as a part of historic record. I have often been astonished that the chroniclers of national temper during the

War years, and during the steadily heightening tension before 1917, have mostly drawn their newspaper quotation from the solemn editorialists. But in those days, when anything important happened, I give you my word most of us didn't consult the leading editorials to know what to think. The almost universal reflex, in New York at any rate, was "Let's see what Don says about it." I'm not saying that I always agreed, then or now, with Don's notions; but every now and then he would turn on some particular fog of hooey and cut it with a blade that would divide floating silk. Some of those old clippings, yellowed with more than twenty years, I still keep. One was at the time of the great revolution in Russia. The Bolshevik *coup d'état* was accompanied, as the bloodiest revolutions usually are, by paregoric announcements of universal brotherhood and peace. Don's comment was brief and piercing: "A kind word was seen on the streets of Petrograd, attempting to butter a parsnip." And though it ran counter to my own private hero worship, I chuckled and still do at a comment on Woodrow Wilson about the time of the Peace Conference:

An ocean rolls all pebbles interned within it or abutting upon it; but it may be difficult for an ocean, upon request, to roll any one particular pebble a measured and certain twenty inches north or west on any particular beach. President Wilson (with his great tides) may move all the pebbles of mundane statesmanship, and trace with his ebbs and flows impressive and cryptic and everchanging symbols upon the agitated sands; but we have often felt that when it comes to picking up any one designated pebble and putting it into any one designated little red pail upon a beach President Wilson fumbles. [Sun Dial, August 7, 1919.]

There is a whole generation of newspaper readers around New York who will remember as long as brain cells hold together those occasional flashes of magnesium. With a magic that seemed like that of Alice going through the mirror, suddenly we saw the whole furniture of affairs from the other side. When President Wilson brusquely dismissed his secretary of state, Mr. Lansing, for instance, and Marquis burlesqued it by dismissing archy. Or when Mr. Henry Ford was catechized on his knowledge of history by a congressional committee. There had been no such commentator on public affairs since Mr. Dooley; they don't come often.

But it is only too characteristic of the Solemn Skullworkers that because many of Marquis's most pungent comments on the human comedy were put in the form of soliloquies by the Old Soak or by archy the roach, they could not recognize their high coefficient of seriousness. I was amazed to discover that Max Eastman's *Enjoyment of Laughter,* a book with a depressing picture on the jacket showing the author roaring with mirth, and including diagrams analyzing the various phases of a joke, made no mention whatever of the most philosophical humorist of our time. That was, to me, the biggest laugh in the book.

I remember from college days that there was someone called Democritus, of Abdera, nicknamed the Laughing Philosopher. What was there about Abdera that encouraged humor? Was it the fact that its inhabitants became proverbial for stupidity? Perhaps it was there that someone first became aware of the deep truth that the great things, even the best laughters, happen unpremeditated. The notion of the office cockroach butting the typewriter with his head was not, to begin with, very promising or even very original. (John Kendrick Bangs tried a similar idea with a June bug a good many years ago, and abandoned it.) The use of nothing but lower-case font, and no punctuation (because the roach couldn't manage the shift key) once adopted had to be continued, and was probably worth while as a stunt, though that—like the typographical tricks in *Tristram Shandy*—is a primary kind of waggishness. It has resulted in some of Don's subtlest comment and some of his most humorous bits of verse being buried in irregular strips of print not easy to read. I think for instance of the superb fragment of Shakespearean criticism *The Parrot and Shakespeare,* in *archy and mehitabel.* I succeeded some time ago in getting this adopted as practically required reading in a Shakespeare course at Smith College, but it is still too little known:

> i got acquainted with
> a parrot named pete recently
> who is an interesting bird
> pete says he used
> to belong to the fellow
> that ran the mermaid tavern
> in london then i said
> you must have known
> shakespeare know him said pete

poor mutt i knew him well
he called me pete and i called him
bill but why do you say poor mutt
well said pete bill was a
disappointed man and was always
boring his friends about what
he might have been and done
if he only had a fair break
two or three pints of sack
and sherris and the tears
would trickle down into his
beard and his beard would get
soppy and wilt his collar
i remember one night when
bill and ben jonson and
frankie beaumont
were sopping it up

here i am ben says bill
nothing but a lousy playwright
and with anything like luck
in the breaks i might have been
a fairly decent sonnet writer
i might have been a poet
if i had kept away from the theatre

yes says ben i ve often
thought of that bill
but one consolation is
you are making pretty good money
out of the theatre

money money says bill what the hell
is money what i want is to be
a poet not a business man
these damned cheap shows
i turn out to keep the
theatre running break my heart
slap stick comedies and
blood and thunder tragedies
and melodramas say i wonder
if that boy heard you order
another bottle frankie

the only compensation is that i get
a chance now and then
to stick in a little poetry
when nobody is looking
but hells bells that isn t
what i want to do
i want to write sonnets and
songs and spenserian stanzas
and i might have done it too
if i hadn t got
into this frightful show game
business business business
grind grind grind
what a life for a man
that might have been a poet

well says frankie beaumont
why don t you cut it bill
i can t says bill
i need the money i ve got
a family to support down in
the country well says frankie
anyhow you write pretty good
plays bill any mutt can write
plays for this london public
says bill if he puts enough
murder in them what they want
is kings talking like kings
never had sense enough to talk
and stabbings and stranglings
and fat men making love
and clowns basting each
other with clubs and cheap puns
and off color allusions to all
the smut of the day oh i know
what the low brows want
and i give it to them

well says ben jonson
don t blubber into the drink
brace up like a man
and quit the rotten business

i can t i can t says bill
i ve been at it too long i ve got to
the place now where i can t
write anything else
but this cheap stuff
i m ashamed to look an honest
young sonneteer in the face
i live a hell of a life i do
the manager hands me some mouldy old
manuscript and says
bill here s a plot for you
this is the third of the month
by the tenth i want a good
script out of this that we
can start rehearsals on
not too big a cast
and not too much of your
damned poetry either
you know your old
familiar line of hokum
they eat up that falstaff stuff
of yours ring him in again
and give them a good ghost
or two and remember we gotta
have something dick burbage can get
his teeth into and be sure
and stick in a speech
somewhere the queen will take
for a personal compliment and if
you get in a line or two somewhere
about the honest english yeoman
it s always good stuff
and it s a pretty good stunt
bill to have the heavy villain
a moor or a dago or a jew
or something like that and say
i want another
comic welshman in this
but i don t need to tell
you bill you know this game
just some of your ordinary

hokum and maybe you could
kill a little kid or two a prince
or something they like
a little pathos along with
the dirt now you better see burbage
tonight and see what he wants
in that part oh says bill
to think i am
debasing my talents with junk
like that oh god what i wanted
was to be a poet
and write sonnet serials
like a gentleman should

Archy the roach began as a "dee-vice" of scoff against the vers libre poets who were pallidly conspicuous some twenty years ago. But that idea was soon forgotten. Mehitabel the corybantic cat, with her doctrine of *toujours gai,* came on the scene to provide lyric spasms; archy became less the clown and more the skeptical commentator. I don't propose to maxeastman the matter by avoirdupois analysis, nor insist that these two grotesque false-faces provided just the mechanism Marquis's genius required. We could suggest that archy is the Mickey Mouse of the highbrows, but the kind of people who have enjoyed him do not need to have it rubbed in on them that there is much more there than sheer enjoyment. The right sort of reader, unspoiled by painful palaver, feels that sort of thing by sensitive instinct—and resents pedestrian footnotes.

Anyhow, the roach and the cat, by their humble station in life and the lowliness of their associates, provided an admirable vantage for merciless joshing of everything biggity. Those who only noted archy's doings in the hasty reading of the daily papers, or in *Collier's,* which he afterward infested, may scarcely have realized the precision of his best spoof. The last book of the three (*archy does his part,* 1935), though it contains some of the best stuff, also was more carelessly edited, or photostatted, than the others. A lot of irrelevant matter got in that obviously should have been dropped; but as a journeyman student of such affairs I do not regret this. It shows the author laboring, as everyone in such a task must often labor, under the stress of deadline and fatigue, mechanically going through the motions of assembling a batch of copy—and then there used to happen to Don what only happens to the man gifted by the gods. The automatic motions were replaced by the authoritative inward heat; his magical and stupendous fecundity took charge, and some totally unexpected gorgeousness would explode. As an instance I offer the whinnying absurdity of archy climbing Mount Everest, in the course of which he meets the Dalai Lama, mehitabel, the Taj Mahal, and the Czar of All the Russias (who is living on canned heat). Among any number of exquisitely abominable belly laughs in this piece, the one that most cruelly besets me is the Czar's explanation why the sun never set on his dominions. "They were too cold to hatch." Archy discovers a "virgin gold mine." How do you know it is virgin, mehitabel wants to know—she is expertly skeptical in such matters. "Give it the benefit of the doubt," says the Dalai Lama, but archy is sanguine—

> well it seems reasonable said i
> there is a snow slide
> over it every twenty minutes

Or, in the precious album of things that Really Are Funny, see archy's radio interviews on the Roach Paste Hour, or his ribbing of the Experts in Washington.

Like all old troupers, Don has always been delightfully shameless to use a familiar chestnut when (in the words of mehitabel in one of her best pieces) "he doesn't feel it here" (putting paw on bosom). He has the unerring instinct for things that are universal sure-fire, recognized all the world over as comic. Green vegetables are always funny, and bad poets, and winter underwear, and feet. He does not scruple, in extremity, to use the dreadful antique of the passenger who takes off his shoe just as the streetcar is passing the glue factory (the first glue factory was probably in Abdera), and he uses again and again certain little whimwhams of his own of which he has grown fond. The flea that brags about having bitten the lion and made him cower; the bullhead that learns to live out of water; the man who pulls out his glass eye in the subway car and eats it, explaining that it's a pickled onion—what frolic the sedentary psychologist might have in computing some soul dynamic on the frequent reappearance of these episodes. (Freuds rush in where angels fear to

tread, as archy once said.) The practising journalist smiles affection-
ately and says, "Good old boy, that day he was hard up for copy." And
then, among routine comedy, there stream rockets of cold fire—

>   that stern and rockbound coast
>   felt like an amateur
>   when it saw how grim the puritans
>   that landed on it were

Or the egotistic lightning bug that said

>   all I need is a harbor
>   under me to be a
>   statue of liberty

But archy took him down:

>   you ve made lightning for two hours
>   little bug but i don t hear
>   any claps of thunder

If you want to see archy in his best philosophic vein, examine the
fable called *The Robin and the Worm,* in *archy and mehitabel.* Like
the Uncle Remus fables of Don's old boss, it has superb social analo-
gies that are being illustrated all around us every moment. Exactly
like the absorption of the worm (both gastric and psychic), a placid
economic peristalsis is now taking effect in the United States—almost
unsuspected by some digestees.

So I ask myself again, what was the happy quiddity of Abdera that
gave its first citizen this richest gift of all—this incalculable unpredict-
able joy of the grotesque, the magic to show us truth in the very shout
of laughter. First the mirthquake, as Don said long ago, and then
the still small voice. In a riotously absurd piece of kidding, the
"Preface to the Prospectus of a Club," Don was talking about
Brooklyn:

Walt Whitman used to live over there and edit the *Eagle* and go
swimming in Buttermilk Channel, two points off the starboard bow of
Hank Beecher's church. Once an old Long Island skipper sunk a harpoon into Walt's haunch when he came up to blow, and the poet, snort-
ing and bellowing and spouting verse, towed the whaler and his vessel
clear out to Montauk before he shook the iron loose. Is there a bard in
Greenwich Village that could do that?

What I'm suggesting, and the whole gist of this little tribute, is that this casual comic paragraph, in the very guts and gusto of its Munchausenism, contains more shrewd criticism of Walt than many a whole solemn tome by the serious little people who write books about Moby Walt.—If you don't discern that, there's no use your reading Don Marquis—or Walt Whitman either.

I want to say a word of Mr. Marquis as divinity student. This came back to me the other day when a friend told me he was going to attend a kinsman's graduation from theological seminary. The thought occurred to me—but I did not say it, for it would have required some explanation—that the ideal graduation gift for a young parson (with a sense of humor) would be two of Don Marquis's books: *The Old Soak's History of the World* and *Chapters for the Orthodox.*

The Old Soak became folklore during the Bootleg era. He was not merely the denizen of "a nose-red city, pickled half the time," if Bartlett will pardon us. You will remember that beautiful portrait (as pathetic as comic) of the old boozer's fumbling mind, his incoherent attempts to express the simple kindliness and good humor he had known in the reputable saloon—to say nothing of its stimulus to art ("hand-paintings"), politics, and home life. Mr. Clem Hawley was also no mean student of Holy Writ. His retelling of Old Testament stories, in his *History of the World,* is to me some of the most genuinely laughable stuff ever written. And in the course of his exegetics the Old Soak makes a profound remark which must be remembered by those who find themselves shocked by Mr. Marquis's apparent levity. The Old Soak vigorously objects to Mr. Hennery Withers, the "dam little athyiss," laughing at the fable of Jonah. "Only its friends," he says, "got a right to laugh at that story." The laughter in *Chapters for the Orthodox* is sometimes cerebral, sometimes violently of the midriff, but those who will take pains to explore under the superficial shock will find it always the laughter of a friend.

The Old Soak, incidentally, always stood up for his trinity of fundamentals: the Bible, calomel, and straight whiskey. Mr. Marquis himself has been equally conservative in his choice of apostolic matter. It has come down to us by unbroken laying on of hands. The literary genealogy of Mr. Hawley was suggested with gorgeous impudence when Mrs. Quickly's deathwatch for Falstaff was echoed in the hired girl's epitaph on the parrot. I'm ashamed to say I had forgotten this colossal jape until I heard it again recently in the talking picture. They've been trying Al's homemade hootch on the parrot:

He's gone, Mr. Hawley. He's d-d-d-dead! Seriously dead! It happened a half hour ago. I think it was his constitution undermined itself with that hootch Al brought here the other night, and I never will forgive myself, I won't. But he kept coaxin' and coaxin' for it that pretty that I couldn't refuse him. . . . And he kept drinking of it till he deceased himself with it. He called out to me about a half hour ago, he did. "Fair weather," he says, and then he laughed. Only he didn't laugh natural. Mr. Hawley, he laffed kind of puny and feeble like there was somethin' furrin weighin' onto his stomach. "I can't give you any more Peter," I says to him, "for there ain't no more," I says. And then he stretched his neck out and bit the wire on his cage and squawked, for he says in a kind of sad voice: "Nellie was a lady, she was," he says. And them was the last words he ever give utterings to. (*Exit Hired Girl, weeping.*)

Chapters for the Orthodox, perhaps Marquis's most brilliant and least known book, I have always felt restricted from discussing on account of the author's affectionate partiality exhibited in the dedication. However, the formal phobias mean less and less as time shortens, and because I am fond of parsons and wish them well I set scruple aside. A man who has been through the anxieties of the seminary, and emerged with his Bachelorhood of Sacred Theology, is surely grounded in faith to stand a few jolts. That book was timidly published (1934) and timidly dealt with by the Trade. My own feeling about it was that its only chance was to be offered as a translation from some other language, in which case it might perhaps have been a sensation. It would be hard to find anything more in the spirit of Voltaire than the first story—"Miss Higginbotham Declines"—with its glorious opening sentence: "It was Jehovah's custom, when he came to New York, to put on the material appearance and manner of a member of the Union League Club; indeed, he used the club itself a great deal."

I remember offering (don't laugh) to translate that story into French and try to get it published in that language, but could persuade no one—not even the author. But its delicate and reverent ribaldries would shock no one under the screen of a different tongue. The barb of the parable, as the new Bachelor will soon perceive, is a prickly one. Jehovah, brooding on the problems of humanity (and especially New York City), decides that what the world needs is another Begotten Son. This implies the necessity of finding for the purpose . . . but perhaps you'd better read it yourself.

In short, the book is devout to the point of scandal. Semireligious people are always horrified by completely religious people; ethical ideas, as every philosopher has observed, are loaded with dynamite and perilous indeed for every kind of establishment. The world (said Santayana in a fine passage) is always a caricature of itself, always pretending to be something quite other than what it actually is. And to pretend to take those pretences literally is always horrifying. Nothing disturbs, or surprises, man so much as the discrepancy between his professions and his actual behavior; in that discrepancy lies the mother lode of intellectual comedy. Marquis once remarked that he had a great idea: he was going to dramatize some of Bernard Shaw's plays. What he did in *Chapters for the Orthodox* had something of the same double-edged riposte: by taking ticklishly beautiful things with simple seriousness he explodes (in shattering laughter) the towering falsehoods of our genteel imposture.—And then humorously rebuilds them, knowing well that by make-believe we live.

This book, which ranges from tender and moving fable to the most outrageous catcalls and trombone raspberries (uproarious, deplorable, with such blasphemous farcing as a Police Commissioner would not tolerate for even one performance) does actually come somewhere near expressing the blaze and belly laugh of life. The Prosecution of Jesus by the swine dealer of Gadara (for having damaged the pork business), with Jehovah on the bench and Satan as prosecuting attorney and a number of well-known contemporaries as jurymen, is a fair example of Marquis's audacious method. As a characteristic spoof of Britain, one of the demons (when called on to testify) speaks in a strong cockney accent. But it is impossible to give any idea of a book like this without frightening or scandalizing the casual reader. Are they so few, I have sadly asked myself, who can see beneath this cosmic clowning the flash of its genial piety? Indeed, as Don said in his preface, he sports "in spiritual essence like a porpoise in the Gulf Stream."

It is in this book, apropos of nothing in particular, that Marquis pays his great—I wish I could say famous—tribute to Mark Twain. I can think of nothing truer to say of *Chapters for the Orthodox* than this: it is the book Mark Twain must often have talked, and would have liked to write, but was too canny to do so.—That one-act skit of Faust in Hell . . . really, Mr. Marquis, really . . . .

Welladay! (as Don says in the sonnets)—it's futile to try to suggest—in the cold sobriety of the platform—the quick-change paradoxes, the chameleon flicker, of a sultry mind.

Let me mention one more noble paradox. Marquis's finely realized play of the crucifixion, *The Dark Hours,* was produced, largely at his own charges, from profits made on the hokum of the dramatized *Old Soak*.

Briefly to recapitulate, for the benefit of our imagined research student, the lines of parallelism where you will find in Marquis and Mark Twain temperamental affinity. You will observe it in their fundamental comedian's instinct to turn suddenly, without warning, from the beautiful to the grotesque, or vice versa. You will find it in a rich vein of anger and disgust, turning on the genteel and cruel hypocrisies with the fury of a child or an archangel. You will find it in a kindly and respectful charity to the underdog: they are both infracaninophiles. You will find it in their passionate interest in religion and philosophy—with which is joined a blandly mischievous delight in shocking those for whom shocking is good. You will find it—though I can't help you in this just now—in their habitual employment of a devastating Anglo-Saxonism of speech and epithet. And finally you'll observe that both had a keen (and somewhat ham) dramatic sense, which Marquis expressed in plays and Mark Twain in his superlative performances on the lecture platform.

But there is one quality in Don that Mark never had—or at any rate it was only latent in Mark. Don is a poet, and a poet of high technical dexterity. He remarked once that publishing a volume of verse was like dropping a rose petal down the Grand Canyon and waiting for the echo. One reason why the echo has been little audible is that he has puzzled the critics by writing verse of so many different kinds. His gamut has run from lyrics of the most serious and tender mood to the genial fooling of *Noah an' Jonah an' Cap[n] John Smith* or the farcical *Famous Love Affairs* or the sardonic ferocity of the

Savage Sonnets. The sensitive little folks who make a business of collecting and admiring current poetry don't understand such chameleon shifts of color—also, Don has made a lifelong habit of spoofing the Poetry Societies and anything that had the aroma of cult. You remember that lovely verse of Ralph Hodgson—

> Reason has moons, but moons not hers
>   Lie mirrored on her sea,
> Confounding her astronomers,
>   But O! delighting me.

Read Don's "Preface to a Book of Poetry" (in the volume called *Prefaces*) if you want to see how he used to harpoon the solemn, self-appointed custodians of the Muse.

"Write sonnet serials like a gentleman should," he said in the Shakespeare piece. I assign you as homework the reading aloud of the sequence called *Sonnets to a Red-Haired Lady*—where, after thirty-two stinging cocktails of song, he turns on us with four concluding sonnets that—as William Rose Benét has said—might well have been written by the earliest of our great sonneteers, Wyatt or Surrey—

> The poet blots the end the jester wrote:
> For now I drop the dull quip's forced pretence,
> Forego the perch'd fool's dubious eminence—
> Thy tresses I have sung, that fall and float
> Across the lyric wonder of thy throat
> In dangerous tides of golden turbulence
> Wherein a man might drown him, soul and sense,
> Is not their beauty worth one honest note?
>
> And thee, thyself, what shall I say of thee?—
> Are thy snares strong, and will thy bonds endure?
> Thou hast the sense, hast thou the soul of me?
> In subtle webs and silken arts obscure
> Thou hast the sense of me, but canst thou bind
> The scornful pinions of my laughing mind?

"Thou hast the sense of me, but canst thou bind The scornful pinions of my laughing mind"—I tried once in verse of my own to bind those pinions. This was written more than a dozen years ago: I'll quote briefly:

Well-mingled spirit, rich with savory earth
Of humor; poet, jester of fecund mirth
So masterfully simple that it shows
No minim speck of sham, pretence, or pose—
So lit and winged with antic mimicry
That conies of the upper cults, or casuals of the press
Are scarcely competent to guess
Behind that gusty offhand ribaldry
The full control and pressure of great art—
Satire so waggishly disguised
Its victims would have been surprised
To know themselves were being satirized—
Satire that loved them even while it skinned them,
And chloroformed them first, before it pinned them. . . .

A reverent doubtful spirit
And opal-minded, where an inward red
Burns in the milk and moonlight of the gem—
Humble and defiant as all men are,
(Falling, as we do, from star to star),
Droll tragedian, lip pouted to consider
Life's technicals, so crooked and so slidder,
With such strange prizes for the highest bidder—
Old curly cherub, with the poker face, not always shaven,
But with such prankish pensiveness engraven,
You, in an age when almost everyone is clever,
Never declined—No, never—
Into the easy triumphs of the smart,
Old Goldenheart.

. . . I think that those inherit
The bitter coronal, who can most finely wear it:
Shuddering and abased,
But not disgraced;
Proud, proud to have outfaced
The champion stroke, the merciless dirty wit
Of the Player Opposite.
And honor, wine and sunlight yet remain,
Clean wind and washing rain,
And that gigantic mirth that men so need,
And loneliness indeed,
Loneliness, which I rate high,

> And the love of friends,
> And by and by
> Silence, the end of ends.

There's an infinitely touching little poem, toward the end of *The Almost Perfect State,* called *Lines for a Gravestone.* It concludes as follows:

> Speed, I bid you, speed the earth
> Onward with a shout of mirth,
> Fill your eager eyes with light,
> Put my face and memory
> Out of mind and out of sight.
> Nothing I have caused or done,
> But this gravestone, meets the sun:
> Friends, a great simplicity
> Comes at last to you and me!

On this note of lovely kindness, humility, courage and laughter, I should like to close. Of this man, more than of any I have known, the great seventeenth-century words apply—words three centuries old this year and still the most expressive of masculine love and fellowship. I change only the name—*O rare Don Marquis.*

American Drama versus Literature

by WALTER PRICHARD EATON

IN A RECENT CRITICAL ARTICLE ABOUT THE PLAYS OF EUGENE O'NEILL, Professor Homer E. Woodbridge, of Wesleyan University, remarks that "up to the Great War we (i.e., the United States) produced almost no plays of more than immediate contemporary interest— almost none which had literary value or prospect of permanence." He speaks of Quinn's collection, *Representative American Plays,* as "depressing," and concludes: "To get up much interest in the American theatre before O'Neill one must consider it from the historical or sociological point of view."

Well, why not? Is it not perhaps true that in our study of the drama, certainly our academic study, we have put an emphasis on the literary side which neither the nature of the drama nor the function of the theatre wholly warrants, and dismissed as unworthy of study much which, properly considered, is interesting and important? Is it not true, for example, that a great deal of Elizabethan drama has lived as literature (though some of it I venture heretically to hazard is less exalted literature than I was taught in college) by virtue of its poetry, when actually as permanent drama, as stuff capable of being acted in a theatre today and holding an audience, it is quite as dead as the earlier American dramas which so depress Professor Woodbridge? I was taught, and trustingly believed, that *The Way of the World* is one of the most brilliant comedies in our language, in spite of the fact staring me in the face that it failed in Congreve's own day. It was not till I became a worker in the theatre myself that I realized a failure before one's contemporaries means a failure before posterity, and not till I saw *The Way of the World* produced that I realized not only that it isn't the most brilliant comedy in the language, but is actually a very bad play. It has passages of dazzling dialogue—yes. The literary style is brilliant in the extreme. There is a charming female character, and one scene for her of delicious comedy on the stage. But the play pursues a long, confused, and tedious way in getting to it. In plain language, it is a bore. Congreve's contemporaries were right. So why, I now ask myself, should I bow down to this play, which is a bad play, because the dialogue has literary charm? Literary charm is an accident, or overtone, of drama, not its end. The end of drama is the emotional excitation of an audience in a theatre. If that fails, all fails. If that is achieved, even without the aid of literature, we have at least a living playhouse.

In recent years I have had numerous opportunities to see revivals of all sorts of plays, from various languages and periods. Among them have been dramas more or less famous in the annals of English literature, and several of the earlier American plays which so depress Professor Woodbridge (and, lest I seem to single him out, many other commentators on our native literature). It is, I assure you, a fact that something of theatrical verve and effectiveness still lives in certain of these American works which is painfully absent from their resounding literary rivals. Making all due allowance for the greater historical interest, to a native audience, in an American play, it is still impossible not to find the audience response to *The Contrast* or *Fashion* much more warm and spontaneous than to most Restoration comedies, and certainly than to such a Restoration tragedy as *Venice Preserved*. Indeed, an American tragedy in the heroic verse drama tradition, Boker's *Francesca di Rimini,* is far more effective in the theatre today than *Venice Preserved* or any of its companions, even though it is included in Quinn's "depressing" collection of Americana.

It is not my purpose, however, to defend these plays as enduring works of art. It would be as difficult to do that as to defend as enduring works of art nearly all the plays produced in England from the end of the Restoration to the days of Gilbert, Wilde, and Shaw. If you left out two plays by Sheridan and one by Goldsmith, what collection of eighteenth-century English plays could you honestly read without depression? And how about a collection of English plays from 1800 to 1860? We must rule out entirely the closet dramas of the great poets, for their theatrical future is admitted. Who now could read, let alone sit through, without depression, *London Assurance, Money, Richelieu* (unless Booth came back to play it), *Virginius, The Lady of Lyons,* or even perhaps most of Robertson's comedies and Gilbert's *Pygmalion and Galatea?* The fact of the matter is that only in widely separated periods do playwrights arise who combine with enduring theatrical situation an enduring literary style, and hence create for posterity.

It is not entirely true, as Somerset Maugham implies in his latest book of craftsman autobiography, that poetry is essential for survival. Sheridan has certainly survived, or at any rate until very recent times, as a living dramatist, not a mere historical curiosity. But it is undoubtedly a fact that in the majority of cases true survival—that is, the ability to meet the test of paying audiences in the theatre of commerce, generation after generation—is dependent on romantic timelessness of theme, and on poetry, on a heightened speech which transcends its own hour and still sings to the hearts of later ages. And such poetry is so infrequently written by men who can also write plays, and only in periods when it is a fresh and natural expression, not a traditional mold, that the chances for survival of any plays in the theatre are slight indeed.

This is particularly true of the realistic plays characteristic of our generation and the years just preceding it. Indeed, we might almost say that the better they met the exacting test of realism, the slighter were their survival chances; for what gave to the modern drama, i.e., the drama since Ibsen, its vital appeal and its great creative dignity was its newly found technical ability to comment seriously on the contemporary scene, to be a weapon, consciously employed, of social criticism and even of reform. You may if you like call it journalistic, in the sense that it was deliberately contemporaneous, and deliberately discarded all "fine writing" and "bookish" or "literary" language in favor of the actual conversational vernacular of the hour. Not to have done so would have defeated its own ends, shattered the illusion it sought to create. But by so doing it paid the price of impermanence.

Until the coming of modern realism, the life of a successful play in the theatre could often be reckoned by half centuries, at least. Most comedies were based on farcical intrigue. You recall Pinero's definition of a classic comedy—"A successful farce by an author who is dead." It is the farce in *The Rivals* which has given it a superior theatrical vitality to *The School for Scandal.* Molière is farcical to such an extent that in translation his plays, unless acted with the utmost skill, seem almost burlesque. Blank-verse tragedy established a tradition which was accepted for generation after generation, and the theatrically effective plays written in that tradition were the vehicles for actors age after age. *Venice Preserved,* to us a dreary waste of pretentious bombast and unmotivated incident, gave tragediennes a chance to snuggle bloody ghosts and go pathetically mad from 1682 until well into the nineteenth century. It had dropped from the repertoire after the Civil War, but was revived at Booth's Theatre in 1874, in a new version made by Dion Boucicault, with a long speech for Pierre incorporated from Byron's *Marino Faliero.* John McCullough played Pierre, and Fanny Brough, later noted as a comedienne, played Belvidera, evidently very badly. The revival did not succeed. Postwar taste had definitely dated the old play.

From still farther back, Massinger's *New Way to Pay Old Debts* survived into the repertoire of numerous nineteenth-century tragedians, until the last quarter of the century. But when Walter Hampden attempted to revive it in this century, he speedily discovered it an old way to contract new debts. In general, we may almost say that a thoroughly successful play could, until comparatively recent times, count on at least half a century of theatrical life.

But plays in our day, as successful at the time of first production, and I venture with no hesitancy to say often superior in technical construction and intellectual point, even sometimes in emotional appeal, can hardly count on more than a decade or two of theatrical life. It is true that Ibsen's *Doll's House,* an opening gun in that author's campaign for the modern drama, first produced in 1879, was successfully revived in New York last winter. But even that seemed, as we say, a trifle "dated." After all, Nora won her battle some time ago. We all admit women are people now—or Heaven help us if we don't. The play had a job to do; it did it; and that's that. Its permanence is not on the stage, but—shall we say?—in the ballot box. And how about *The Second Mrs. Tanqueray?* How well I recall the tears I wept over Paula's fate in the nineties—and how distressingly uninterested I was in it at a recent revival, by which time society had something else to think about more important than Victorian taboos. Another illustration from the nineties is Henry Arthur Jones's comedy of manners, *The Liars,* a brilliant play, beautifully constructed, and in its day deliciously amusing. But why does the heroine have to lie to her husband, and induce all her friends to lie, also, in her behalf? Because she has gone to dinner with another man! Since, today, she would simply call her husband up and tell him to leave the front door unlatched, the present generation finds no validity in the premise, and hence no fun in the play. It is hopelessly "dated" because once it was dated so accurately.

Shaw (like Ibsen) was wiser in his generation. He dated his plays ahead. But even he, a wit as keen as any Restoration writer, a literary stylist who has to be considered in the same class with Swift, an intellect far deeper and incomparably more earnest of purpose than Congreve or Wycherley, did not date his plays, perhaps, far enough ahead for immortality. Already we have made many of his ideas our own, and the young even call him "old fogy." *Candida,* which does not deal with social ideas as much as with emotions, *Saint Joan,* which is an historical work, and possibly *Heartbreak House* because it is so closely and subtly connected with one of the world's most shattering events, the Great War, may survive a long while. But the others seem already slipping from our repertoire. Who of my hearers, I wonder, recalls that one-act masterpiece by J. M. Barrie, *The Old Lady Shows Her Medals?* Barrie was moved, as we all were, by the psychology of wartime, by the mass urge to do each his bit. He had that psychology to rely on in his audience—he knew exactly the extent and direction of potential response; and with sure, quick strokes of mingled comedy and pathos (the ideal stroke to use if you can master it) he drew our tears. But a whole new generation of theatre-goers has grown up since the War. They know nothing of that psychology which Barrie relied on, which was so important a contemporary element in the success of his play. Would it have the original effect on this new generation? Certainly only in part. In another generation it may be quite forgotten.

Only a little over a decade ago an American play was produced which aroused great interest. It was called *What Price Glory?* and was a lusty, bawdy, disillusioned yet oddly heroic story of a company of American marines, "hard-boiled" professional soldiers, in the

Great War. No one questioned its realism, which went, of course, deeper than expletives and mud-caked uniforms. It caught the spirit of bitter disillusion in most of us at the time, and simultaneously gave us a kind of grimly comic insight into the ironic contrast between amorous instincts deeper than battle lust, and doggedly courageous devotion to duty. It was a fine play, full of color, excitement, humor, truth. But when have you seen it revived? Its theatrical life was two or three brief years. Another enormously effective play produced in 1926 was *Broadway*. It was the saga of the prohibition era, it swirled madly, to a jazz rhythm, through the back rooms of a "speak-easy," with gangsters and "hoofers" and cheap girls and gunfire and murder keeping you on the edge of your seat. It was realistic, and, as a play has no way to be "literary," so far as the academic critics seem to apply the term to drama, save through its dialogue, I suppose *Broadway* was quite without literary merit. One touch of "literature" would have sent illusion reeling. It would have been as out of place as a bar of Beethoven from the "speak-easy" saxophones. But it was capital theatre, and enjoyed a huge success. Where is it now? It has vanished with the Noble Experiment which it so ironically hymned. Its realism both gave it its life, and took its life away.

But there is no need to labor the point further. Even were our theatre conducted as it used to be, with resident stock companies everywhere, slapping a great number of plays on to their stages, in repertoire, with the minimum of cost and scenic originality and fitness, and of course depending largely on constant revivals, it would still be impossible for modern realistic plays to enjoy the length of life successful dramas could formerly anticipate, especially if they were written in verse and ignored contemporary themes. The greater the faithfulness of the realistic play to the speech, the customs, the ways of thinking and still more of feeling, of its hour—in other words, the better it very often is as a realistic play—the less its chance of survival. And, we may add, the more difficult for a critic of a later date to judge its merits from any ordinary academic, or literary, standards. It can only be estimated fairly by taking, in Professor Woodbridge's phrase, "the historical or sociological point of view," and also, I fear, the theatrical point of view—something which, alas, too many academic critics are incapable of doing.

Let us now try to take these points of view in considering a certain very famous American play, to be found in Quinn's "depressing" collection. It is a play made from an even more famous piece of literature, but of literature in the printed play you will find a great dearth. Perhaps only one line. That line begins, "Are we so soon forgot?" And the speaker is Rip Van Winkle.

Irving's story of Rip Van Winkle contains scarcely two hundred words of dialogue, and its entire narrative could be condensed into a couple of pages. But through the magic of literature, the creation of atmosphere, it has so saturated the Catskill Mountains with a legendary haze that all the water-system tunnels and cement roads and filling stations and boardinghouses cannot dispel it. Irving's Catskills, for most Americans, are more real than the reality. But what is there dramatic in all this? Only the satisfaction of a human curiosity to learn what would happen to a man if he slept twenty years, and then came back to his home. The character of Rip in Irving's sketch is lightly drawn. It scarcely moves out of the second dimension. His expulsion from home is the hint of drama, not the realization. To the playwright, for whom that legendary haze created by Irving is largely impossible, the material is thin and baffling. It proved so baffling, indeed, that from 1829, when the first stage version was made, until 1865, when Joseph Jefferson called in Dion Boucicault to help and produced, in London, the famous version which was to serve him the rest of his life, no play about Rip satisfied either the actors or the public. Yet both actors and public hungered for such a play, the actors because they felt in the part the opportunity for rich and picturesque character delineation and emotional possibilities, the public because the story gave them, the children of a new raw country, a sense of the past, a background of legend.

Now, Joseph Jefferson was an actor who combined a delicate and highly trained craftsmanship with an enormously winning personality, and both were peculiarly adapted to the potential demands of Rip. He could be entrusted by himself to develop the character into three dimensions on the stage without violence to Irving, but he couldn't do it without more framework of plot and dialogue than Irving had provided. Atmosphere doesn't make a plot. Boucicault gave him the plot, devised the progressive situations in which Rip's character could be revealed and developed, the sleep accounted for, and the return illustrated by incidents which would bring out its pathos and round the story to a happy close. If you read the text of this Boucicault–Jefferson play today, you will not be impressed with much of the dialogue; you will feel, perhaps, that the trumped-up business of the deeds and the villainy of Derrick in Act I is a sad descent from Irving's delicate art; you will think Rip's expulsion from home a bit like a comic strip; and for most of the scene in the mountains (so magically evoked by Irving) you will be confronted only by stage directions, which, unless written by Shaw or Barrie, are among the least literary of human word arrangements. You will, perhaps, be depressed, and deem all this unworthy of attention.

Yet the fact remains that from 1865 until after 1900, Jefferson played Rip in every city in the land; to see him was a part of the education of every American child, and not to have seen him was to have missed one of the most charming, the most moving, the most enchanting experiences the theatre of that, or any other day, afforded. From the point of view of American cultural history, this play can hardly be ignored. But from the theatrical point of view, also, it should not be ignored, and so considered its merits are much greater than the literary approach can disclose. Far from being depressing, it is highly stimulating.

Its greatest and most obvious merit, of course, is in the opportunity it gives the skilled actor to enlarge Irving's pale figure into a living character, a lovable character whose amiable virtues are his weaknesses, who can resist anything but temptation, and in whose mind a mingled shrewdness and humor and naïveté were forever resulting in the most delightful of surprises.

Here is one of his speeches, when he recalls his wedding day: "My! My! Yah, we was a fine couple altogether." And he holds out his cup for the schnapps Nick Vedder is dispensing. But when Nick starts to add water, he cries, "Stop! I come along mitout that, Nick Vedder." Then his mind reverts to Gretchen again, but the mood has shifted from past to present. "Good licker and water is like man and wife . . . They don't agree together." And now he has rounded the years of his married life, and completes his speech with a laugh: "I always like my licker single." A speech like this was not devised with any thought of its effect in print. It was devised to give the actor opportunity to illuminate character, to create that undercurrent of emotion, of life in process, which is the heart of theatre. The extraordinary charm and vitality of Jefferson's Rip testifies to how well the playwrights succeeded.

Because we loved Rip, because we wept to see him driven into the storm, because he had become endeared to us as a living person, the pathos of his return and his bewilderment at being unrecognized took on, with Jefferson, a dignity almost like Lear's. But that mood was not long to be sustained. This is a happy play, as Irving's is a happy story. But, because it is a play, and Rip is the hero, he must on the stage do something volitional. He foils the villain. He tries and fails again to resist temptation. His final words are the familiar toast gurgled into his tankard.

In the mountain scene, when Rip encounters the ghostly crew and drinks the potion, the theatre was able as early as 1865 (and would be far more able today) to create by costumes, lights, and scenery its equivalent of Irving's magic description. This scene, in which Hudson's crew never speak, thus emphasizing Rip's growing loneliness and terror, was of Jefferson's own contriving. Rip's humor was not in complete abeyance till the end, which intensified the uncanny strangeness. Naturally, when you read the stage directions without willingness or power to visualize them carried out in terms of theatre, and read Rip's monologue without power to visualize the solemn, nodding, sinister crew who pressed close around him, or the actor's changing expressions and the tones and inflections of his voice, you are not moved as you are by literature, and there is little for your mind to get hold of. Yet dramatic literature is there, if by that term we may be permitted to mean something which can create that responsive emotion peculiar to the theatre, roused by situations in which character is truly displayed and the imagination of the audience released. It is there as surely as music is in the black lines and dots of a Mozart score.

Many of you will say, I know, that I am finding in the play of *Rip Van Winkle* rather more my memories of the great actor who played it than its actual merits. The merits were those of Joseph Jefferson. Booth was almost equally regnant as Hamlet from 1865 to 1892, but others have shone as Hamlet since: no one has succeeded in making Rip live again, or only sporadically. That last is true, and for more than one reason. *Hamlet* is a great play from every angle, written in a poetic dialogue seemingly as enduring as the English language. Much of the secondary dialogue of Rip is as old-fashioned as a black walnut hatrack. Jefferson held the play so exclusively his own for forty years that it seemed to die with him. Finally, there is no longer in our theatre public the urge for the comfort of legend to give us background. The play's mission in our social history has been fulfilled. But because it was—and still is—a theatrical framework which enables a skilled actor, with the right temperament, to fill in a humorous and tender and touching character study, and imparts stage vividness to one of humanity's famous folk tales, *Rip Van Winkle* cannot justly be dismissed as either depressing or insignificant. Properly considered, it gives us considerable respect for the American theatre of our fathers.

Let us go back now to the decades before the Civil War, and consider a form of American theatrical entertainment which cannot be represented in any collection of American plays, but which I think can be shown to have greatly influenced the plays, or perhaps we had better say the audiences, which followed. I refer to the so-called Negro minstrels. In any serious academic study of the drama as a literary art, the minstrels have, I'm sure, no recognition. They came about in the early forties as a result of the success of certain men, whom we would now call vaudeville performers, blacking up and imitating Negro singers and dancers. A group of these performers got together and by pooling their resources were able to give an entire evening's entertainment. Soon the country was flooded with minstrel troups, and for at least two decades the Negro minstrels were undoubtedly the most widely popular form of entertainment in America. Their popularity endured, in diminishing degree, until the present century, and the curious theatrical form they evolved is still employed by amateurs. The Elks probably gave a minstrel show in your town last winter.

In general, the minstrel show was divided into three parts. Part one, the olio, found the whole troupe in a semicircle on the stage, with the Interlocutor in the middle, and the two chief comedians as Bones, or End Men, and between jokes the rest, solo or in chorus, sang, danced, and played their banjos. Finally they all marched out to a stirring tune called a "walk-around." Part two was an interlude, which often contained as its meat a satirical political stump speech.

Part three was a short play, not necessarily with Negro characters (but played in black face).

The initial appeal of the minstrels, of course, was in their exploitation of African rhythm and the warm, simple humor of the Negro. Their employment of these things was but partial and imperfect, yet it gave us our best-loved American songs, the songs of Stephen Foster. *Oh, Susanna* so captured the country that it was the marching song of the forty-niners across the continent. *Old Folks at Home* still remains the most beautiful song composed by an American. *Dixie,* now the national song of the South, was written by Dan Emmet (whose parents were ardent Abolitionists) as a minstrel "walkaround." The black faces were burlesqued, the songs were often sentimental and imperfectly negroid, the jokes were often those of the Negro only in the dialect in which they were spoken. Nevertheless, something peculiarly American, and something familiar to all of us, was at the base of the appeal.

But there was something else. The minstrel shows were intimate, contemporaneous, they made the audience a part of the entertainment. Here were not actors removed across a void and living imagined lives apart, but jolly men facing you directly and aiming their songs and gags right at you. More than that, the gags were changed from night to night, from town to town. The Interlocutor and the End Men made it a point to learn something harmlessly funny about leading citizens of any town they played in, and nobody in the audience knew when he or his neighbor would become the butt of laughter. Similarly, comment on contemporary events of national scope were constantly incorporated into the text of the entertainment, particularly, of course, in the burlesque stump speech. There were, too, among the minstrels, a surprisingly large number of genuine artists, who could develop their interludes into character studies. One such typical minstrel character interlude survives to this day on the radio— the Amos and Andy skits. But even these character interludes were a part of the contemporaneous appeal, because they were based on a realistic observation of Negro life. There was no hint of literary creation about them, no likeness to the classic repertoire the elder Booth may have been playing across the street, or to Forrest's thunderously rhetorical Indian chieftain, Metamora.

Now, there is a profound psychological difference between sitting across the gulf of the orchestra pit, watching actors move and declaim in an imagined story, and sitting ready to chuckle when a black-face Bones on the stage looks right down at you and tosses off a gag about your next-door neighbor. And there is an equally profound difference between your response to satire, however witty, directed at Bob Acres or a Restoration husband, and satire, be it ever so crude, directed at the man in the White House at the moment, or whatever event or fad might be uppermost in the national consciousness. Passing over the musical appeal of the minstrels, which in their earlier years, at least, was deservedly great, their appeal by the spoken word, and by interludes of character delineation, was to a considerable extent revolutionary, because it brought intimacy into the playhouse, and the pleasurable excitement of contemporary comment, and a genuine, if crude, conception of realism. Negro life was too close to us, bulked too large in our consciousness, to permit any grave tamperings with its more obvious aspects.

In 1829 Edwin Forrest, the American-born tragedian, offered a prize of $500 for a play on a native theme, and the result of this first prize-play contest in our history was a drama by John Augustus Stone, called *Metamora,* which was concerned with the Indian Wars in Rhode Island. Unfortunately, the full text of this work has not survived, although the drama was played by Forrest for many years. But the actor's own part is treasured at the Forrest home in Philadelphia, and causes us to wonder how even Forrest could have poured forth these surges of heroically rhythmed prose without being a trifle ridiculous—although, to be sure, they are no more bombastic and inflated than the speeches in the great Sheridan's version of *Pizzaro,* which Mrs. Siddons thundered in Old Drury.[1]

Here is a fair sample of how John Augustus Stone and Edwin Forrest represented the speech and character of a Narraganset chief in the Colonial days:

The pale faces are around me thicker than the leaves of summer. I chase the hart in the hunting grounds; he leads me to the white man's village. I drive my canoe into the rivers; they are full of the white man's ships. I visit the graves of my fathers; they are lost in the white man's corn fields. They come like the waves of the ocean forever rolling upon

[1] After this paper was read, a text of *Metamora* was discovered in Salt Lake City, complete except for the fourth act (there are five acts), and this text has been printed in Volume XIV of the "America's Lost Plays" series, Princeton University Press, 1941.

the shore. Surge after surge, they dash upon the beach, and every foam drop is a white man. They swarm over the land like the doves of winter, and the red men are dropping like withered leaves.

There was in this sort of language, and in Forrest's manner of delivery, undoubtedly an emotional release for our ancestors difficult to understand today. But even for some of them it had its humorous side, and John Brougham's famous burlesque of *Metamora* and all the Indian plays which followed it, which he called *Pokahontas* and produced in 1855, was one of those important burlesques of the mid-century that both here and in England played a leading part in laughing stale tradition out of the theatre. When, four years later, Dion Boucicault produced his drama, *The Octoroon,* he put an Indian into the play, and played the rôle himself. But this Indian did not speak like Metamora. In fact, he did not speak at all. He merely grunted.

The Indian, however, was a minor figure in *The Octoroon.* What counted most heavily were the Negro slaves, and of course the Octoroon herself, whose tragic predicament was, and still is, the stuff of drama. The play opens with a little plantation genre picture which even today has humor and charm and truth; and the later scene of the enforced slave auction held audiences tense only two years ago, in a summer theatre production which I witnessed. The rôle of Old Pete was almost always played by some actor trained in the minstrels, and was long looked upon as a choice part in our native repertoire. If you will bear with me for a moment, I should like to include here the opening scene of *The Octoroon.* It opens on a view of the plantation of Terrebonne, in Louisiana. A branch of the Mississippi is seen winding through the estate. A low-built but extensive planter's dwelling, surrounded by a veranda and raised a few feet from the ground, occupies the left side. On the right stand a table and chairs. Grace is discovered sitting at the breakfast table with the Negro children.

(SOLON enters from the house.)

SOLON. Yah! you bomn'ble fry—git out—a gen'leman can't pass for you.
GRACE. (Seizing a fly whisk) Hee!—ha, git out. (She drives the children away: in escaping they tumble against SOLON, who falls with the tray; the children steal the bananas and rolls that fall about)

(Enter PETE, who is lame; he carries a mop and pail.)

PETE. Hay! Laws a massy! why, clar out! drop dat banana! I'll murder dis yere crowd. (He chases the children, who leap over the railing at back. Exit SOLON.) Dem little niggers is a judgment upon dis generation.

(Enter GEORGE from the house.)

GEO. What's the matter, Pete?

PETE. It's dem black trash, Mas'r George; dis ere property wants claring; dem's gettin' too numerous round: when I gets time I'll kill some on 'em, sure!

GEO. They don't seem to be scared by the threat.

PETE. Stop, you varmin! Stop till I get enough of you in one place!

GEO. Were they all born on this estate?

PETE. Guess dey nebber was born, dem t'ings! what, dem? Git away! Born here, dem darkies? What, on Terrebonne! Don't b'lieve it, Mas'r George; dem black t'ings nebber was born at all; dey swarmed one mornin' on a sassafras tree in de swamp; I cotched 'em; dey ain't no count. Don't believe dey'll turn out niggers when dey're growed; dey'll come out sunthin else.

GRACE. Yes, Mas'r George, dey was born here, and old Pete is fonder on 'em dan he is of his fiddle of a Sunday.

PETE. What? Dem tings—dem?—get away. (Makes blow at the children.) Born here, dem darkies? Don't believe it, Mas'r George. No. One morning dey swarmed on a sassafras tree in de swamp and I cotched 'em all in a sieve—dats how dey come on top of dis yearth— git out you, ya, ya! (Laughs) (Exit GRACE)

(Enter MRS. PEYTON from the house.)

MRS. PEYTON. So, Pete, you are spoiling those children as usual.

PETE. Dat's right, missus, gib it to old Pete! he's allers in for it. Git away, dere! Ya! if dey ain't all lighted, like coons, on dat snake fence, jest out o' shot. Look dar! Ya, ya! Dem debils Ya! . . . Git down dar. I'm arter you! (Hobbles off)

MRS. PEYTON. You are out early this morning, George.

GEO. I was up before daylight. We got the horses saddled and galloped down the shell road over the Piney Patch; then coasting the Bayou Lake, we crossed the long swamps by Paul's Path, and so came home again.

MRS. PEYTON. You seem already familiar with the names of every spot on the estate.

GEO. Just one month ago I quitted Paris. I left that siren city as I would have left a beloved woman.

It is apparent, is it not, that when Old Pete leaves the stage, he takes with him something recognizably real and recognizably illusive as we know the theatre today. Pete talks something like a Negro. George, and to a lesser extent his Mama, talk like the stage characters Boucicault had been maneuvering in half a hundred plays before. We must not forget, of course, that *The Octoroon* had been preceded by *Uncle Tom's Cabin,* which had prepared us to find pathos and humor in Negro life. But that hardly explains the superior realism Boucicault displays in handling his Negro characters over his treatment of his whites. In handling his whites, he was working in a convention. In handling his Negroes he was working with material familiar in daily life, but comparatively new in the theatre—only a generation old. And that generation had seen the Negro chiefly represented by minstrels, i.e., intimately and with a crude and kindly realism. It is hard to avoid the belief that the minstrels had a definite effect upon the best parts of Boucicault's best play on an American theme. And it is impossible to avoid the belief that they had an effect upon American audiences, making them perhaps subconsciously dissatisfied with too much aloofness in the theatre, eager for the delights of the contemporary reference and the tang of the moment's reality, and hence in the long run preparing them for the advent of the modern realistic drama. In fact, I have a suspicion that if the Civil War had not suddenly intervened, we would have evolved a modern drama for ourselves and not been forced to get it by importing the comedies of Tom Robertson.

Nothing is more futile, though we all indulge in the pastime, than predicting the immortality of contemporary works of art. Any one of us, who has reached middle age, can recall evenings of high excitement in the theatre, or books which roused him to a burning pitch of enthusiasm, and yet, today, those plays, those books, are accumulating dust. What of it? If in their day and hour they accomplished well what they set out to do, that is enough, and their immortality is to be found in the effects they had on those who saw or read them, and on the artists who followed. Who of my generation can forget the enormous excitement with which we pounced upon a new story by Kipling? Today the young read him, if at all, either with apathy or resentment at his "Empire complex," as they call it. I fear I do myself.

But that isn't to say that he was not a great force in the nineties. Can anyone, I wonder, recall James A. Herne at the end of *Shore Acres,* when he fixed the old kitchen for the night and went upstairs to bed? All the humble, homely, and heart-warming quality of rural New England life was in that scene, and the sweet simplicity of brave old age. It was the beginning, too, of American realistic drama, but we didn't know that (though Herne did). We accepted it as touching and tender, a poem of the familiar. But I dare say *Shore Acres* would prove depressing to the literary critic today. It has no permanence on the printed page. It was compounded of an actor's art, pantomime, a stage setting, and the spirit of 1893.

If you had been present some night in a minstrel hall when the black-faced comedians on the stage tuned their banjos, paused a moment for silence, and then began to sing "Way down upon the Swanee Ribber," would you have known that you were present at the birth of something immortal? Would you have cared? The minstrels, you may be sure, had no thought of immortality for their songs. They thought only of entertaining the paying customers. I was myself present at the birth (at least the birth in Boston) of a now seemingly immortal work, *The Mikado.* To be sure, I was a trifle young to be thinking of immortality, but I cannot recall that any of my elders talked about it, either. They were too busy singing "The flowers that bloom in the Spring, tra-la—." We all had a wonderful time— and waited for the next one. But at how many other plays have you and I been present when we had as wonderful—well, *almost* as wonderful—a time, but which have not achieved permanence either in the theatre repertoire, or on the printed page? Their number is considerable, even for those people who are not yet old. We know that those plays, as performed in their day and hour, had an artistic validity which made them important. And we are bound to assume, therefore, that if later critics find them "depressing" it is because those critics are not able properly to appreciate them in their social, historical, and above all their theatrical setting.

Hence it is that the study of drama solely, or chiefly, from the printed text and the literary point of view not only results in failure to understand many interesting and important examples of playmaking, but actually sometimes in a distortion of the real progression and direction of dramatic art. For a long time (and I fear sometimes even today) Goldsmith and Sheridan were represented as the apex to which British drama climbed in the eighteenth century. But, as a matter of fact, they were both throwbacks. The future was not with either man, though the literature was. It was far more with Lillo and his *London Merchant,* which as a literary production is certainly depressing. The future, in the nineteenth century, was not with *Richelieu* or *Virginius* or *London Assurance,* but with the burlettas produced by Madame Vestris. In America the future was not with Boker's *Francesca,* which has definite literary merits, but with *Mose the Fireman,* the Negro minstrels, and *Yankee Hill.* In fact, to study the history of drama from a collection of the literary highlights of various periods may very easily result in missing almost completely the true line of evolution, and never seeing the sources of even the master works themselves.

Think for a moment of the present situation in the theatre. Apparently a fresh creative style soon reaches its maximum effectiveness, becomes universally accepted, and then declines—all in a space of two generations. It was so with Elizabethan drama, with Restoration comedy, and it now seems to be true of realism. We in America, mastering the medium later, did not reach our peak till the 1920's; Europe's peak came before the War. But already the decline is evident. Our drama is obviously entering a period of eclecticism, of almost random experiment, and finding outlets, too, on screen and radio hitherto unknown. Maxwell Anderson writes in verse, combining realistic tight construction with the diffusion and freedom in speech of an older poetic tradition. A play without scenery, employing a combination of Greek chorus, Chinese property man, and Josh Whitcomb, wins the Pulitzer prize. Out-and-out realism wins the Critics' Circle prize—*Of Mice and Men.* Ireland's leading playwright, Sean O'Casey, deserts realism, of which he was a master, for a curious jumble of symbolism and poetry which defies classification. The screen's greatest popular triumph this year is an animated illustration of a Grimm's fairy tale. The radio seeks to rouse your imagination purely by sounds and spoken words. Somewhere here is the germ of the future, but who can say where? One prediction is as good as another. Some day in the future it will be known. But what if it were in a play, or series of plays, or in a picture or a radio broadcast, which had little or no literary merit, which is quite unlikely to be printed in an anthology, between O'Neill's *Strange Interlude* and Anderson's *Masque of Kings?*

O'Neill's *Strange Interlude* contained a new kind of stage soliloquy, spoken while other characters were present, and supposed to represent the subconscious thought of the speakers. Many critics declared that here was a new dimension added to drama, that in the future all dramatists would be forced to employ the device. So far as I have noticed, no dramatists have, not even O'Neill himself after one subsequent and disastrous attempt in *Dynamo*. Verily, Cassandra's robe is a perilous garment.

I profoundly hope that none of you is assuming that I therefore attach no importance to *Strange Interlude* as a work of art or a subject for study, and still more that I am advocating any neglect or minimizing of the intellectual and poetic approach to playwriting. No student, and certainly no artist, should be unaware of the best that has been done in the past, and no artist can have too much to say, nor say it too well, for his generation. But to succeed in his generation (which he must do, or he is no dramatist at all) the theatrical artist must say things which are understandable and vital to his contemporaries, and he must say them in a speech they can accept. He must rouse emotional interest and create illusion. And what all along I have been trying myself to say is simply this:—that in many, if not most periods of the theatre, emotional interest has been aroused and illusion created by plays, even by mere entertainments, which may not evoke any such responses from us today, which may lack the literary savor to keep them enduring in print and the intellectual pith to survive the changing years. Because this is true of so much American drama before the turn of the current century, we have almost completely ignored any study of our native playhouse; we have dubbed it depressing and unworthy. We have been unwilling to study it, not as printed literature, but as a score from which our actors made music for your parents and mine, as a precious (and, when so studied, fascinating) record of the emotional responses of our forebears which constitutes perhaps the subtlest and surest clue for a spiritual reconstruction of the past.

No more than you and I today, did our ancestors go to the theatre to be educated, or to do right by literature. Even as you and I, they went to be entertained. An understanding analysis of what plays most entertained—for there can really be no drama without audiences —will not only explain them, but will disclose as nothing else can the true lines of theatrical evolution, the true steps by which drama advances—or, if you like, recedes. Such study will, alas, sometimes call for more historical sympathy than literary acumen. It will entail some knowledge of stage practice, and the imagination to visualize a printed direction into an emotional effect. It will entail the reading of some texts painfully deficient in enduring literary value or intellectual robustness. But it will vitalize the past of the American theatre for anyone who honestly attempts it, and will in the long run cause neither depression nor a sense of wasted time.

When I think of the time many and many a student has spent upon dead dramas from England because they were "literary"—i.e., too often because they were Elizabethan or Restoration—it is I who am depressed. The style of those plays, the weight of their tradition, was a back drag on the English as well as the American stage for generations. There is something stirring and fine about a poor, crude little Yankee comedy, brashly unconscious of its depressing lack of literature yet rousing our ancestors to gales of laughter by its native tang and truth. I see the Future there. I see the plays which are most important and interesting to you and me today; just as only that is really vital today which is not imitative, traditional, but which speaks to us frankly in our own idiom. The past of the American theatre does not depress me. It couldn't;—I saw Joe Jefferson play Rip Van Winkle. You may take your *Duchess of Malfi* and go off with her in a library corner or a classroom if you like. I find Rip far more congenial.

The First American Man of Letters:
Benjamin Franklin

by Carl Van Doren

Iᴛ ɪs ᴀ sᴛʀᴀɴɢᴇ ꜰᴀᴄᴛ ɪɴ ᴛʜᴇ ʜɪsᴛᴏʀʏ ᴏꜰ ʟɪᴛᴇʀᴀᴛᴜʀᴇ, ᴛʜᴏᴜɢʜ ᴏɴʟʏ
one of many strange facts in that enormous record, that Benjamin
Franklin should so often have been overlooked as a man of letters
when he was that, on the whole, before anything else. His autobiography has been more widely read than any other. His proverbial
sayings have passed into the general language of mankind, in un-
counted tongues. He wrote with masterly skill in the fields of science,
economics, diplomacy, politics. A great moralist, he was an equally
great humorist. He belongs among the supreme writers of familiar
letters. Of all writers he perhaps best combines in his style a felicitous
elegance with a happy vernacular, the grace of philosophers and wits
and the wit of the people. If he was not a man of letters it is difficult
to say what man ever was. It sometimes seems that literary criticism
has passed Franklin over because he had so many things to say and
said them so well.

He himself knew that "prose writing has been of great use to me
in the course of my life, and was a principal means of my advancement." But it must be borne in mind that Franklin, like most good
prose writers, began with verse. At twelve he wrote ballads which,
printed by his elder brother, were sold by the boy himself in the
streets of Boston, where they made a stir which flattered his vanity.
At sixteen he was laughing at bad poetry in his review of an imaginary
elegy on Mehitabel Kitel of Salem and his *Receipt to Make a New
England Funeral Elegy*. He did not, however, escape verse by
parodying bad poems. Two years later, in Philadelphia, his three

closest friends were all poets. "Many pleasant walks we four had together on Sundays into the woods, near Schuylkill, where we read to
one another, and conferred on what we read." Franklin had come to
approve of "amusing one's self with poetry now and then, so far
as to improve one's language, but no farther," and he probably wrote
fewer verses than his companions. But these poets were the friends
he chose out of all the young men in Philadelphia, and it was with one
of them that he made his first voyage to London, where the prose
writer supported the poet till they quarreled, like either poets or prose
writers, over a woman.

Then for something like twenty years Franklin had little to do
with verse, so far as is known, except for the homely rhymes he
credited to Poor Richard in his annual almanac. But he printed or
reprinted as much verse as prose in *Poor Richard*. When Franklin
was thirty-eight, writing to London to order books for his shop, he
asked that he be sent a dozen copies of anything James Thomson
might publish. "I had read no poetry for several years, and almost
lost the relish of it, till I met with his *Seasons*. That charming poet
has brought more tears of pleasure into my eyes than all I ever read
before. I wish it were in my power to return him any part of the
joy he has given me." When within a year or so Franklin began to
withdraw from business and to think of the leisure toward which
he had long been working, he turned again to verse in drinking songs
which became famous in his circle.

> The antediluvians were all very sober,
> For they had no wine and they brewed no October;
> All wicked, bad livers, on mischief still thinking,
> For there can't be good living where there is not good drinking.
> *Derry-down*

> 'Twas honest old Noah first planted the vine,
> And mended his morals by drinking its wine;
> He justly the drinking of water decried;
> For he knew that all mankind by drinking it died.
> *Derry-down*

So ran one of the liveliest of Franklin's songs, in a casual meter
designed for alcoholic voices. Here as elsewhere he matched his art
to the occasion. Nor did he forget his belief, founded on his own

experience, that a way to learn to write prose is to write verse. In his plan for the English school of the Academy which became the University of Pennsylvania he proposed in 1750 that the pupils write "sometimes in verse, not to make them poets, but for this reason, that nothing acquaints a lad so speedily with variety of expression as the necessity of finding such words and phrases as will suit with the measure, sound, and rhyme of verse, and at the same time well express the sentiment."

In prose Franklin at sixteen was already the most charming writer in America, as he remained for the nearly seventy years he had yet to live. Because his amazing faculties kept green to his old age it is often forgotten that he had been very precocious. In a classic passage he tells how he taught himself to write, by imitating the *Spectator*. He would read one of the papers, make a brief note on each sentence, lay the original aside, and after a few days try to write it from his notes. "Then I compared my *Spectator* with the original, discovered some of my faults, and corrected them." Finding his vocabulary small and not varied enough to suit him, he "took some of the tales and turned them into verse; and, after a time, when I had pretty well forgotten the prose, turned them back again." Or he would jumble his notes into confusion, and weeks later try to arrange them in the best order before he began to write. "This was to teach me method in the arrangement of thoughts." Now and then he had "the pleasure of fancying that, in certain particulars of small import, I had been lucky enough to improve the method or the language, and this encouraged me to think I might possibly in time come to be a tolerable English writer, of which I was extremely ambitious."

In the Dogood papers, written before he was seventeen, he exhibited most of the qualities he was to have when, maturer, he decided that writing should above all be "smooth, clear, and short." In the journal which Franklin kept at twenty, on his voyage from London to Philadelphia, he was all but full-grown as a writer, though he still lacked the sharper edge and clearer freshness which experience afterwards gave him and the rich tones of his later wisdom. Compare his entry for this last day with the entry he wrote in another journal, fifty-nine years later, on the next to the last day of his last voyage. He wrote in 1726:

This morning we weighed anchor with a gentle breeze and passed by New Castle, whence they hailed us and bade us welcome. It is extreme fine weather. The sun enlivens our stiff limbs with his glorious rays of warmth and brightness. The sky looks gay, with here and there a silver cloud. The fresh breezes from the woods refresh us; the immediate prospect of liberty, after so long and irksome confinement, ravishes us. In short, all things conspire to make this the most joyful day I ever knew.

In 1785 he wrote:

The wind springing fair last evening after a calm, we found ourselves this morning, at sunrising, abreast of the lighthouse and between Capes May and Henlopen. We sail into the bay very pleasantly; water smooth, air cool, day fair and fine. We passed New Castle about sunset and went on near Red Bank before the tide and wind failed; then came to an anchor.

The simple perfection of Franklin at eighty was of course beyond Franklin at twenty, but the youth had outgrown most of the self-conscious awkwardness customary at his age and was beginning to write as by second nature.

It was characteristic of Franklin that when, on that youthful voyage, he drew up a plan to regulate his future conduct, he said: "Those who write of the art of poetry teach us that if we would write what may be worth reading we ought always, before we begin, to form a regular plan and design of our piece; otherwise we shall be in danger of incongruity. I am apt to think it is the same as to life." He would plan his life as he might plan a poem. Thirty years later he could still draw a similar image from literature. "Life, like a dramatic piece," he wrote to George Whitefield, "should not only be conducted with regularity but methinks it should finish handsomely. Being now in the last act," as Franklin may then have thought, though actually he had most of his great years still ahead of him, "I begin to cast about for something fit to end with. Or if mine be more properly compared to an epigram, as some of its lines are barely tolerable, I am very desirous of concluding with a bright point." And he put into the mouth of Poor Richard a saying which throws light on Franklin's constant sense of the interplay of literature and life. "If you would not be forgotten, as soon as you are dead and rotten, either write things worth reading, or do things worth the writing."

This sense of interplay between writing and doing kept Frankin from looking upon his writing as an end in itself. Writing with him was an applied art. In part because he did not talk readily, and throughout his life delivered few speeches, he made use of writing to gain his ends. He would write a paper for his club, the Junto, founded when he was twenty-one and kept alive by him for thirty years, to bring his ideas before his friends. He would publish the paper in his *Pennsylvania Gazette,* taken over when he was twenty-three, and carry his ideas further to the public. When, along with the other debtors, traders, and workmen of Pennsylvania, he decided that the province needed a new issue of paper currency, he wrote—at twenty-three—his first public pamphlet, on that topic. "Bills issued upon land," he said in the earliest of his memorable phrases, "are, in effect, coined land." Not only did his arguments help bring about the new issue, but his grateful friends in the legislature "thought fit to reward me by employing me in printing the money: a very profitable job and a great help to me. This was another advantage gained by my being able to write." In the neighboring province of New Jersey Franklin was once at Burlington when the legislature wanted to draft an answer to a message from the governor, but did not trust their own skill. Franklin drafted the answer for them, and they made him printer for that government as well. It was notably by writing that he introduced and furthered the many civic interests he was devoted to: the fire companies, the militia, the Academy, the Hospital. Side by side with these pieces went the little satires and hoaxes which he wrote to entertain both friends and public, out of the tireless energy which flowed up in him at times in a broad, sly humor.

Franklin's efforts for the general welfare included a wide range of services to literature. With the Junto he founded the first permanent subscription library in America. The books he gave to it on its first list were a black-letter Magna Charta and Montaigne's essays. Franklin printed its catalogue. As busy as any man in Philadelphia, he served for three months as its librarian, in attendance from two to three every Wednesday and from ten to four on Saturdays. Against the wishes of his utilitarian associates he enriched the Library Company's collection with early Americana which few Americans besides him then valued, though these books and pamphlets have become the proudest treasures of the library. Franklin chose with what seems like prophetic tact to print his great Indian treaties, between Pennsylvania and the Six Nations, in folios which make them as monumental as they are important. He published James Logan's *Cato Major,* the first Latin classic both translated and printed in America, and Richardson's *Pamela,* the first novel printed here. In 1744 Franklin had in his shop what must have been the most distinguished array of books on sale anywhere on the continent. That same year, in a letter to an English friend, he forecast the relations of English and American literature. "Your authors," he said, "know but little of the fame they have on this side of the ocean. We are a kind of posterity in respect to them. We read their works with perfect impartiality, being at too great a distance to be biased by the fractions, parties, and prejudices that prevail among you." Franklin was later to convince Hume that the increase of English readers in America must affect the future of English as a literary language, and Hume's persuasions had perhaps something to do with Gibbon's decision to write history in English, not in French, as he had first intended.

In Franklin's prospectus for the Academy he laid much stress on history as the subject through which other subjects might be studied. It would "fix in the minds of youth deep impressions of the beauty and usefulness of virtue of all kinds." He included American history, then unknown to American curriculums, and histories of nature and commerce. Far from confining himself to merely practical education, he wanted the Academy, while training the boys to make a living, also to help them become literate and philosophical, with "that benignity of mind which shows itself in searching and seizing every opportunity to serve and oblige, and is the foundation of what is called good breeding." Not for nothing had the self-made Franklin learned to read Latin, Italian, Spanish, French, and German, and gone through books on every subject of interest to mankind. Though he seems to have cared less for purely imaginative literature than for other forms, it is hardly safe to say that there was any given book he had not read.

In the almanac which he began at twenty-six and edited for twenty-five years he followed a fashion already set and already prosperous.

But no other almanac has ever been so famous as *Poor Richard,* or so influential. Franklin created the character of his Richard Saunders as a contemporary novelist or playwright might have done. Poor Richard had the look of existing outside his almanac. He told about his tiffs with his wife Bridget, who also seemed real. He talked about his poverty and his profits, and admitted he could not write good verse. His neighbors, he complained, were forever teasing him for private astrological information. "Will my ship return safe? Will my mare win the race? Will her next colt be a pacer? When will my wife die? Who shall be my husband, and how long first? When is the best time to cut hair, trim cocks, or sow salads?" Poor Richard said he had ceased to have either taste or leisure for such impertinences. But he never lost his taste and leisure for the pungent sayings that run through his almanacs, printed in the crowded margins wherever there was space.

Franklin is in a sense to blame if the prudential maxims have come to be thought of as his only ones. When, crossing the Atlantic in 1757, he wrote the preface for the next year's almanac, he had more time than usual on his hands and wrote at greater length. His preface for 1758 was long enough to be separately printed, first as *Father Abraham's Speech* and thereafter as *The Way to Wealth,* the title it still bears. Because Franklin himself loosely spoke of "bringing all these scattered counsels thus into a focus," it has been taken for granted by most readers that *The Way to Wealth* contains the whole of his sayings. Not a few scholars have found it easier to accept this than to go to the trouble of hunting out the rare original almanacs and running through them. But whoever does it will find that the prudential maxims are by no means the whole. Franklin in *The Way to Wealth* was writing dramatically, putting his sayings in the mouth of an old man whose specific theme was economy. Father Abraham chose Poor Richard's economical adages because they proved a point. He left out many times more than he chose. And those he left out range over wide regions of wit and understanding.

Who would have expected a provincial almanac maker to say: "Thou hadst better eat salt with the philosophers of Greece than sugar with the courtiers of Italy"? Or: "The brave and the wise can both pity and excuse when cowards and fools show no mercy"? Or: "Hast thou virtue? Acquire also the graces and beauties of virtue"?

Or: "The muses love the morning"? It was not Poor Richard so much as the inquiring young Benjamin Franklin who came to this reasonable view of the nature of sin: "Sin is not hurtful because it is forbidden, but it is forbidden because it is hurtful." It was a Franklin on the way to becoming a great sage who said: "Cunning proceeds from want of capacity." "A lie stands on one leg, truth on two" was a pointed saying, but it had less moral weight behind it than: "Half a truth is often a great lie."

A good many of the sayings had to do with good manners:

He is no clown that drives the plough, but he that doth clownish things.
Having been poor is no shame, but being ashamed of it is.
He is not well bred that cannot bear ill-breeding in others.
It is ill manners to silence a fool, and cruelty to let him go on.
What's proper is becoming; See the blacksmith with his white silk apron.

There are sayings about too much talking:

None preaches better than the ant, and she says nothing.
The worst wheel of the cart makes the most noise.
Proclaim not all thou knowest, all thou owest, all thou hast, nor all thou canst.

But there are also sayings about not talking enough:

Sloth and silence are a fool's virtues.
As we must account for every idle word, so must we for every idle silence.

There are sayings against avarice:

Avarice and happiness never saw each other. How then should they become acquainted?
Poverty wants some things, luxury many things, avarice all things.

There are even sayings against prudence and economy:

Never spare the parson's wine nor the baker's pudding.
There's more old drunkards than old doctors.
An egg today is better than a hen tomorrow.

Poor Richard might speak of almost anything:

He that drinks fast pays slow.

Where there's marriage without love there will be love without marriage.

The family of fools is ancient.

The rotten apple spoils his companions.

A countryman between two lawyers is like a fish between two cats.

Write with the learned, pronounce with the vulgar.

The ancients tell us what is best; but we must learn from the moderns what is fittest.

Keep your eyes wide open before marriage, half shut afterwards.

He that falls in love with himself will have no rivals.

Light-heeled mothers make leaden-heeled daughters.

The most exquisite folly is made of wisdom spun too fine.

What maintains one vice would bring up two children.

Many foxes grow grey, but few grow good.

We may give advice, but we cannot give conduct.

'Tis against some people's principle to pay interest, and seems against others' interest to pay the principal.

The bell calls others to church, but itself never minds the sermon.

In the affairs of this world, men are saved not by faith but by the want of it.

The almanac was of course an anthology, and Franklin took his sayings where he found them, as freely from books as from his experience or reflection. But many of the sayings were his own to begin with or were made his own by the flavor he gave them. Something of what that flavor was appears from a comparison of certain classic maxims of Poor Richard which Franklin did not invent with others which he apparently did.

Fools make feasts, and wise men eat them.

Keep thy shop, and thy shop will keep thee.

God helps them that help themselves. [To this one Franklin gave its final form.]

These were not Franklin's but those of many men before him, and had already been polished to almost abstract antithesis. Franklin's own sayings were more likely to be based on precise images from the common life.

'Tis hard for an empty bag to stand upright.

The sleeping fox catches no poultry.

The used key is always bright.
Three removes is as good as a fire.

He had a knack at improving older proverbs, which in his hands became more direct and more graphic than they had been before. There was a Scottish proverb, "Fat housekeepers make lean executors," which he sharpened to "A fat kitchen, a lean will." Another Scottish proverb, "A gloved cat was never a good hunter," had an English variant, "A muffled cat is no good mouser." Franklin bettered both of them: "The cat in glove catches no mice." As far back as Plautus it had been said that no guest is welcome after three days. Lyly in his *Euphues* had said that "Fish and guests in three days are stale," and Sancho Panza in *Don Quixote* had agreed with him, and Herrick in the *Hesperides*. Franklin may have come upon the saying in John Ray's *English Proverbs* (1670) as "Fresh fish and new come guests, smell by they are three days old," or in James Kelly's *Scottish Proverbs* (1721) as "Fresh fish and poor friends become soon ill sar'd"—that is, ill savored. In Franklin's handling the proverb settled at last into its vernacular idiom and cadence: "Fish and visitors stink in three days." In all these improvements, it should be noted, the cadence Franklin gave his sayings added as much to them as his change of words.

While he was writing as Poor Richard with point and edge Franklin was writing as himself with increasing grace and homely ease. Publisher, editor, citizen active in all the affairs of Philadelphia and Pennsylvania, clerk and then member of the Assembly, secretary of the American Philosophical Society he had organized, soldier on the frontier, postmaster general for North America, author of the first plan for intercolonial union and of farsighted plans for a new status for America in the British Empire, scientist renowned throughout the learned world for his discoveries in electricity: in all these capacities Franklin was habitually if not primarily a writer, almost always applying his art to immediate ends, to communicate and persuade. He seems to have had no impulse to create new forms. Maxims were as old as literature, and older. Newspapers had standard types of essay, tale, dialogue, or letter (real or imaginary) to the editor. Pamphlets were common. Franklin practiced all these forms, content if he could give each of them, as he did, fresh matter in fresh language. Two kinds at which he was especially adept were far apart. One was the hoax. He wrote a circumstantial account of a witch trial at Mount Holly that had never taken place, reported a speech that no Polly Baker had ever made in defense of her unlicensed fecundity. In a letter to himself, as editor of the *Gazette,* he circumstantially proposed that if the British government persisted in sending convicts to the Colonies, the Colonies should pay their debt by sending rattlesnakes to England. It amused him to write his hoaxes with such a straight face that readers might be taken in. There was a strong vein of fiction in Franklin, if he had ever worked it. But he was as excellent in his scientific papers, which were perfectly lucid and utterly honest, clear of technical jargon, sensible, humane, and exciting.

Franklin's stylistic range was greater than has been realized. It is possible that he deliberately experimented, long after his youth, with different styles. There is, for example, the exordium to *Some Account of the Pennsylvania Hospital,* in which, without false eloquence or toplofty language, without in the least turning aside from the plain business of the narrative, Franklin by his sustained and linked cadences produced an effect of homespun splendor.

About the end of the year 1750 some persons who had frequent opportunities of observing the distress of such distempered poor as from time to time came to Philadelphia for the advice and assistance of the physicians and surgeons of that city; how difficult it was for them to procure suitable lodgings and other conveniences proper for their respective cases and how expensive the providing good and careful nurses and other attendants for want whereof many must suffer greatly, and some probably perish, that might otherwise have been restored to health and comfort and become useful to themselves, their families, and the public for many years after; and considering moreover that even the poor inhabitants of this city though they had homes were therein but badly accommodated in sickness and could not be so well and so easily taken care of in their separate habitations as they might be in one convenient house, under one inspection and in the hands of skilful practitioners; and several of the inhabitants of the province who unhappily became disordered in their senses wandered about to the terror of their neighbors, there being no place (except the house of correction) in which they might be confined and subjected to proper management for their recovery, and that house was by no means fitted for such purposes; did charitably consult together and confer with their friends and acquaintances on the best means of relieving the distressed under those circumstances.

Such a style is nearly as far apart as it could be from that in which Franklin, in his *Reflections on Courtship and Marriage,* described a slattern:

Let us survey the morning dress of some women. Downstairs they come, pulling up their ungartered, dirty stockings; slipshod, with naked heels peeping out; no stays or other decent conveniency, but all flip-flop; a sort of a clout thrown about their neck, half on and half off, with the frowsy hair hanging in sweaty ringlets, staring like Medusa with her serpents; shrugging up her petticoats, that are sweeping the ground and scarce tied on; hands unwashed, teeth furred, and eyes crusted—but I beg your pardon, I'll go no farther with this sluttish picture, which I am afraid has already turned your stomach.

This was as harsh as Swift, and racier.

And Franklin had a third style, remote from both these two, which he used in the will he wrote in 1750. When he had done with his bequests, he wrote:

And now humbly returning sincere Thanks to God, for producing me into Being, and conducting me hitherto thro' Life so happily, so free from Sickness, Pain & Trouble, and with such a Competency of this World's Goods as might make a reasonable Mind easy; That he was pleased to give me such a Mind, with moderate Passions, or so much of his gracious Assistance in governing them; and to free it early from Ambition, Avarice and Superstition, common Causes of much Uneasiness to Men. That he gave me to live so long in a Land of Liberty, with a People that I love, and rais'd me, tho' a Stranger, so many Friends among them; bestowing on me, moreover, a loving and prudent Wife and dutiful Children. For these and all his other innumerable Mercies and Favours, I bless that Being of Beings who does not disdain to care for the meanest of his Creatures. And I reflect on those Benefits received with the greater Satisfaction, as they give me such a Confidence in his Goodness as will, I hope, enable me always in all things to submit freely to his Will, and to resign my Spirit chearfully into his Hands whenever he shall please to call for it; reposing my Self securely in the Lap of God & Nature as a Child in the Arms of an affectionate Parent.

In April 1757 Franklin wrote a letter to his youngest sister about his oldest, then near eighty. She must, he said, be allowed to go on living in her own house. When old people "have lived long in a house it becomes natural to them; they are almost as closely connected with it as a tortoise with its shell; old folks and old trees, if you remove them, it is ten to one you kill them." This was in Franklin's familiar style, which he used in letters and which became in time his essential style: the true style which was the man. The letter was the form which his art took more often than any other. Most of his writings on science were letters to his scientific friends. Though he wrote more or less formal pamphlets for the public, his private correspondence is richer than they in speculations on politics, economics, religion, morals, aesthetics. He told many of his best anecdotes in letters, and frequently wrote his bagatelles as letters. Even his autobiography began as a long letter to his son. His surreptitious writings —no longer surreptitious—were cast in that form: *Advice to a Young Man on the Choice of a Mistress; A Letter to the Royal Academy of Brussels.* Franklin, one of the greatest of public men, had what may be called a kind of private mind. He liked the sense that what he wrote was being written for some actual definite person, rather than for a general audience.

This accounts for the variety of his letters: they were to a variety of persons. The letters of his American years, up to 1757, were more often related to business or science or public affairs than to pleasant friendships. Only after he had met Catherine Ray and had written her the earliest of his famous letters to women (American, English, and French) did he fully enlarge and enrich the uses he put letters to. In time he knew how to be as stately as in his great letter to Washington, written from Paris in 1780:

Should peace arrive after another campaign or two, and afford us a little leisure, I should be happy to see your Excellency in Europe and to accompany you, if my age and strength would permit, in visiting some of its ancient and most famous kingdoms. You would, at this side of the sea, enjoy the great reputation you have acquired, pure and free from those little shades that the jealousy of a man's countrymen and contemporaries are ever endeavoring to cast over living merit. Here you would know, and enjoy, what posterity will say of Washington. For a thousand leagues have nearly the same effect with a thousand years. The feeble voice of those grovelling passions cannot extend so far in either time or distance. At present I enjoy that pleasure for you, as I frequently hear the old generals of this martial country (who study the maps of America and mark upon them all your operations) speak with sincere approbation and great applause of your conduct; and join in giving you the character of one of the greatest captains of the age.

Then Franklin went on in a set piece, a large Homeric simile.

I must soon quit the scene, but you may live to see our country flourish, as it will amazingly and rapidly after the war is over: like a field of young Indian corn, which long fair weather and sunshine had enfeebled and discolored, and which, in that weak state, by a thunder-gust of violent wind, hail, and rain seemed to be threatened with absolute destruction; yet the storm being past, it recovers fresh verdure, shoots up with double vigor, and delights the eye not of its owner only but of every observing traveller.

This was in Franklin's grand style for letters. He had another style in which he could write like a wise imp. In 1777 he drew up a model letter of introduction, at a time when he was unendurably harried in Paris with requests for such letters to America.

The bearer of this, who is going to America, presses me to give him a letter of recommendation, though I know nothing of him, not even his name. This may seem extraordinary, but I assure you it is not uncommon here. Sometimes, indeed, one unknown person brings another, equally unknown, to recommend him; and sometimes they recommend one another. As to this gentleman, I must refer you to himself for his character and merits, with which he is certainly better acquainted than I can possibly be. I recommend him, however, to those civilities which every stranger of whom one knows no harm has a right to; and I request you will do him all the good offices, and show him all the favor, that on further acquaintance you shall find him to deserve.

There is no evidence that Franklin ever gave this model letter to any actual person. He wrote it to relieve himself, and perhaps to entertain his friends, as a poet might have written a humorous lyric.

A still better instance of this practice appears in the letter Franklin wrote to William Strahan in July, 1775. They had been friends for more than thirty years, Strahan as eminent among printers in England as Franklin in America. Now Strahan was a member of Parliament, Franklin of the Continental Congress. All America was aroused over Lexington and Concord. Franklin on the day he wrote his letter, the 5th, met with the Pennsylvania Committee of Safety at six in the morning, moved on to the meeting of Congress at nine, and sat till four in the afternoon. Some time during the day, it may be guessed, he thought of writing to Strahan, to whom he owed a letter. But when he set his pen to paper Franklin did not begin with "Dear Friend" or "Dear Straney" as he usually did, but with "Mr. Strahan." His formality was a reproach, as his first sentence was. "You are a member of Parliament," he began, "and one of that majority which has doomed my country to destruction. You have begun to burn our towns and murder our people." Suddenly Franklin's strong feeling rose to a bitter image. "Look upon your hands! They are stained with the blood of your relations." Then Franklin remembered: "You and I were long friends." And at that he was himself again, and tempered his final sentence with its deft conclusion: "You are now my enemy, and I am   Yours, B. Franklin." This was stern, but it was in Franklin's true idiom and true form. Two days later Franklin wrote Strahan a friendly letter to which he had a friendly answer.

Not many of Franklin's letters have the perfected structure of these three. He was a busy man, and in his letters had commonly to transact one kind of business or another and convey information. But he seldom wrote a letter in which there was not some graceful or witty turn of language or sentiment. His letters are in effect his conversations, of which few records have survived. He ordinarily wrote them straight off in his clear, running hand, without many erasures or corrections, but often too he made first drafts and copied them. For Franklin was a writer who took pains with his prose, as poets do with verse. In a letter to a friend who had asked for advice about writing Franklin in 1789 recommended the method which he himself had followed for a lifetime:

Before you sit down to write on any subject . . . spend some days in considering it, putting down at the same time, in short hints, every thought which occurs to you as proper to make a part of your intended piece. When you have thus obtained a collection of the thoughts, examine them carefully with this view, to find which of them is properest to be presented first to the mind of the reader, that he, being possessed of that, may the more easily understand it, and be better disposed to receive what you intend for the second; and thus I would have you put a figure before each thought, to mark its future place in your composition. For so, every preceding proposition preparing the mind for that which is to follow, and the reader often anticipating it, he proceeds with ease, and pleasure, and approbation, as seeming continually to meet with his own thoughts. In this mode you have a better chance for a perfect production; because, the mind attending first to the sentiments alone, next to the method alone, each part is likely to be better performed, and I think too in less time.

Words are the tools of a writer as well as his materials, and good writers may always be known by the care they take with the words they choose. To the end of his life Franklin was extremely scrupulous, both as to diction and cadence. His last speech in the Constitutional Convention was the Convention's literary masterpiece and was so considered at the time. Various colleagues asked Franklin for copies of it. It was printed in several states while the legislatures were deciding whether or not to ratify. The variants show how ready he was to better his text at any time. A copy in his own hand, now in the Library of Cornell University, shows him at work. He began: "I must own that there are several parts of this Constitution which I do not at present approve"; then he crossed out and added till the opening stood: "I confess that I do not entirely approve of this Constitution"—eleven words in place of eighteen, and simpler words. He had often, he went on, in a long life found himself obliged "to change opinions . . . which I once thought right, but found to be wrong." This apparently seemed to him too blunt, and he changed "wrong" to "otherwise." Every few lines throughout the manuscript there is some change, generally slight, now and then considerable. "When," he said, "you assemble a number of men . . . you assemble with these men all their prejudices, their passions, their errors of opinion, their local interests, and their selfish views." In the following sentence he first wrote: "From the fermentation of this heterogeneous mixture can a perfect production be expected?" The figure of speech seems to have displeased him, and for "the fermentation of this heterogeneous mixture" he substituted "such an assembly." A minor scientist might have held to the scientific image. Franklin was an artist, and he knew that the simpler form was better.

Any number of his manuscripts remain to show how systematically he might plan his compositions and how delicately he might revise his language. But even for Franklin there were only so many hours in a day, only so many days to live in however many years. In the midst of great affairs he found time to write letters, notes, pamphlets, but no histories or treatises. For something like thirty years he hoped he might some day complete a work to be called "The Art of Virtue." He never began it, though he lived it. His sixteen years in England, his eight years in France saw no essential alteration of his literary habits, except that his prose grew wittier and sweeter. His hoaxes came to have as a rule a definite political bearing. He ridiculed British ignorance of America by telling the English about whale and cod in the upper lakes: "Whales, when they have a mind to eat cod, pursue them wherever they fly; and . . . the grand leap of a whale in that chase up the fall of Niagara is esteemed, by all who have seen it, as one of the finest spectacles in nature."

He ridiculed the British claim to America by gravely printing an alleged edict by the King of Prussia, who, according to the document, claimed the right to rule Great Britain because its people had formerly emigrated from Germany. Outraged over the use by the British of Hessian mercenaries in America, Franklin chose to rouse European opinion against it by a hoax. And during the peace negotiations, when Franklin was demanding reparations for the damage done to innocent Americans along the coast and on the frontier, he produced his most circumstantial hoax about the American scalps which had been taken by Indians in the pay of the British. No matter how deeply Franklin might be moved, he could not long go without his organic humor and never without his native grace.

As *The Way to Wealth* does Franklin's wisdom less than justice, so does his *Autobiography* do less than justice to his life. It brings his story down to only 1757 or so, and deals rather with his beginnings than with his achievements. The time he gave to writing it had to be snatched from crowding affairs. When he began it, at Bishop Shipley's country house in late July or early August 1771, he expected to have "a week's uninterrupted leisure." He may have had more than that, for he remained at Twyford nearly two weeks. But Franklin was a genial guest, and it is hardly likely that he gave more than a few hours a day to his book, writing in a study on the grounds. He is said to have read it to his hosts and their children, possibly in installments as he wrote them. It may have been suggested to him by their questions, about the young adventures of the renowned philosopher who had begun life as a tradesman—a kind of life so remote from the Shipleys'—and in America—a country so remote from England. And Franklin himself, he told his son in the first sentence, had always "had pleasure in obtaining any little anecdotes of my ancestors." The first third or so of the book, written that week or so at Twyford, is richer in anecdotes than the rest, more easygoing and lighthearted. Franklin took the manuscript with him to America, and left it there when he went off on his dangerous winter voyage to France. Good luck preserved it through the Revolution. When Franklin resumed his story at Passy in 1784 he had no copy of what he had already written and was not quite sure where to begin again. Now a famous sage, he began with an account of his youthful experiments at perfection, and went no further.

At home once more, retired for ever from public office, he undertook at last in 1788 to carry his memoirs to their conclusion. But he was old and suffering. Many of his papers had been lost or mislaid. He would not trust his memory—accurate as it really was—or, in time, his judgment. He was not even sure that he should go on with the book or allow it to be published. He almost certainly made late revisions in what he had written, occasionally preferring academic phrases to his earlier homely ones. His *Autobiography* remained a fragment—strictly speaking, four fragments. As history it needs to be supplemented from his letters, his diplomatic journals and dispatches, his scientific writings, and many private records.

But it is not to be wondered at that Franklin is on the whole best remembered from his *Autobiography*. He was an autobiographical man. He never, like little men, valued secrets for themselves. Nor did he, like self-conscious men, make half-modest half-vain efforts to conceal what he had done. Though he punctiliously gave his associates, in business, science, politics, and public welfare, whatever credit was due them, he no less frankly took the credit due him. If that was vanity, people could make the most of it. He knew he had led a great life in the midst of great affairs. He had a story to tell and he enjoyed telling it. So many of his friends had enjoyed hearing it that he could assume the world would enjoy it too. He could not foresee the immense popularity of this book. Before him the autobiography as a literary form hardly existed. Rousseau and he at almost the same time took the first steps toward creating it. Unlike as these two were, they had in common a prophetic sense of the future's interest in the lives of individuals, whether passionate and romantic like Rousseau or realistic and honest like Franklin. Rousseau was primarily a writer. He could turn inward and pour his total self into his *Confessions*. Franklin could not stop making history long enough to write it. His bent was outward and he worked through actions and events. And yet in the part which was all he wrote of his *Autobiography* he somehow managed to indicate the outline of the unwritten whole. Most of his readers barely realize that he has told so little of the story, because he has revealed to them what seems to be so much of the man.

It is not the whole man. The outline is hinted at, but the colors are not filled in. They must be filled in from other sources, some of them still undiscovered. Discovery after discovery rounds out the picture of a man greater than any of the things he did. Master of himself, he was a master in the physical world, and a master of men. But none of these masteries, or all of them, can explain his accomplishments or his magic. He had also to be a master of living and lasting words. In him life made literature and literature perpetuated life. The first great American man was the first great American writer.

The American Tradition in
Contemporary Literature

by HENRY SEIDEL CANBY

Too much has perhaps been said of new departures in american literature. Like the New Deal, they are new in America only in so far as twentieth-century man has encountered new problems and invented new ways of thinking about them. This nation has been incredibly urbanized by the factory, the automobile, the moving picture, and the radio. Racial minorities, with traditions other than Anglo-Saxon, have become articulate and given to American literature, not so much a new accent, as new materials upon which the imagination can work. Yet it is questionable whether American literature owes much that is distinctively American to these influences. Joyce has worked more powerfully in our fiction than the radio broadcaster; New York Jews, Minnesota Scandinavians, Mississippi Negroes, Boston Irish, when they begin to write, prove to be more American than foreign, sometimes, I think often, more American than the Anglo-Saxon strain. If we are to seek for a national character in American literature, giving it qualities not dependent upon its English backgrounds and the doctrines of the twentieth century, it must be in the American tradition. This is not a dead hand reaching from out of our past, but a force that is alive and, like all living things, growing and changing, while preserving a pattern that can be recognized and defined.

There have been many attempts to define the American tradition, but the best have been protests against some other definition, and have suffered from oversimplification. Turner's famous exposition of the frontier spirit was a correction of an overemphasis upon our

European origins; Parrington's study of democracy in American literature was an attack upon the New England successors of the Federalists, who had been indifferent to democracy. The recent Marxian school has lit obscure corners of economic influence without supplying any formula broad enough for an Emerson, a Cooper, or a Whitman. In a brief paper like this one, I cannot hope to analyze, and much less to challenge, all these explanations of what it means to be an American. Yet it is possible to break down some of this conflicting testimony, and describe a group of traits that we can all agree are distinctively American, and then see how far they continue to live in the vivid, vigorous, if often disorderly, and sometimes noisy, literature of our own contemporaries in the twenties, thirties, and forties.

I shall not try to be original in this portrait of the American tradition, unless in a fresh application to books and people of our time. Probably the job could be done with different classifications, and certainly more classifications are possible. That is not important. If the traits I describe are true and significant, they are enough for an experiment in literary criticism. If anyone wishes to deny that the categories that follow are intensely American he will need a powerful argument. Some of them are English or French or Russian traits, also, but not to the same degree, not in the same way, not so significantly. Taken together, they spell in outline the name of our country when it thinks, feels, imagines, judges, expresses itself in literature.

The first and probably the most deep-lying of these characteristics is expansiveness. Naturally, our conquest of a continent conditioned us to expansiveness, but the inheritance goes much further back. It is probably true that the vast majority of immigrants to these shores, from the seventeenth century on, came because they felt they had to come. But it is not so often remembered that an equal, and perhaps a much greater number of Europeans, under like compelling circumstances, stayed at home. We got the restless, we got the seekers, we got the rebels, we got the oppressed who were willing to escape. When the first Swedish colonists landed on the Delaware, they brought with them some Finns who had been jailed for their undue energy in girdling and burning Her Majesty's forests in Sweden. Criminals at home from too much expansiveness, they became ace settlers on the Delaware, where burning, girdling, and chopping were the preliminaries to every crop of corn. The story is typical. And if, by the eighteenth century, expansiveness on land had subsided east of the Alleghenies, the burst through to the west, and the conquest of sea routes, renewed it in full vigor. Franklin's *Poor Richard* is intended as a brake on expansiveness. With Jonathan Edwards, hell itself became expansive. *Rip Van Winkle* is a serio-comedy of expansiveness. Cooper's Natty Bumppo symbolizes the conflict between the expansive soul seeking the freedom of the wilderness, and an expanding civilization always at his heels. Emerson is a spiritual expansionist. Thoreau wrote *Walden* to turn expansion inward. Mark Twain's boys are always going places, and Whitman's *Song of Myself* links Brooklyn, human nature, the West, and the universe.

But how vitally this trait persists in our literature today! If there is one trend, for example, in American fiction that has amounted almost to a folk lore in this decade, it is the historical novel, which has pushed for its sources backward and left and right across the continent. And note that these novels, from *Northwest Passage* and the innumerable narratives of prairie settlers to *Gone with the Wind,* have been stories of expansion, of conflict, and of building. It is the re-creation, the expansion, of the new South after the war that is the original and memorable part of *Gone with the Wind,* and both hero and heroine are identified with salvage and reconstruction, not with memory and loss. Note again the contrast of this school of history in fiction with the great European novelists of a century earlier. It is lost causes, defeated countries, or heroes in their last stand that Sir Walter Scott chooses for subjects. With him and with Dumas the vane points always to the past. The theme in the American books is preparation for a future expansiveness.

Or let us choose an individual writer, regarded by many of the younger generation as their leader, Thomas Wolfe. Here is expansiveness incarnate, even as in Whitman, even as in the westward pioneers who lived for frontier experience and moved on when stability caught up with them. Wolfe could write only one book and that was his whole expanding life. His work has a beginning and many middles but no end anywhere. Its faults are apparent, its virtue is an insatiable zest for experience, an expanding ego to which every happening seems important because it happens to Tom Wolfe.

Asheville, the railroad, the Harvard library, New York, and love and hate and human nature, all open illimitably when he reaches them. Everything is continental to his view, and he is as immune to classical restraint as a Mohawk chieftain, or Anthony Wayne, or Colonel Sellers, or Moby Dick. He ravaged his country for words, as the lumbermen ravaged its forests—leaving desert wastes and blacked confusion behind, but also roads and magnificent vistas. This is expansiveness run wild in the fourth century of our exploitation of a continent, in the second century of our national literature.

I could add many more examples, John Dos Passos, Faulkner in his way, Hemingway in his, Benét's *John Brown's Body* in its way, Hervey Allen, Robinson Jeffers emphatically and, like Wolfe, to his own damage, Marc Connolly's *The Green Pastures,* or Richard Wright's recent *Native Son,* a study of expansiveness thwarted and poisoned by racial prejudice.

I dislike applying a term such as equalitarianism, with its strongly European connotations, to the next American trait to be discussed, but I can think of no other word so applicable. Nevertheless, American equalitarianism is very different, both in origins and in results, from the European variety. It had to wait for no French Revolution in order to flourish. The first Swedish governor in Delaware complained that he could not keep his peasants within the stockade: they insisted upon establishing themselves in the forest, where they could become landholders like their superiors at home. The Quakers of Pennsylvania were radically equalitarian, and even when many of them grew rich, remained so within their own sect. The eighteenth-century aristocracy of Virginia and New England came from small people seeking equality with their betters in the old country, and was submerged in New England and segregated in Virginia by new waves of equalitarians. Given easy access to land and water, if not at home then just over the hills, an equalitarianism was as inevitable as an increase in national wealth. We have been conditioned by it in our formative centuries.

One result of this long-continued and dangerously successful attempt to make the Smiths as good as the Joneses is the dominantly bourgeois nature of the American tradition. Where so many have had—in the past at least—an opportunity to rise in the economic scale, there will be neither an aristocracy nor a plutocracy with that sense of security which produces a class. Equalitarianism and exclusiveness are mutually incompatible, and privilege, which has supported aristocracies elsewhere, becomes a reward of ability, not a heritable right. Plutocracy is less vulnerable here than aristocracy, but it is clear that even our plutocrats have been forced to establish foundations rather than families, in order to perpetuate their names.

But I am using "bourgeois" in no unfavorable sense. "Middle class" is the more usual term, and, indeed, fits perfectly the economic aspirations of the American millions since we began. It is too narrow a word, however, to apply to literature. Our literature has had the bourgeois virtues, which are real and valuable. It has never been successfully heroic, although intellectually it has reached, especially in our earlier New England, formidable heights. But on the austere pinnacles of thinking an Emerson and a Thoreau, if not a Hawthorne, wrote definitely for the community of all men of good will, and believed them capable of good will. So did Jefferson, although himself a product of our Southern experiment in making an aristocracy by the plantation and slavery system, an experiment already failing in his time. It was, indeed, the so-called Virginia aristocracy which founded the political party which has made a political program of equalitarianism.

Could anything be more bourgeois in a good sense than the books of Mark Twain? I do not refer to the obvious leveling of *A Connecticut Yankee in King Arthur's Court,* but to more instinctive because less conscious expressions of equalitarianism. Consider the theme of *Huckleberry Finn,* which must certainly be regarded as one of the most typical as well as one of the best creations of the American imagination. The theme of that book is the conversion of Huck to the bourgeois virtues. He has inherited an outmoded equalitarianism, the faith of his poor-white father that he is as good as any man—and indeed he is, in a frontier society where good hunting and good fishing and a body inured to cold and bad whiskey guarantee independence. But Hannibal is not frontier any more. The border ruffian is out of date. All he can do is to boast and go to the lockup. If Huck is to climb on the American bandwagon, he has to learn how to keep up with a new set of Joneses, and his difficulties and backslidings make the story. Mark Twain doubts the values of Hannibal society, and it is possible to read both *Tom Sawyer* and *Huckleberry Finn* as satires of that society, but he never doubts—or never doubted until toward the end of his life—the duty and privilege of every good American to become as rich and independent and successful as the Judge Thatchers, whoever they might be, of the time. Huck grown up will be a better bourgeois than the rest.

How strong this equalitarian *motif* is in the majority of American books need not be emphasized here. The difficulty is to find American books of vitality in which it is not a moving force. Poe, who belongs to another phase of the American tradition, is one example. Melville may be regarded as another, Hawthorne as a third, Henry James as a fourth. But Poe was a pathological romanticist, Melville and Hawthorne were skeptics, and James an internationalist. And even these men were all specialists in that inevitable accompaniment of bourgeois equalitarianism, the emphasis upon the individual and individualism. Far from having subsided with the closing of the frontier and the economic changes which have so clamped down on American opportunity, this trait has merely changed its metabolism in the imagination.

The novels of Sinclair Lewis, for example, are essentially studies in the pathology of American ambition. In every important story, from *Main Street* on, he has described the American passion to get on, to be as good as the current Joneses, to conform to success and share it. But the societies that Lewis describes have got their values wrong. They want, like Babbitt, tokens of success, which prove to be only tokens. They have lost sight of valuable ends in contriving efficient means. Or, as in *Arrowsmith* or *Elmer Gantry,* they have paid a heavy price for an equality of low ideals and an unworthy success. It is never the right of the American to have what the best have, which Lewis questions. His heroes are all go-getters in their own right. But Americans have gone after the wrong values. He scorns them, *not* because they are going places, but because they have lost their way. In all of this, though with less satire and more philosophy, Thoreau, in *Walden,* was his predecessor.

A less important but very cogent instance may be found in a book just published, which, with its renewal of the theme of *Huckleberry Finn,* shows how heavily this national problem still weighs upon our imagination. Jesse Stuart, the Kentucky poet of the mountains, has written a novel in poetic prose called *Trees of Heaven*. It is a notable contribution to those books sprung from the American soil, styled by it, and rich in essential character, which prove that the virility and energy of the new American fiction are not to be confined to ideology, sophistication, or fictionized history. But *Trees of Heaven,* unlike *The Yearling* with which it may be compared, has a theme. Anse, the mountain farmer, is an equalitarian determined to lift his family to economic security. In contrast, the squatters, who once had been free pioneers, are poor whites on the way out to relief or vagabondage. Boliver, whose daughter is so beautiful, is Huck's father over again, with a difference. He can work, he can create a good life, but the particular bourgeois ideals that Anse has acquired from the Joneses of his neighborhood send Bolly back to drunkenness, with his bare feet hanging over the porch. This American type must have freedom to enjoy life, as his ancestors had freedom to live their own life in the woods. The wrong kind of equalitarianism makes him into a bum.

The will to be equal, which is so strong in the American tradition, has become a critique of equality; but the will is still there. You will find it as the motive of Richard Wright's Negro story, *Native Son.* You will find it, subtly displayed, in Thornton Wilder's *Our Town,* you will find it dramatically spoken by Mrs. Joad in *The Grapes of Wrath.* We are mature as a nation, but this obsession is the same as in our youth.

Picking and choosing among the other outstanding attributes of the American tradition, I take next its most puzzling element. Not puzzling in how and why it came about, but puzzling in its action and its unexpected strength and weakness. We are a humanitarian nation, even more so than the British—one might say, the tougher we are, the more humanitarian.

Our record for tough ruthlessness is not a pretty one. If fewer Indians were massacred in Anglo-Saxon than in Spanish territories, it is chiefly because there were fewer Indians to massacre. If we did not reduce the remainder to slavery, they were equally exploited and much more thoroughly dispossessed. The type badman of modern literature comes from our West. The gunman and gangster were American specialties until Germany capitalized them for political purposes. If the factory system at its beginning was more ruthless in England, that was simply because British men, women, and children were more helpless. There was less room and less food. The most influential humanitarian book in English, one of the most effectively moving books of all time, *Uncle Tom's Cabin,* was inspired not so much by slavery as such, as by the ruthless exploitation of the Negro for quick profits in the cotton lands of the frontier. We have never been slow with knife, pistol, or whip.

And yet never was a nation so readily touched emotionally to humanitarian ends as the American since the nineteenth century made the idea of humanitarianism familiar. The North took back the South after the Civil War without a proscription, an unheard of thing then, before, or after, in a civil war. If there was oppression and exploitation later, that came from the other strain in our make-up. Our foreign-mission effort, of which at least two thirds was humanitarian in its appeal, has been vast in proportion to means and population. No cause that awaked pity or sympathy has ever failed of support in this country, and, as we grow rich, our contributions to world suffering have expanded out of proportion. The type political machine of the United States, Tammany, to whose methods the Nazis owe much, was built upon a basis of genuine humanitarianism combined with exploitation without scruple.

The cause, of course, of this deep-set trait is no superior quality of mercy in the stocks that settled America. The fact of settlement itself made them will to re-form themselves and their circumstances. Newcomers, torn from a settled environment, facing new conditions of living, separated from the tradition of stable communities upon which law and custom are based, they *had* to re-form themselves, and sooner or later re-form their neighbors. The frontiers of the United States have usually been advanced by pioneers who, having re-formed themselves once to the freedoms and necessities of the wilderness, did not choose to re-form themselves again to suit an approaching civilization. Reform in its broadest implication is in our blood because we have been conditioned by it for generations. It has become traditional, and this tradition the experiences of the latest immigrants into our industrialized society has not invalidated. They also have had both the opportunity and the necessity of re-forming themselves.

But this reforming habit of mind did not have to become humanitarian. It did not have to become moral. It was the influence, undoubtedly, of the strong Protestant tradition of a reforming ethics which made our tradition of reform so moral in its implications. An interesting comparison can be made here between the re-forming of Latin civilization in both North and South America, and our own. With the Latins, the ethical element in reform was weak, even though the religious element was durable. They sought a rich life rather than a good one.

And it was the influence of abundant opportunity in a continent working upon this ethical prepossession that seems to have made the peculiarly American blend of humanitarianism. It is more sentimental than the English because, except perhaps in the area of slavery, it has never been harshly tested. It is notably more widespread, being not confined to a class, as in the humanitarianism of the Victorian middle class, but even more characteristic of the worker than of the *rentier* or successful exploiter. It is more generous among men and women of small means because our opportunities have been more generous. We have never had to be stingy or mean, at least as a nation. Economically it may ruin us yet, for it is behind the easy good nature that, quite as much as predatory politics, is responsible for such disastrous handouts as our pension system and the uncritical character of much of our relief.

To stretch out the long list of notable American books which carry on the tradition of this humanitarianism is quite unnecessary. There are, as a matter of fact, few really hard-boiled books in the American tradition. Those which appear to be so, usually under scrutiny show, like Poe's stories of terror, a shrinking sensitiveness to pain, or like Hemingway's tough episodes, a defensive mechanism against fear. But in the main stream of tradition, the trait is self-evident. Curiously enough, the two great men of Concord, Emerson and Thoreau, have the least of it. They have good will toward all good men, yet—Thoreau especially—are not easily moved to emotion by ills not spiritual in origin. But there is passionate and uncritical humanitarianism in Walt Whitman. There is sentimental humanitarianism in Bret Harte, whose stories of the easily aroused pity of gold-diggers and camp prostitutes seem to have had sufficient base in reality. There is a passionate and unsentimental humanitarianism in Mark Twain—at its best, I think, in *Huckleberry Finn,* where it is veiled by irony. And, coming to our own times, regard again for an instant Sinclair Lewis, whose *Babbitt,* felt at the time of its publication to be a document in reform, seems now to be not so much a satire as a lament for the good American warped by the irresistible pressure of commonplace ideals. Or consider Theodore Dreiser's *American Tragedy,* which, for all its appearance of callous documentation, is at base pity for an ordinary man caught in tragic circumstances and doomed by his public's pathological craving for sensation to relieve its own dull lives.

No better example, however, could be found of the persistence of this tradition in what we profess to think is a new and different America, than the resounding success of John Steinbeck's *The Grapes of Wrath.* Here is a book which breaks the laws of the genteel Medes and Persians who, until this decade, have always dominated our literature. It offends decency, not only by deeds, which has always been permissible, but by words. Its language sets new standards of realism for the American novel. Here, also, is a book which attacks the economic theories which have been orthodox in American literature, and attacks them, not by argument, but by precisely that kind of sentimental generalization upon a society of mutual love and help which has always driven the practical American business man into a contemptuous fury. Nevertheless, in spite of some natural local objection in the communities described, the book has made its way wherever a book can in America. And why? Its sometimes uncertain art aside, I am sure its success is due to a reforming humanitarianism in the exact American tradition which produced *Uncle Tom's Cabin.* We may shrug our economic shoulders over the problem of migratory labor, but we cannot guard our imagination against Mrs. Joad, who wanted only to make good Americans of her family, and could not. We are sorry for the Joads because they were deprived of what has made our tradition a generous one—opportunity. And this pity stirs on to reform.

I shall choose for my last earmark of the American tradition—youth. With more time and analytical shrewdness, it might be possible to distinguish a dozen more, but this one cannot be neglected. Perhaps it is the most important, probably it is the most determining characteristic of all. I am not so naïve as to speak of America as a young nation politically and economically. Politically we are matured, though, one hopes, not crystallized. Only the British regime shows an equal correspondence between the will of the people and the direction and control of government. And this constitutes maturity in politics, even though strains and stresses show the vital need of more growth and adaptiveness. France is still experimental by comparison. The totalitarian states are in the crude youth of violence and compulsion, where evolution has scarcely begun its work, and order comes from forced obedience, not from custom and free acceptance. Nor are we young economically. On the contrary, our capitalist system, slowly absorbing ideas and practices of socialism, is certainly the most developed of its type, and, if it lags behind the industrial revolution, has not found it necessary to change our ways of life in order to survive.

But in literature—and the arts in general—we are still extraordinarily young. In fact, it is obvious that we have been growing younger and younger as decade by decade we have wrenched further and further away from European, and especially English, tradition. Jonathan Edwards and Benjamin Franklin were European minds only slightly affected by a new environment. Irving and Cooper are still old minds functioning with new material. Emerson and Thoreau are full of new sap, but their youthfulness is not in manner; it is hope in the one and rebellion in the other. With Mark Twain and Whitman a raw kind of youthfulness appears—brash, vulgar, disregardful of the rules. They write like youngsters even when they are old. Energy begins to be the chief attribute of great Americans, a crude and wasteful energy, not regardful of the labor-saving devices of classicism. Such men write both badly and well, and on the same page. The vigorous, pushing imaginations grow more and more experimental, more and more indifferent to anything but quick expression. It is not literature that excites them any more, but the country. They go to it for news, and their reporting in prose or poetry is news, with the quality of journalism, which becomes an American art. The proportion of the writers who work in the great literary tradition to the innovators and expressionists grows steadily less. Finally, in our own time, the public taste itself changes and readers fall avidly upon the sensations of their own land.

What is young here is, of course, the imagination, which at last is beginning to construct its images in terms of a new continent. And there are many other signs of youth in this imagination besides its reckless and untiring energy. American writing for a half century has tended to begin everything and finish it fast. In fiction, the short story has been its chosen form, and its very best writers—even such classicists as Willa Cather—have been at their best in briefish stories. Others, like Caldwell, Faulkner, Hemingway, Wilder, Steinbeck, Sherwood Anderson, have begun to falter every time they have tried to sustain their work in the dimension of a complete novel. Their great success is in the short story, single or compounded. It may be that this results in part from the unheroic character of the equalitarian American mind, but that is not enough explanation. Our social structure is, apparently, still too youthful, too fluid, to bear the weight of a great reconstruction in terms of art. Light craft go better.

Another trait which seems to me characteristically youthful is the curious duplex quality of the American imagination. Ever since the beginnings of our national literature this has been manifest. In the upper story we tend to be cheerful, generous, optimistic, humorous. But downstairs, writer after writer has been caught, sometimes fatally, by the macabre, the satiric, the sardonic, the horrible. It is surely strange that Poe and Ambrose Bierce and the Twain of *The Mysterious Stranger* and James of *The Turn of the Screw,* and Faulkner who wrote that terrible book *Sanctuary,* and Hemingway who specialized in cruelty, should all be Americans! Not strange, however, if one remembers the contrasts between freedom, success, degeneracy, and violence, all existing on the frontier, or in a boom industrial city. Not strange either, if one considers the hurry of our development, which has been built over bog and cesspool, as well as good firm ground.

And, indeed, these almost hysterical relapses into fear and disgust, so characteristic of American writing, are certainly aspects of a youthful imagination that, until recently, has never had to take stock. If it assumed a culture as its basis, it was a European culture, and in this it was like a youth who assumes his parents' stability as groundwork for his own activities. And as with that youth, when America showed itself as not according to European specifications, there has been a quick disillusionment and a tendency to rush into extremes of despair or abuse. It is hard to tell where one gets the most untrustworthy pictures of American life—in the too wholesome, too complacent books of the Age of American Confidence, or in the hysterical studies of disorganization, depression, exploitation, and violence, so current today.

The truth is, that since the American imagination really began to busy itself with America as a subject for literary interpretation, it has been going places with such youthful and nervous rapidity that relapses into pessimism or distrust or plain hysteria were inevitable. It has, as I have said, been primarily engaged with news, and what has been found has been described more often than interpreted. Mark Twain and Whitman were like that. Thoreau's *Walden* was a protest against going places until you know your own, and if there had been a more vigorous literature extant might very well have been aimed in that direction instead of at mercantilism. Much as he admired Whitman's passionate individualism, Thoreau took issue with him on just this point. Why praise the hurrying crowds until we know the man?

Look once again at Thomas Wolfe. Could anything be more youthful in good and bad senses, or more illustrative of the American way of attempting a great theme, than his work? His achievement is to describe Tom Wolfe going places and recording his reactions in contact with a continent. His writing boils with energy, it is all news, it descends from ecstatic enthusiasm to the macabre or the despairing, it has, as I have said, beginning and middle, but no sign of the ending which to an older imagination would have been implicit in the first chapter. Not a truly successful writer, Wolfe, in his faults and in his virtues, is symptomatic of what we are imaginatively, and that is the reason for his powerful grip upon young artists of this generation.

I might add, of course, to this picture of youth, the moving picture, an American art, still dominated by Americans, as a more complete and even more cogent example of the young imagination of America, although the tight grasp of profit makers has almost, but not quite, suppressed relapses into disgust or despair. Particularly when the American movie is not literature at all, which is usually, the mental age of its imagination can scarcely be more than twelve. And that, of course, is because the producers, however sophisticate in techniques, have spiritually and morally not yet reached adulthood, and so welcome the immature as well as the energetic in the American imagination.

The moral I have tried to draw in this paper is a very simple one. In our culture, we are definitely a nation in the making, and this is our tradition, and still governs us. This culture has had two climaxes. The first was just before the Civil War, when, still largely English in civilization but feeling our new environment, we broke into extraordinary waves of duplex energy, some material, some spiritual. The second climax, I suspect, we are living in now, and European chaos may hasten its movement.

In both climaxes the formative elements of our tradition are powerful. We have lost little from these, and are steadily adding to a distinctive heritage. It is not a literary culture to boast about yet, as one can boast of our political and economic progress even while deploring our errors. But it is still expansive, and perhaps never so interesting to a student of criticism as now.

You get one aspect of it today in the cheaply optimistic magazine, which is all wish psychology, like the pioneer. You get another in our ironical, sophisticated books, and magazines like the *New Yorker,* where idealism is handled skeptically by a good-natured fellow who does not intend to be fooled. You get still another in deadly serious reformers, like Steinbeck. You get still another in brutal tough guys, who easily turn tender. Still another in the vulgar smartness of gossip columns, the trim emptiness of Broadway plays, the mechanical short story.

But make no mistake. The expansiveness of a hearty America, good-willed, hopeful, energetic, is not dead. Tom Wolfe echoes Whitman; Steinbeck, Harriet Beecher Stowe. When this generation gets through with going places, we may expect another period like that really great New England stir of the imagination which was frustrated by materialism and war. Unfortunately, there is another war on, but I doubt whether any European involvement can now change the direction, though it may add to the qualities, of our American tradition.

On Counting Your Chickens
before They Hatch

by EDWARD WEEKS

YOU REMEMBER THE STORY OF THE CHICKEN FARMER? ONE NIGHT HE heard a fearful rumpus in his chicken yard. Seizing his shotgun, he ran out to the wire, where he thought he saw a figure lurking in the corner. "Who's there?" he shouted, "Come out! Come out, or I'll shoot!" Dead silence. Then a soft voice said, "Ain't nobody here, boss, 'ceptin' us chickens." On this occasion I knew that I should have the opportunity of speaking face to face to a group of people who were just as interested in writing as I am. There would be nobody here but us chickens.

I have noticed that writers and editors have this much in common with people who raise chickens—they love to count their chickens before they hatch. I believe it is second nature for writers to do so. When I was in college I wrote what I thought was a good story in which my parents were the central characters. My teacher in composition said it should be published, and after the manuscript had been returned to me by the *Saturday Evening Post,* I contributed it to the *Harvard Advocate.* But even before it appeared in print I was receiving congratulations—at least in my mind—not on that particular short story but on the volume of them which at that moment I was confident I should write in the next six months. If I had written such a book, I am sure you would have heard of it, but it still remains one of those chickens I haven't had time to hatch.

All writers, small and great, are nourished by such illusions. I don't think they could live without them. When John Keats realized that he was in love with Fanny Brawne and could not afford matrimony, he decided to get away by himself and write for money. We know from his letters that *La Belle Dame sans Merci* was almost the least of the arrows he thought he had in his quiver. He was going to write plays, great smashing tragedies which would make his reputation, and he thought he already heard the applause before he had finished the first act of *Otho the Great.* The notebook of any honest writer will tell you the same thing. Think how often Samuel Taylor Coleridge got set for some great, ambitious project—and how seldom he laid the egg. Xanadu stands for that superb but fleeting vision which entrances every one of us who try to write. While the spell is on us we see our short story instantaneous, vivid, and complete; we see our poem an epic to stir the country; we see our novel so thick— and over 100,000 copies! We all share in this experience when we have the vision and feel the power that goes with it, and our only wonder is whether we shall have life enough to accomplish the limitless and magnificent work we see ahead. Were it not for this recurring illusion, writing would be a drudgery too disappointing for most to endure.

II

Those of you who have been competing for the Hopwood Awards this year must have had moments when you asked yourselves whether it was worth the doing. What chance is there for a beginning writer in a world so full of tension and belligerency? Or, to put it specifically, what chance will *you* have to practice what you have learned when a year from now you may be in a training camp or up to your ears in defense work? It seems to me that perhaps the friendliest service I can perform this afternoon is to describe the climatic conditions under which I see writers working today and to foretell as accurately as possible the demands which any young American author will be expected to meet in the near future. I am not speaking as a prophet but as an editor of a magazine who has been trained to observe the changing currents in literature.

In the first place, what effect has the emergency upon those who are going to read your work? To what extent have the tastes and needs of the American reader been altered since the summer of 1939? Let me give you a close-up of the American reader in action. Fresh from his shave and with all the vigor of the early day, he comes down to breakfast to be greeted by the morning newspaper. After some quick sparring with the headlines he reads the baseball scores, follows along with the local murder case, and then, since he can't escape it, he stands up to the war news as delivered by the A.P., the Berlin dispatch, Walter Lippmann, Alsop and Kintner, Boake Carter, Pearson and Allen, Dorothy Thompson, and Westbrook Pegler. Round One. The challenger is still fresh, but a little off-balance. On the way to the office he is asked what he thinks of the President's speech. He puts up the best defense he can by quoting what he can remember from Walter Lippmann, Alsop and Kintner, Dorothy Thompson, and Westbrook Pegler. Round Two. On his desk at the office is the Whaley-Eaton Foreign Letter, and the Kiplinger Letter from Washington—full of portentous details about the defense program. The challenger is still boring in. Round Three. On the way to lunch he sees a scare-head and buys the extra. At lunch he is asked what he thinks of the British chances in the Middle East. He leads with his chin. Round Four. On the way home from the office he reads the afternoon edition, and before dinner his wife turns on the broadcasts from the foreign capitals. Round Five. Challenger still upright but wobbly. After dinner he looks through the illustrations in *Life*—which dent him a little. And as he is trying to get up courage to read the *Atlantic,* the family says to come along with them to the movies. When he gets there, the first thing he sees is the newsreel. Round Six—and the challenger is on the ropes. Joe Louis would be child's play for a mind that goes through such daily battering—and that is the kind of mind you've got to cope with for the duration!

Most Americans I talk with today are groggy from the effects of journalism. But that's not the only reaction I observe. In their self-defense they have become much more determined about what they want to read in their free time. What I mean by determination is this: the American reader is impatient with big words—those India-rubber words which have been stretched too far and too often by propagandists, orators, and politicians. It is my custom to make at least two long trips from East to West each year, and always I return from them with an amazement that a nation so widespread and composite can manage to settle its local problems and at the same time pull together. I think that is the kind of thing our American reader wants to know. The word "democracy" is not enough: he wants to be told how it works.

Second, he knows he is living in a world of violent change and that, like a gambler, he must take his chances with the rest of the country. He has learned to be much more resilient since That Man in the White House showed us the need. Third, he is eager for leadership. He is hopeful of finding a way out of this mess. He is waiting for a Democrat to provide a better solution than Hitler's. But he is not prejudiced—it might be a Republican.

And, finally, the American reader has more respect for his way of living. What do I mean by that? Well, let me show you. My office is a five-minute walk from my home on Beacon Hill. To get to it I skirt the Boston Common and cut a diagonal across our Public Gardens. On these late spring afternoons I find myself looking up into the sky and thinking, "My lord, what an easy target this open city would be for a bomber." The contrast between the pond with its swan boats, the blazing beds of tulips for which our Gardens are famous, and the fine old trees which were planted here on the clam shells by Charles Sargent—the contrast between this serene picture and what the place might look like when a squadron of heavy bombers had done their work has this effect upon me: it makes me realize how much I love life and how much I want to remain the kind of individual I am. I have been bombed before, and this new approach of danger sharpens my respect for individuality. I know that in my own case I am reading novels with avidity these days because I find they refresh my mind and restore my confidence in what the individual can do. In our novels it is the individual, not the system, which carries our hopes of the future. That is certainly true of Ma and Tom Joad as they are revealed to us by John Steinbeck. It is equally true of old Pilar in *For Whom the Bell Tolls*. No civil war, no cruelty, will ever shake her faith in life.

III

If these changes are apparent in the American reader, what can be said of our writers? The first thing an editor notices is that our chickens have all come home to roost. Novelists from Wisconsin and Ohio no longer need the sunlight of the Riviera in which to do their work. The expatriates who were once so busy finding—or losing— themselves in Paris have come home. With them have come many talented exiles who, as they struggle to adjust themselves to American life, may help us to a better appreciation of what American life should be. One result of all this is that the condescension toward things American has disappeared, I suspect for good.

With the disappearance of the expatriate there has also disappeared that by-product of the cosmopolitan, the book which was fashionable because it was odd. I am sure that there would be no incentive today which would prompt Gertrude Stein to write that first freak of hers entitled *Tender Buttons*. The impulse which led James Joyce away from *Dubliners* and into his maze, *Finnegans Wake,* is dead and buried with the past. So is the fashion which produced *Gadsby,* a novel of over 50,000 words, written without the letter *e.* The author, E. V. Wright, tied down the *e* key on his typewriter before he began to compose. For your own fun sometime just try to write an engaging sentence of twenty-five words without once using the letter *e.* Oddities like these shrink to the size of very small buttons indeed when writers are faced with the magnitude of what is now going on. There will always be need for experiments. There will always be a proving ground in literature for those young writers who must seek new directions. But, for the time being, the cult of unintelligibility finds no takers. That cult has gone with the silly sophistication which once made it popular.

And going, going, gone is that much more serious influence, the cult of the negative, a philosophy with which our novelists lived for twenty years, a philosophy which urged them to point out what's wrong without the glimmer of hope for what's right. "A mood of desperate unhappiness reigns in the world," says Van Wyck Brooks in his recent address "On Literature Today," "and this is marked especially in most of the writers. The temperamental cards of our time are all stacked in favour of despair. It seems as if our writers passively wallowed in misery, calling it fate; as if the most powerful writers, from James Joyce to Hemingway, from Eliot of *The Waste Land* to Eugene O'Neill and Theodore Dreiser, were bent on proving that life is a dark little pocket. Even where, as in many cases, these writers are fighting for social justice, they still picture life as hardly worth the trouble of fighting for it. You know the picture of life you find in the novels of William Faulkner, Dos Passos, James T. Farrell and so many others, who carry the day with their readers because they are writers of great power. They seem to delight in kicking their world to pieces, as if civilization were all a pretence and everything noble a humbug." I agree emphatically with Mr. Brooks. This attitude began as a direct reaction to the First World War, it settled into a habit, and it ended by becoming a pose. I do not mean for a moment that our writers will cease to be realists. But I do mean that writers and readers both have had a bellyful of despair and that as a daily diet it is simply not good enough.

IV

You won't remember the books on which this country was feeding as it made ready to take part in the First World War. But I do. I remember them vividly, because they were the books which eventually inflamed my mind and propelled me into the French Army. When I volunteered at the end of 1916, I stood five feet five and weighed exactly ninety-eight pounds. The French Army was the only army then willing to take a soldier of that size. Let me give you a bird's-eye view of what our literature was like at that time.

Begin in the spring of 1914—we were perfectly oblivious to the thunderstorm that was coming. We were like cows in a happy pasture, munching on lush novels which, I suspect, would turn your stomach if you tried them today. Remember that 1914 was the end of an epoch, the climax of peace and prosperity. In 1914 a struggling young American poet named Robert Frost published his collection of poems, *North of Boston,* but he did not publish it in Massachusetts. He published it in England, where he had gone in search of the recognition and encouragement denied him in America. In 1914 a young man who was having a hard time trying to write plays, a young man by the name of Eugene O'Neill, brought out his first book, *Thirst and Other Plays.* In 1914 Theodore Dreiser published his novel, *The Titan,* and I doubt if two thousand people in this country took the pains to read it. The reason we did not have time to discover the talent of Robert Frost and Eugene O'Neill and Theodore Dreiser was that we were absorbed in the best sellers. We were reading *Pollyanna* by Eleanor H. Porter, which sold more than a million copies; *Laddie* by Gene Stratton Porter, which sold a million and a half copies; *Tarzan of the Apes* by Edgar Rice Burroughs, *The Eyes of the World* by Harold Bell Wright, and *Penrod* by Booth Tarkington—all in half million lots. I don't hold these up to you as models for imitation, but if you will compare those titles with our 1940 best sellers you will see how our taste has improved.

The outbreak of the war stunned our writers. But not for long. The same prevailing optimism, the same belief that right would triumph, and that life would always have a happy ending, rose again to the surface in the first crop of war books, and it was reënforced by the passionate belief that the Hun was all black and that we were all white and that no personal sacrifice was too great for Democracy. I read every one of those war books I could get my hands on. I read Guy Empey's *Over the Top.* I read *The First Hundred Thousand* by Ian Hay, in which you saw the eager spirit and good humor with which English civilians were converted into fighting men. I read *Kitchener's Mob* by James Norman Hall—who was one of that Mob —and that second book of his, *High Adventure,* in which he describes the almost idyllic chivalry of a war pilot. There were no dive bombers in those days.

It would be impossible to make you feel the electricity which passed from books like those into the minds of us who were still under twenty. If you write those books off as English propaganda, you miss the point. They were written by men who were actually in the fighting, not by bureaucrats in the Home Office. They were written by men who volunteered to fight because they believed it was the only way to save what they valued. Later, as the novelists swung into action, I read *Sonia* by Stephen McKenna, one of the great best sellers in England, in which the hero comes back blinded—but he does come back! And I read *Mr. Britling Sees It Through,* the novel by H. G. Wells which typified what the head of any household should be willing to sacrifice. I cannot overemphasize the importance of that word "sacrifice." The men in the Army never used it. But it meant something to them, and even more to the people back home. And if any one word was ever a seed, you can say that this word "sacrifice" was the seed from which grew the novels and poems which were written during the war. It is the idea which lies behind Edith Wharton's *A Son at the Front;* it is the idea which Edward Streeter kidded and made laughable in his *Dere Mable;* it is the idea which runs through that exceptionally good novel of Willa Cather's, *My Antonia*.

But by 1918 a change was discernible. The poets were the first to reveal it, being, as I suspect, thinner-skinned than most novelists. At the outbreak of the war the poets had marched off singing. They could not wait for commissions—the war would be over too soon. They were like Rupert Brooke. And his war sonnets stand for the ardor of that time as no others we have:

> If I should die, think only this of me:
>   That there's some corner of a foreign field
> That is for ever England. There shall be
>   In that rich earth a richer dust concealed;
> A dust whom England bore, shaped, made aware,
>   Gave, once, her flowers to love, her ways to roam,
> A body of England's, breathing English air,
>   Washed by the rivers, blest by suns of home.
>
> And think, this heart, all evil shed away,
>   A pulse in the eternal mind, no less
> Gives somewhere back the thoughts by England given;
>   Her sights and sounds; dreams happy as her day;
> And laughter, learnt of friends; and gentleness,
>   In hearts at peace, under an English heaven.

Siegfried Sassoon wrote in the same vein. But Sassoon survived the first two years of the war, as Brooke did not. And it was he who first marked the change. It was Sassoon who came out flatly with the statement that the sacrifice was too great; it was wanton; it was more than civilization could endure. Sassoon was an infantry officer who had been awarded the Military Cross and who, so rumor has it, had been recommended for the Victoria Cross. But at that moment he did what every hard-driven Englishman is prompted to do under stress —he wrote to the *London Times*. His letter was an eye-opener, and after its publication he threw his medals away and withdrew from the British Army. His friends kept him as quiet as they could. But Sassoon was aching to say then—and did say later in his poetry—what another infantry officer was already writing in his notebook. I mean Captain Wilfred Owen, who died of wounds just before the Armistice, and whose poems in their bitter beauty mark the despair which had risen in men's minds since Rupert Brooke:

Let the boy try along this bayonet-blade
How cold steel is, and keen with hunger of blood;
Blue with all malice, like a madman's flash;
And thinly drawn with famishing for flesh.

Lend him to stroke these blind, blunt bullet-heads
Which long to nuzzle in the hearts of lads.
Or give him cartridges of fine zinc teeth,
Sharp with the sharpness of grief and death.

For his teeth seem for laughing round an apple.
There lurk no claws behind his fingers supple;
And God will grow no talons at his heels,
Nor antlers through the thickness of his curls.

Coming back to this country for our demobilization, what did we veterans read? We read *Through the Wheat* by Thomas Boyd, *Toward the Flame* by Hervey Allen. We enjoyed *What Price Glory?* —the play which was so shattering to our parents—and eventually we read the greatest novel of the war, the story brewed from defeat, *All Quiet on the Western Front.* By that time the transformation was complete. Germans and Americans alike, we had been through the mill: the ardor had gone, we had seen what the sacrifice was worth— and despair was creeping in.

v

Today the habits of twenty years are still with us. It is still the method of our writers to shock the reader into awareness. The in- grained skepticism still makes our Zolas report what they see and question what they know. It also makes them slow, perhaps it makes them incapable of being sure that a better way is available. In short, we face this new war with the despair left over from the last. If we are to have any feeling of ardor, any self-confidence, any exhilaration about what we are to do, that feeling is still to come. Can despair sink any lower in literature? Can the attitude of our writers be any more discouraging than it has been in the past two years? Why, of course it can. You have only to look at France today to realize how far the tide has ebbed in that silent country. But even in France there must be people who take consolation in the thought that men have been through this despair in times past and have risen from it. At the end of the French Revolution, a Frenchman said something like this: "Now we must begin to build again on the bedrock of despair; we must entertain no illusions, we must recognize the worst—and then build."

On this side of the Atlantic writers are trying to shake off their gloom. They are trying to write constructively about what is to come. But, you will ask, what is there that we can positively believe in at this moment? There is a new feeling of responsibility in the air and this will inevitably affect your writing. First, I am positive that as a nation we can do the things we set our minds to. We are a dynamic people and we hate to mark time. We have set ourselves an enormous job and I am confident that we can do it. If some of you go into defense work, you will have a chance to see the job at first hand— and there may be books in it. Secondly, don't forget the millions of middle-aged and elderly people—your parents and mine—people who run out of breath, who find it hard to keep up with what's happening. Someone has got to bridge the understanding between your generation and theirs—and that bridge will be built of books. Thirdly, we have got to decide for ourselves whether we really are a united people. I am positive that we are. But according to Goebbels we are divided. Where does the truth lie? Have we been able to absorb thirty-eight million newcomers in a hundred years? Are they Americans? No one man knows enough to say. The truth can only be testified by hundreds of writers in their short stories and novels about our American communities.

"Sure, sure," you say to yourself. "I have heard something like that before. What I really want to know is how I am to get any writing done if I am packed off to a training camp." Well, that is up to you. T. E. Lawrence—Lawrence of Arabia, only he then called himself T. E. Shaw—managed to translate the *Odyssey,* write his forbidden novel, *The Mint,* and carry on the most voluminous correspondence—all this as a private in the English Tank Corps. James Norman Hall, who graduated from Grinnell College, Iowa, wrote his first two books in intervals between being a machine-gunner and a pursuit pilot. They had no more time than you will have. Nor should you dismiss the possibility of what can be done in a letter. I remember reading last winter a famous letter in which W. T. Donald, the Australian adviser to Chiang Kai-shek, describes the enor-

mous tenacity and infinite patience with which the Chinese transported their factories, their schools, their hospitals, and their homes,
brick by brick, object by object, all the way up to Chungking, knowing even while they rebuilt their capital that it would be a target
for the Japanese bombers. Letters with a tenacity like that will live.
So may yours, if you are part of a great movement.

If writing is really in you, you will not lose the habit of counting
your chickens before they hatch. Your real problem, it seems to me,
is not whether you will be able to write, but rather what form of
writing is best suited to the nature of your work and the time you
have available. For example, if you are going to camp or if you are
going to be tied up for nine hours a day in some heavy industry,
then obviously the kind of writing which you can most readily putter
along with is that which grows out of the first person singular. Read
your own experience, see what it is good for, and then see how vivid
you can make that experience to the stay-at-home. That's what Jim
Hall did. That's what John Dos Passos did. That's what Hervey
Allen did.

If you are a poet, you are in luck, because poetry hits quickly and
a whole poem can often be captured in an afternoon off. If you are
a poet, remember what I said about the cult of unintelligibility. If
you have got something worth saying, make it count. And if you
are a poet, don't spend all your substance on the lyric or the didactic.
Remember that not since *John Brown's Body* has anyone really taken
the trouble to exercise the narrative poem. People are hungry for
narration today—just as hungry as they are for poetry they can understand.

If you are a novelist, I suggest that you do not burn up your free
time trying to write a long novel. If you have got to make every minute count, and if you are weary—as I am—of that novel which begins
with the hero in his cradle, carries him through his school days,
through his college years, through his unhappy marriage and finally
pushes him into the grave, take a day off and refresh your knowledge of what can be done within the compass of the short novel.
See what Conrad Richter did in that intense and lovely story of his,
The Sea of Grass. All told it measures less than 36,000 words. See
what Willa Cather did with her *Lost Lady*. See what Wilder did
in his *Bridge of San Luis Rey*—that story is less than 50,000 words.

See what Steinbeck did in *Of Mice and Men*. See what Robert Nathan does, year after year. These are brilliant performances, these short novels, and the form is a very exciting one with which to work. You haven't room to build year upon year; you haven't room for any elaborate descriptions. You have got to begin in the middle of things and then, shuttling your story back and forth, by balancing your passages of introspection against the forward movement, you shape a story which, if it be really good, will carry the reader's thoughts far beyond the last period.

VI

I know no more than you do whether we shall go all the way down the road to intervention until we are at last openly and irrevocably at war. Or whether by some surprising turn we may be able to tip the scales in favor of a negotiated peace. If peace comes now, I wonder if it can be any more than an armistice until our job is done. For whether we like it or not, we have been challenged to stand up and tell the world what we mean by American democracy. We can't do that overnight. It will take time. And as we work out the proof in our own way, there will come with it, I firmly believe, an upsurge in American writing. I look for good historical novels; I hope for a revival of the Mark Twain–Will Rogers humor we need so badly; I expect contemporary novels with courage and zest for the present. Where is the man who will write the novel that ought to be written about skilled labor? Will Steinbeck do it, or will someone we have never heard of? I have often speculated as to how it might be done. Suppose the father of the family was a railroad engineer and a member of the brotherhood. Suppose his son has thrown in his lot with motors, and is just as rabidly C.I.O. Here are men drawn together by their love of machines and their love of doing things with their hands, and yet set in opposition by systems over which they have little control. Were such a story told in human terms, it would stir us as no novel about our mechanical genius has yet done.

Or looking still further ahead into the future, who will tell the story of the resettlement of this country as it is now going on, as the new factories spring up and the boom towns grow? We are doing more than simply forge new weapons. We are forging new communities, many of which will become permanent when at last the time comes to live in peace.

I have often wished that I might have seen this country as Audubon saw it, when the trees were in the forests and the birds were in the trees. And kindred to that desire is a hankering to have lived at the time of the American Revolution and to have seen our first great leaders in action, to have seen Washington's farewell to his officers at Fraunces' Tavern, to have heard what Thomas Jefferson thought of the French Revolution, to have known men like John Adams and Hamilton. These men pulled the country together; to have lived in their time, we think, would have made bigger men of us. Time is kind as we look back. We remember the clear thinking, the manliness, and the grandeur of the old days; we forget the uncertainty, the persecution, and the despair which made them dark. Again as we approach the perspective of a full century we begin to appreciate the size and the depth of the men who came, most of them from nowhere, to wrestle, in the 1860's, with the problem of whether this country could be united: Lincoln, Grant, Sherman, Jackson, and Lee.

Now for a third time the country is being put to the test. Seventy-five years from now will people say to themselves, "By God, that was the time to have lived! How I'd like to have had a hand in it!" It could be.

Poetry as Primitive Language

by JOHN CROWE RANSOM

A FRIEND OF MINE SAID HE HAD BEEN DRIVING IN THE NEIGHBORHOOD of Memphis. The new highway was in places a sort of causeway built up above bayou water, and right at the base of it on one side an old Negro was fishing. Thinking that the water was too near the slag and the noise of the highway for this sport, my friend stopped his car and had the following conversation with the fisherman:

Good morning, Uncle, are you fishing?
Yessir, Cap'n, I'm fishin'.
Have you caught any fish yet?
Nossir, I ain't yet.
Have you had any bites?
Nossir, I don't believe I has.
Have you had any nibbles?
Nossir, I can't say I is.
Do you think there are any fish in that hole?
Cap'n, I don't much reckon there's any fish there nohow.
Well, Uncle, why do you keep fishing there?
Well, Cap'n, this is the hole I'se always done my fishin' in, 'cause that's my house right up yonder on the rise.

This anecdote has several possible morals, and I may have used it in the past to suit the occasion. The one I read from it today is the truest of all its meanings, and has to do with a spiritual affinity between the fisherman and Mr. T. S. Eliot of *The Waste Land*. The big new road symbolizes modernity. It had killed out the fish in this particular hole, but the old man went on fishing there just the same. The fact is that fishing is not a single action like a science, but an ambiguous activity like an art. It means to take fish and be effective, just as poetry means to carry on a rational argument and say something. But it means also to sit on the ground, smell the water, watch the snakes and dragonflies, slap the mosquitoes, feel the sun, and smoke a pipe—all of which together amount to a diffuse, delicious context which goes with fish-taking, and parallels most precisely the splendid contextual detail of poetic language. But in the forms of modern life the colored man and Mr. Eliot have found it so hard to attach the old familiar contexts to the new effective actions that they have decided to take the contexts and let the effective actions go. Modern art tends that way. It does a pretty piece of fishing, and allows for all the business that belongs to fishing except the taking of fish.

Let that wait a moment. My topic is not the ineffectiveness but the primitivism of poetry, and they do not necessarily come to the same thing, though sometimes they may. By primitivism I mean an antique or outmoded cast of thought, so that the poetry is likely to seem heroic as compared with contemporary thought, or to seem pastoral, agrarian, medieval, Pre-Raphaelitish, or merely old-fashioned and quaint. After some progress of civilization comes a movement of regress, with poets in charge of it. But I have generally labored this point in large or philosophical terms, with the result that I seemed to myself profound but not very pointed, and academically correct but, as a student of poetry, not really close to the topic. Today, in your honor, I will talk about the primitive quality that appears in poetry as language. This version of critical theory is brand-new for me, and experimental, since I have not worked it out, but it seems more streamlined and presentable than any other I have hit upon.

Literary criticism is not identical with philosophy at large, but it occurs to me that it may well be identical with linguistic. Or, if you prefer the term, it may be identical with semantics, one of the newest, most capable, and sharpest of analytic tools. The advantage is that in applying it, whether to a poetry or to a science, you can uncover a lot of philosophical elements that belong to your topic, and escape from uncovering a lot of philosophical elements that do not belong to your topic. I am at the moment a sort of convertite to linguistic, and am trying to translate into its forms such theoretical notions as I have otherwise arrived at.

I have assembled my observations not too systematically under the head of a numerical series of "points." This is logically a bad style, but it is a fast one, and great statesmen have recommended it to your favor. I will not say how many "points" appeared in my notes, but they were too many; they greatly exceeded fourteen. I have now reduced them slightly below that number. I proceed:

1. A primitive language is one whose standard discourse, in trying to be *conceptual* (or rational), is obliged also, and whether or no, to be *imaginal* (or substantival). That is, in trying to make useful formulations about things, relating them by virtue of some common or class property, it is obliged to refer to the many-propertied or substantial things themselves, the things as wholes. Primitive languages are sometimes called *radical* languages: they consist almost wholly in root words, each one denoting a whole thing or whole event. In discourse these roots are jumbled together, and it devolves upon the hearer to figure out the properties in which the things named are related, and by elimination to read into the jumble a consecutive argument. Here is the famous ambiguity of language. You still have it in poetic metaphor, for example, and in all unskillful speech. Does your metaphorical word refer to the single property which makes it logically fit for the argument, or does it also evoke an image and refer to the independent substance? Homer was fond of the "wine-dark" sea, and used the locution again and again; ostensibly he meant a shade of color, but incidentally his readers and singers were sure to receive a fleeting image of the substantial and very good thing named wine.

2. A language develops out of its primitive or radical condition in at least two ways. First, it improves its vocabulary, finding words which denote the several properties of the thing and not having to keep on denoting every time the whole manifold of properties which make up the substance—adjectives for the leading aspects of the thing, adverbs and highly restricted verbs for aspects of the event. They are relatively abstract, technical, scientific, and useful. Second, the primitive language develops syntactically. It learns to place the parts of predication in a definitive order expressive of their relation; it invents inflections, prefixes and suffixes, and relational words like the conjunction and the preposition. It is improving the precision of discourse, and more and more squeezing imagination, which looks for its substantial images, out of the action. I do not mention as a

syntactical development the device of compounding or hyphenating words; that is generally the crudest primitivism, though poets are given to it, and it either antedates or repudiates the close syntactical articulation.

In short, suppose an American Indian plenipotentiary, knowing his English only to the extent of a few root words like those of some primitive language and treating with the white invaders, who know even less than that about his language, as follows: "Heap big Indian hunting go, heap big paleface firewater come." Against its particular background this discourse might just be intelligible. But now conceive the plenipotentiary as having behind him a modern Indian's college studies and the whole recent development of the English language, and phrasing his proposition like this: "The designated territories are obviously extensive and valuable, and my government would require in compensation for them a fully proportionate volume of distilled liquor of acceptable alcoholic content." But to phrase the bargain in this way seems to insult the intelligence of the party of the first part and the honesty of the party of the second part, and we should remark that linguistic precision illuminates the values offered in a bargain, or anywhere else. I do not think poets, Indians, heroes, demigods, or any other primitives could look out for themselves in a society whose advanced prose precision they could not master.

3. An advanced language is one in which the standard discourse is perfect or nearly perfect conceptually, and the imaginal or substantival range of meaning has all but disappeared. At this stage language conquers its involuntary ambiguity. It becomes fit for big business, technical science, and all other abstract forms of thinking. This is the kind of language that seems exclusively to be coveted by some semanticists, such as Korzybski. Kenneth Burke wrote to me that all semanticists of his acquaintance were naturalists, meaning that they tolerated only discourse after the scientific ideal, and in his view were bad people; that is, they would like to impose this ideal upon all discourses regardless of its suitability. I for my part just now referred to conceptual discourse as the standard of language; and certainly, as language improves its prose, it approximates more and more to that standard; even if we include its literary prose. Sir Thomas Browne sustained his imagistic magniloquence proudly as

something that in his day would be set to the credit of a writer. It is significant that we have no Brownes today; but we do have, for instance, Mr. Logan Pearsall Smith, whose phantasies are one sentence or at most several sentences long, whose mock seriousness represents an author with tongue in cheek, and who denominates his pieces as *Trivia*. But I think not all semanticists are uncompromising partisans of science for all occasions, and my acquaintance with them has been a little more fortunate than Mr. Burke's.

4. As a language develops, and discourse becomes more rigorously conceptual, and the imaginal fringe of substance is obliterated from view, poetry intervenes. Poetry recovers to language its imaginal or substantival dimension, almost as fast as language loses it, though of course not quite. That is probably what poetry is for, as nearly as we can state it. It is a special and artificial kind of discourse fighting for excuse to live in a society which has proscribed it. Naturally it might court the more primitive groups of this society and claim to speak their language, and Wordsworth offers a doctrine of poetry as the language of common men. But if it is not more regressive and braver in its diction than that, it will not have for common men the value of a poetry, and on the whole I think it needs to be maintained that poetry has a value only for those who are familiar with the advancement of contemporary language and disaffected by the failure of its imaginal dimension. The imaginal dimension in language is something you did not know was there till it is gone, and then you turn to poetry in order to get it back. The primitive character of the poetic language will show, of course, in the radical quality of its terms and in the looseness of its syntax.

5. Our own present language is highly advanced, so that its prose standard enforces a conceptual purity that would be simply fabulous for a primitive mind. The need for poetry is probably all the more imperative. But evidently the difficulty is greater than usual, perhaps greater than ever. It is harder to go primitive in your language when you are bred up to maintain its rationality; and at the same time it may be harder to palm poetry off upon a public that has come under an aggressive educational establishment and learned something about linguistic duty and linguistic destiny; the whole artifice of poetry becomes transparent, and a little shabby. What will the modern poet do? Mr. Eliot has advised him to "dislocate language" if necessary,

and in his own verse has practiced many violences. That is a bold strategy, and does not appeal to the middling public, which, from its casual acquaintance with older poetry, is not used to outraging the contemporary modes of discourse so recklessly. But Mr. Eliot is a wise man and a veteran of the wars, and we should not dismiss his counsel hastily. Poets appear to be faced with a crisis of language, the critical difficulty being that the imaginal element of language is now so slurred and abridged that there is not room enough in reputable discourse for poetry to begin its usual procedures.

6. The style of poetic discourse has always been outwardly loyal to the purpose of primitive language (indeed to the ruling purpose of any language) in preserving the impression of being a conceptual discourse intending to say something rather clear and useful. But now there appear exceptions: poems in which no binding argument is visible supporting the images of the poem. There are, for example, the poems of Eliot, of Hart Crane, of a school of surrealists, and there is the poetic prose of James Joyce. In France, where there is more consciousness of language than elsewhere, the exceptions began with the Symbolists far back in the nineteenth century. But in general these poems are highly modern, and still under question. I advert again to my colored fisherman who achieved the fishing without the fish: they are trying to provide the body of poetry without providing a skeleton to hold it together. On the whole I think the tactic is wrong. But that does not mean that the situation is not desperate, and I hesitate to offer a general judgment because the poets may really be more subtle and penetrating than I am in their analysis of the poetic situation. I tend to take comfort from the example of William Butler Yeats. His understanding was deep, his strategy perfectly adventurous, so that he tried many experiments that failed; but I am very sure he found an area of language in which images and definitive arguments accommodated themselves to each other. I am not yet sure how big this area was and how much room remains there for further poetic farming.

7. Modern psychology seems to enforce point 6—especially Gestalt psychology, with its studies of the process of attention and the process of learning. I believe it admits scarcely any such thing as a pure image, that is, an image in which our attention diffuses equally upon all the properties. On the contrary, we achieve the image of a thing

only in the process of recognizing the thing, and we recognize it by virtue of detecting in it some dominating surface property or facet property which is obviously valuable. We then apprehend the other properties of the image in a sort of *sub rosa* fashion, thinking we are engrossed or pretending to be engrossed still with the dominant property, but really rioting in that territory of the image which is relatively out of focus and forbidden. However, it remains true that we attend to the image by focusing it, and when it falls out of all focus we cannot attend to it. We get the fringe items by looking out of the corner of our eye; or we turn our eye straight on them, but not for long. Such a technique is probably the one employed by poetry; a way of indirection, but perhaps the only way on earth of realizing the vividness, magnificence, and beauty of the world. A psychology of poetry would work along these lines and show the devices by which poetry permits us to have this truancy without offending the public censor, or even the Freudian censor who presides over our own consciousness. But the Freudian allusion may be misleading. I think the remarkable property of the poetic image, aside from its existence at all, is its innocence. There is no chance of accounting for poetic beauty as a libidinous gratification, nor even as something useful, nor even as something moral. Such accounts have been pushed hard and ingeniously, but they have failed. But perhaps I do not need to declare to you that the poetic beauty survives all the failures of our crude analysis, and we continue to receive it after we confess that it cannot be isolated as easily as we had thought.

8. There is no primitivism in poetry so ubiquitous, so atmospheric, as the primitivism of its language, which is almost identifiable with the process of consciousness itself. But there are primitive characters in it more obvious than this—and, for example, that of its cosmology, theology, or ideology. To be completely contemporary you must give up the *Oxford Book of English Verse,* and you must expurgate large tracts from the corpus of most of the famous poets and some of your favorite poets, because in respect of their ideas you come upon the primitive. Even in their own day they were prepared to commit anachronism. Think of the Christian poets who have restored the Olympian deities, and the Copernicans who have reverted to the Ptolemaic cosmos—a notorious infidelity on the part of the poets, and

they must rate broadly and ideologically, as well as in ways much subtler and harder to remark, as apostates from our achieved culture. We are obliged to remark that there often appears in poetry precisely the mode of primitivism that has the official sanction of the religious establishments. Religion seems fundamentally to be a resistance to the purification of our cosmic conceptions, and in the face of progress a regression to beautiful but primitive dogmas. The new concepts are too pure and emasculated; the old dogmas registered better the contingent density of the actual created world; the concept and the dogma stand for different modes of knowledge. Construed philologically (*religio* = a tying back), religion may be expected, when the issue is joined, to espouse the dogma against the concept. The poetic ideas may likewise show very well the general direction that poetry takes, but they are not strictly my topic. They are a topic for poetic criticism unquestionably, and we know that while it is easy to spot the ideas it is not easy to trace them with precision. But what is still harder, and of a more enveloping importance, and probably more fascinating, is the analysis of the poetic language.

9. Returning to language. It must not be supposed that the poetic regression is merely a matter of finding some actual historic idiom that is now archaic and outmoded. That would be a defiance comparable to the religious recital of the old dogma; but poetry lacks the support of a great institutional establishment to approve an overt defiance, so that would be too bold to succeed, and too simple and literal to rate as a technique. It is true that archaic diction figures in poetry, but it is also true, in my estimation, that the effect is bad. It is possible for poetry to cover up its tracks, and to seem contemporary without conforming to the level of conceptual attainment that is in vogue. Consequently it would be a poor critical project to plan, for example, to discover in the poetic diction of the eighteenth century a diction recovered bodily from the seventeenth century after the latter had vanished from eighteenth-century prose. Poetry must preserve "face." It should sound contemporary, and with the accomplished poets I think it does; it even sounds felicitous, elegant, and fashionable. This requires of the poet the greatest linguistic ingenuity.

10. The diction of fine poetry is always fresh and individual, but there are several broad techniques or strategies which poets have handed down to their successors since time immemorial. They have

become publicly licensed, and no public has been querulous enough to challenge them, unless it is very recently. They make up the only objective institutional establishment there is for poetry to shelter under. I do not know what would happen to poetry if it should be deprived of them, and its tenuous establishment should collapse. I do not know what would happen, but perhaps there is a chance of my finding out before very long, if there is no shift in the linguistic climate. They are rank solecisms, either by nature or by the extravagant manner of their practice.

The first of these strategies is meter. It is a way of enforcing a phonetic imagery upon attention, which otherwise might be completely occupied with the semantic character, or meaning, of the words. That makes a dispersal of attention, enough by itself perhaps to be decisive and to convert reception into an aesthetic experience; the phonetic effect becomes a context round the semantic action. But it has a strange effect upon the semantic action itself which it is important to consider. The meter works upon the poet when he composes, and alters his composition, and then it works upon the hearer, and alters his sense of what he is reading. Look first at the poet. He is not quite free to use the words that express his intended meaning, because these do not automatically fall into the prescribed meter; so he must tinker with them, and try substitutions, till the meter has been realized and the meaning is not too remote. In this process the meaning gets loosened up. He has sacrificed the conceptual precision of his vocabulary, and the cogency of his syntax. If it was difficult to know how to escape from the bondage of a conceptual discourse, his metrical necessities have driven him to do just that, one little step at a time. And now observe the reader. I have observed the reader, many times, and professionally. I have observed that often the reader of a poetry that is perilously on the loose, imaginal, and primitive side is unaware of the fact, because he is fooled by the tidiness of the meter. It takes a reader from one of the science departments of the college to ignore the meter and dig into the obscurities of the discourse. The student from the science department has a harder head than one of our students and is useful to have on hand during poetic studies; but he is rather at the disadvantage of being committed to attending to one thing at a time—first the meaning, then the meter, hardly the two together. Perhaps he has lost his rugged primitive constitution, and is effete. On the other hand, the prejudice of the arts-trained student is all against picking a good thing to pieces; but his habit of taking the whole thing in stride exposes him to blind spots as to just what he is taking. You can hardly persuade him that the elaborate musical development in Swinburne for example, or even in Shelley, went along with, and indeed necessitated, a serious deficiency in the meaning.

11. Another licensed poetic convention, whose loss poetry could hardly survive, is figure of speech, or trope, in all its luxuriant variety. I believe linguistic is prepared to lay down the general rule that any trope represents an aberration from the conceptual ideal of discourse. It is surprising that in collegiate departments of English literature the tropes are not systematically studied as logical or a-logical devices. In this respect the moderns have lapsed from the critical scholarship of the ancients. I would like to write a critical note entitled, "From Aristotle to Longinus to Genung." The point would be that Aristotle made a very close analysis of a great group of tropes under the general head of metaphor, classifying its lawless procedures with at least a show of system; it might be said that he was examining the dodges, or the devices, by which reputable poets, who knew better, imported radicals or imaginal terms into an argument expecting conceptual or abstract terms. Longinus also was more than an ordinary analyst, and should be useful to us because his interest, in part at least and perhaps chiefly, was in the tropes which are purely syntactical and which obscure discourse by jumbling words together without showing their articulation—waiving conjunctions and mixing up tenses, for example. The Greeks recognized both kinds of trope, and a regressive poetry needs both, though we hear today almost exclusively about the first kind, and find the second kind isolated from their poetic occasions and held up to detestation in freshman manuals under such heads as "Uncoördinate Series" and "The *and* Fault." And, last, Genung, American author of a famous textbook of rhetoric, who names and defines most of the tropes with a very pretty scholarship, and appears innocent of any suspicion that the tropes of honored poets were acting with insubordination against the sequence and the unity of their discourses. But Genung flourished years ago, when official studies in English literature were new. The collocation of Aristotle, Longinus, and Genung might prompt the query: What

are the English studies doing? And when will intelligent linguistic come into them?

12. This will be my concluding point. It concerns the over-all or generic motive of the poet, and in the light of his record of apostasy, aberration, sabotage, and furtiveness I should not want to waive that question. I do not like to surrender to that ingenious motive-hunting which finds us doing everything for the sake of something else. We do many things because we must do them, and it only occurs to us later that we probably did them because we wanted to and must have had some "reason." Poetry is a discourse ordinarily in the indicative mode, therefore a mode of knowing, and probably one could say with touching piety that its motive is Truth. But who will tell us what that means? The truth, for the linguist at any rate, is what we know. Poetry is therefore a mode of knowing whose motive is to know. But some illumination is gained if we contrast the poetic language with the scientific language.

If my linguistic orientation is correct, poetic language arises historically because we are not happy over the improvements we make in our scientific language. We are not happy because these improvements require us to abandon progressively the imaginal or substantival elements. But the imaginal or substantival elements characterized a kind of language with which we were familiar by inheritance from our primitive ancestors—an actual and evidently a satisfying kind of language. The linguist will remark, perhaps by a slight departure from his professional duties though with all the more weight because of his disinterest, that there seems to be no testimony on the record to dispute the overwhelming agreement of the poets that these words refer to aspects of the world which are still there and visible in the world, though it may be that our modern linguistic training encourages us to pay little attention to them any more. As a man uses language, so is he. But I do not mean to abuse scientific language in order to praise poetic language. There is as much impulsion upon us to develop our scientific language as there is to protect our poetry. These are two actual and valid languages, though the one is in protest against the other and their fraternal relations become more and more uncomfortable.

I do not know anything further to say on this point, unless I should import into a linguistic discourse for the sake of a final flourish a big word from formal philosophy. The word would be: *ontological*. The poet's motive is ontological, just as is the motive of what we call the pure scientist; he is predicating about a character of the natural world, and it is not the character about which the scientist is predicating—though both might be said to be predicating about some character of The Way Things Are. But "ontological" would add little to the linguist's own nice sense of the poet's strategic situation except an impressive polysyllabic phonetic item. Suffice it to say that for linguistic the poet is in his duty.

The Modern Mode in Literature

by MARY M. COLUM

I SHOULD LIKE TO GIVE AS A SUBTITLE TO THE ONE ABOVE, "THE CHAR-acteristic Literature of Our Age and How to Understand It." But before getting to the core of the subject I have a few general observations to make which may seem platitudinous, but which, unfortunately, are not part of the consciousness of the publishing and book-reviewing worlds.

We have in contemporary writing two classes of product: one belongs to the art of literature and the other to the trade of writing. Naturally, very little contemporary writing belongs to the art of literature. The bulk of it belongs to the trade of writing, and that includes nearly all the books you find reviewed in the literary supplements—novels by people with a competent, or even mild, narrative gift, verses by people with a talent for making syllables at the ends of lines rhyme together, treatises on the lungs and liver by doctors, works concocted out of information dug up in a library, biographies and histories, books written by people who have to employ their time somehow, or to get a Ph.D. or a raise of salary in a college.

The art of literature is something else altogether. Art of any kind —music, literature, painting, or sculpture—belongs to the intellectual and spiritual capital of the world; it has always been a rare product of the human spirit, and a product of the rare human spirit. Now when we discuss the Modern Mode in writing we naturally mean the writing that belongs to the art of literature, that belongs to the spiritual and intellectual capital to which our age has contributed and is contributing. In spite of the confusion, and indeed, I might say, the scrambling of standards that exists in our day, almost unconsciously when it comes to conferring a reputation, it is the artist writers who are placed on the pinnacle, while the others have a different influence and a different position. Publicity and fame are not the same thing and are not conferred by the same public.

I do not imagine that any of you confound books that belong to the art of literature with the lasting books. A book or a poem may be a work of art and not live so very long; it can be simply something that has great significance for its own day. A great work of art, of course, has significance for a very long time, for all time maybe. On the other hand, now and again a book survives that has little or no relation to art—I am not here referring to the jumble of books dealt with in histories of literature not because of their connection with literature but because of their scientific, political or social revelation —a book, say, like *The Origin of Species,* or Newton's *Principia;* I mean books like *Uncle Tom's Cabin,* which has importance through its association with history rather than through its kinship with art. Let me follow up what I have said by stating that the work of our time that belongs to literature may not belong to lasting literature, but that its distinctiveness lies in its being the aesthetic expression of our age. The characteristic literature of any age, let me emphasize, represents the expression peculiar to that age, an expression which did not evidence itself in that particular way in any other age. And so, as we have a modern mode in painting, a modern mode in architecture, a modern mode in warfare, we have a modern mode in literature—a literature peculiar to the period of the last three decades, or the period, roughly speaking, between the last great war and this one.

When we moderns look back at other centuries we can readily see what was the characteristic literary expression of each period. Of the sixteenth century in England and the seventeenth century in France, we say it was the poetic drama; of the seventeenth century in England, the prose comedy; in the eighteenth century, the characteristic literary expression was the essay in prose and verse, for poets of that time often called their poetry "essays"—the *Essay on Man,* the *Essay on Criticism,* and so on. In the eighteenth century we had poetry in rhymed couplets which ran like this:

> Eternal blessings crown my earliest friend,
> And round his dwelling guardian saints attend.
> Blessed be that spot where cheerful guests retire
> To pause from toil and trim their evening fire.

Of course there was far better poetry than this written in the eighteenth century, even far better by the same poet, Goldsmith, but I quote these lines on purpose, for when the characteristic literature of any age shows itself getting obvious and facile like this, we know the change is due, even though it does not show itself for a while longer. The end of the eighteenth and the beginning of the nineteenth century brought the change, as we know.

When we look back on the nineteenth century we see that the characteristic production nearly everywhere was the novel in prose and the lyric in poetry, but especially characteristic of the nineteenth century was the realistic novel; the lyric, of course, had occurred before. Now realism in literature is the revelation of the ordinary man in everyday life, in everyday surroundings. These two literary forms, realism in the novel and also, in some countries, realism in the drama, and lyricism in poetry, so gripped the general imagination that actually many readers and writers have difficulty in realizing that these are not the perennial modes in literature, that they do not give perpetual laws of literary expression. Neither of them, in fact, is the fitting expression of the present age at all.

The realistic novel is the expression in fictional prose of the nineteenth century, when science and the methods of science came into civilization and when literature began to be written from facts, from observation and documentation, when the novelist, instead of drawing primarily upon his imagination, set down what his eyes saw and his ears heard, set down what he observed in everyday life of the everyday people around him.

Taine, the great literary critic and psychologist of the period, supplied the writers with what I might call the literary slogan; he announced that the matter of all knowledge of any kind *was little facts, well chosen, important, significant, amply circumstantiated, and minutely noted*. If anybody wants to write a realistic novel he should head his first page with that sentence of Taine's. Even poetry, according to this critic, was made up of little facts, *les petits faits sensibles,* which may be translated as the "little facts of emotion."

II

The formula of the realistic novel had a sort of scientific precise-
ness: the author picked out characters from the life around him, then
he imposed a story on them with a theme and a problem; there were
ideas associated with each character that tied up with the plot; then
the chief character went through a mental, spiritual, and emotional
stress which first of all helped to build up the story and then carried
it on to a conclusion. It is easy to find this formula at the back of the
great realistic novels like *Madame Bovary, Anna Karenina, Esther
Waters, Sister Carrie, Of Human Bondage, The Old Wives' Tale,*
and the great realistic plays like Ibsen's *Doll's House* and *Hedda
Gabler.* It is also, of course, the formula at the back of a multitude
of lesser novels and plays. Some remarkable works were produced
by this method, and looking back on them we see how characteristic
they were of the nineteenth century and what a genuine expression
of the age they were. The realistic novel then was a characteristic
expression of the nineteenth century as it could not have been an expression of any other age, for it was in line with the scientific discoveries, the social and political outlook of the period.

Now how are we to know what is the characteristic literary expression of our age, what is the modern mode? What are we producing that our descendants will think of as the distinctive expression of our age which is different from the expression of any other
age? Let us take a look at some of the novels everybody was reading
in the last few years. First, let us take *The Grapes of Wrath,* a very
widely read book. It opens with a description on familiar lines:

To the red country and part of the gray country of Oklahoma, the
last rains came gently, and they did not cut the scarred earth. . . . The
last rains lifted the corn quickly and scattered weed colonies and grass
along the sides of the roads so that the gray country and the dark red
country began to disappear under a green cover. In the last part of May
the sky grew pale and the clouds that had hung in high puffs for so long
in the spring were dissipated. The sun flared down on the growing corn
day after day until a line of brown spread along the edge of each green
bayonet. The clouds appeared, and went away, and in a while they did
not try any more. The weeds grew darker green to protect themselves,
and they did not spread any more. The surface of the earth crusted, a

thin hard crust, and as the sky became pale, so the earth became pale, pink in the red country and white in the gray country.

Where have we read this sort of description before? We have read it in every realistic novel whether English, American, French, or German. Was there ever a time when this sort of description was fresh and new and done with rousing art? Yes, it was done exquisitely in the first realistic novel, in the novel that supplied the design for almost all realistic novels, Flaubert's *Madame Bovary,* and, as in every novel of the type, the description comes in one of the first couple of pages:

The rain no longer fell; the day was beginning to dawn, and on the branches of the leafless apple-trees birds were perched motionless, shaking their slight feathers in the cold air of the morning. The flat country stretched away until lost from view, and the clumps of trees around the farms made at long intervals dark violet stains on the great grey surface which became lost in the horizon and one with the gloomy tone of the sky. The warm odor of plaster was mingled with the odor of the morning dew on the grass.

You can easily see now how the Flaubertian manner became the model for all such descriptions. And now I want to give you a sample of the dialogue in *The Grapes of Wrath:*

The six cars stopped. Two bookkeepers moved from car to car. "Want to work?"

Tom answered, "Sure, but what is this?"

"That's not your affair. Want to work?"

"Sure we do."

"Name?"

"Joad."

"How many men?"

"Four."

"Women?"

"Two."

"Kids?"

"Two."

"Can all of you work?"

"Why—I guess so."

"O.K. Find house sixty-three. Wages five cents a box. No bruised fruit. All right, move along now. Go to work right away."

The cars moved on. On the door of each square red house a number was painted. "Sixty," Tom said. "There's sixty. Must be down that way. There, sixty-one, sixty-two— There she is."

Al parked the truck close to the door of the little house. The family came down from the top of the truck and looked about in bewilderment. Two deputies approached. They looked closely into each face.

"Name?"

"Joad," Tom said impatiently. "Say, what is this here?"

One of the deputies took out a long list. "Not here. Ever see these here? Look at the license. Nope. Ain't got it. Guess they're O.K."

This conversation is typical of the conversations in *The Grapes of Wrath:* they all might have been taken down on gramophone records; they have none of the overtones of emotion or characterization that the great realists have in their conversations. A book like *The Grapes of Wrath,* in my estimation, is realism in its decline and petering out into sterility. If I had space I should compare what I have quoted with a conversation out of Flaubert's *Madame Bovary* or out of Tolstoi's *Anna Karenina,* and then you would see the difference between a master novelist who could make every line of conversation vibrate with the emotions behind it, who could show you the interior lives of the people who spoke the words, and a very competent, very intelligent trade novelist who really only got down the external and automatic life of his people. This is not to say but that *The Grapes of Wrath* is a good sociological study in narrative and fictional form, but it simply does not belong to the art of literature. Even as sociology, or representation, better results might have been obtained by a movie camera screening the life of the Joads, the scenes they pass through, and the camps in which they lived, and with a voice-recording machine to take down the conversations.

Let us see if another widely read book of the last few years, *Gone with the Wind,* belongs to the characteristic literature of our age. We look at the opening. Here is a description of the heroine on the very first page:

Scarlett O'Hara was not beautiful, but men seldom realized it when caught by her charm as the Tarleton twins were. In her face were too sharply blended the delicate features of her mother, a Coast aristocrat of French descent, and the heavy ones of her florid Irish father. But it was an arresting face, pointed of chin, square of jaw. Her eyes were pale green without a touch of hazel, starred with bristly black lashes and slightly tilted at the ends. Above them, her thick black brows slanted upward, cutting a startling oblique line in her magnolia-white skin— . . . The green eyes in the carefully sweet face were turbulent, willful, lusty with life, distinctly at variance with her decorous demeanor. Her manners had been imposed upon her by her mother's gentle admonitions and the sterner discipline of her mammy; her eyes were her own.

Now this sort of writing has the charm of the familiar; you have read, more or less, that description of the heroine in many novels. About a hundred and fifty years ago Jane Austen did it first in *Emma*. Here is what she wrote:

Emma Woodhouse, handsome, clever, and rich, with a comfortable home and a happy disposition, seemed to unite some of the best blessings of existence; and lived nearly twenty years in the world with very little to distress or vex her. The real evils . . . of Emma's situation were the power of having too much of her own way, and a disposition to think a little too well of herself; there were the disadvantages which threatened alloy to her many enjoyments. The dangers, however, were at present so unperceived, that they did not by any means rank as misfortunes with her.

You see that Jane Austen manages to tell you a great deal about her heroine without the cluttered detail that is in *Gone with the Wind*. The clutter got in through novelist after novelist, for a century and a half, trying to imitate Jane Austen and improve on her. Of course, *Gone with the Wind* is an entertaining and readable novel, and it saved multitudes of people from ennui and from the trouble of trying to decide what to do with their leisure hours. Of course, *The Grapes of Wrath* is interesting and informing, but both these types of writing are, in one way or another, a hang-over from the nineteenth century.

What is really new in our time, what is really characteristic of our time, has not found expression in these typical and widely read books. We find in them no expression of the new discoveries about the nature of man or the range of his emotions, or the workings of his mind and his memory. For if the nineteenth century was the century of scientific discovery and scientific procedure which naturally found their echo and reflection in literature, the twentieth century has been the century of psychological discovery, of new conceptions of the universe, new conceptions of history, and these, too, are making their entrance into art and literature.

III

When did the characteristic literature of our time begin to show itself? It began in about the second decade of this century when a writer named Marcel Proust realized that the influence of Time on people had never been really expressed in literature, and he wrote a long novel with Time as the hero or protagonist, showing Time as the most influential of all things in human life. He was given a clue as to how to reveal this discovery through the studies in the nature of time of the twentieth-century philosophers and scientists. He learned a great deal from the lectures and writings of Bergson, and he learned not only about time, but he learned about memory, which Bergson called the direct intuition of the past; and he saw how it was all connected with the new studies concerning the nature of man, with the new discoveries in psychology, especially those concerning the importance of the subconscious. His mind fertilized by this sort of knowledge, he set out to write a novel of a kind that had never been written before, and he revealed people in a way that they had never been revealed before. He gave us a whole gallery of personages, all under the domination of ever-transforming Time, characters whom his readers got to know more intimately than the people they knew in everyday life. This long novel in different parts was entitled, as you know, *A la recherche du temps perdu* (*The Search for Lost Time*). The title, as given in English by its distinguished translator—*Remembrance of Things Past*, from Shakespeare's sonnet—actually misrepresents Proust's intention.

And the characteristic literature of our age had another beginning when a writer named James Joyce, under the influence of Freud's and Jung's discoveries in connection with the subconscious, realized that he could reveal the whole past of people by showing everything they did and everything that passed through their minds in a few hours of time. In *Ulysses,* he took about eighteen hours in the lives of a few characters in Dublin, and by representing all their actions in this period and the sights they saw on the streets, in houses, saloons, newspaper offices, hospitals, brothels, and by digging up the content of their subconscious, he was able to evoke the whole past of his characters and suggest their future. He broke down that old stereo-typed form, with its beginning, middle, and end; he threw away the opening description of the *mise en scène,* all that description of the exterior appearance of the characters; and without any exposi-tion he plunged right into the middle of the action. Here is the open-ing of *Ulysses,* and how different it is from the openings of those books which belonged to the realistic literature of the nineteenth century and which, no matter how expert, are now just hang-overs. This is the first page of *Ulysses*—doubtless many of you are familiar with it:

Stately, plump Buck Mulligan came from the stairhead, bearing a bowl of lather on which a mirror and a razor lay crossed. A yellow dress-inggown, ungirdled, was sustained gently behind him by the mild morn-ing air. He held the bowl aloft and intoned:

—*Introibo ad altare Dei.*

Halted, he peered down the dark winding stairs and called up coarsely:

—Come up, Kinch. Come up, you fearful jesuit.

Solemnly he came forward and mounted the round gunrest. He faced about and blessed gravely thrice the tower, the surrounding country and the awaking mountains. Then, catching sight of Stephen Dedalus, he bent towards him and made rapid crosses in the air, gurgling in his throat and shaking his head. Stephen Dedalus, displeased and sleepy, leaned his arms on the top of the staircase and looked coldly at the shak-ing gurgling face that blessed him, equine in its length, and at the light untonsored hair, grained and hued like pale oak.

Buck Mulligan peeped an instant under the mirror and then covered the bowl smartly.

—Back to barracks, he said sternly.

He added in a preacher's tone:

—For this, O dearly beloved, is the genuine Christine: body and soul and blood and ouns. Slow music, please. Shut your eyes, gents. One mo-ment. A little trouble about those white corpuscles. Silence all.

A book like *Ulysses,* when it first came out over twenty years ago, was very difficult for the reader, for not only was the old logical form and matter of the novel displaced, but the reader had to know some-thing about the new discoveries concerning the subconscious and the association of ideas. Something similar could be said about T. S. Eliot's *Waste Land,* which came out within a year or two of *Ulysses.*

These and certain other modern writers made a different kind of demand on the reader than previous writers did: it was as if they said to the reader, "Your mind is composed, not only of the hereditary ideas and emotions common to large sections of mankind, not only of the common physical experiences; it is made up of the books you have read, the music you have heard, the pictures you have seen, the countries you have traveled in, the history you have understood. It is made up of all these in addition to what beliefs you have been taught, the nervous organism you have inherited or that your environment has given you. Your personality at any moment of duration is really composed of everything that has impinged on your consciousness." Until a reader understands the approach a good deal of modern writing will be obscure and may give the impression of a man talking to himself of some experience inside himself of which he alone has the key. But if an intelligent reader with a good training in literature finds after careful attention that a piece of contemporary writing has no meaning for him, it may mean there is no meaning in it, anyway, for as well as serious work a monstrous lot of humbug is being turned out in what purports to be the modern mode.

IV

Joyce's method is far different from Proust's, but both reveal many of the same things: people affected by time, people urged by unconscious and uncontrollable forces within them, people dominated by memory, personal memory and racial memory. As the realistic novel of the nineteenth century was affected by scientific discoveries and scientific procedure, this new writing in prose and verse is affected by psychological and philosophical discoveries. These, as translated into literature, might be summed up as follows:

1. Time is felt duration. We do not think real time, we live it; it is the very stuff of which psychic life is made.

2. In every moment of action there is the influence of our entire past—our character or actions have been shaped by everything that has gone before.

3. Our consciousness is memory; mind is memory; therefore these new novels and much of the new poetry are all a sort of autobiography. This is true, not only of Joyce and Proust, but of Thomas Wolfe, Virginia Woolf, T. S. Eliot, and many others.

4. We change without ceasing; as long as we are alive, we change from moment to moment, but time and memory remain as paramount factors in our existence. The psychic life of an adult human being is a conglomeration of memories though at any one moment our conscious memory picks out for immediate use only a few odd recollections. Life, indeed, might be said to be a continuous process in which new memories are superimposed on already existing ones. And this explains why modern authors do not engage themselves in telling a story; they present the stream of events, thoughts, and emotions that make up the lives of their characters.

I should have to give many lectures to explain in any detail the evolution of the novel from *Madame Bovary* to *Finnegans Wake,* and of poetry from Shelley to our time. It is my business now to give you in one paper some idea of how we have arrived at writing such as is in *Finnegans Wake* and which is beginning to influence all other kinds of writing; you can see its influence not only in the last play of Thornton Wilder's, *The Skin of Our Teeth,* in the last book of poems by T. S. Eliot, but even in up-to-date advertising.

Now, as realistic literature—the realistic novel—had its beginning in France, so the reaction against it started in France. It became not only a reaction against the expression of ordinary everyday life, but a reaction against the use of ordinary everyday language. A poet like Rimbaud, whose name you so often see now mentioned in the literary reviews, declared that literature should not be about external life at all: a writer should force himself outside ordinary experience; the external world, the everyday world, was a deceiving world; there was no reality to it. Now one must remember that these ideas represent very old beliefs of the human race and are at the back of many religions. These ideas later were further developed by Stéphane Mallarmé, who insisted that the world which real writers should express is very different from the world in which one lives, eats, sleeps; true reality, interior reality, is in visions, dreams, even in hallucinations. Literature should express the interior life of man, the interior life of the world, not those physical and material conditions such as our contemporary realistic literature insists on expressing. Mallarmé, like Rimbaud, insisted that in the future writers would have to give their energies to the problems of language, for ordinary language had been developed by the practical intelligence for the needs of everyday life and was of little use any more for high literary expression; words would have to be used with new meanings, for every word had many meanings, not only its objective dictionary meaning—it might even have, according to Rimbaud, a color meaning; words especially had an association interior meaning. It is the use of words in their association interior meaning that has made so much of modern poetry difficult.

The discoveries of the new psychologists and philosophers helped all the new literary ideas along, for they declared that the ordinary everyday man who eats, drinks, and sleeps is only part of the whole man, a small part of him at that. The mind of man was compared by the psychologists to an iceberg of which only about a third or fourth is visible above water and about three fourths is below water. Now the advanced writers, the characteristic twentieth-century writers, said, "Let us express this part of man, this greater part that is, as it were, below water, below consciousness." So writers like Marcel Proust, Paul Valéry in France, Stefan George in Germany, James Joyce, T. S. Eliot, Virginia Woolf, to some extent Thomas Wolfe, also to some extent W. B. Yeats, the greatest poet of our time, tried to express both the little bit of man that is the everyday man and the large part of him that is not everyday but that is submerged in the subconscious. Finally, James Joyce in *Finnegans Wake* threw over the idea of expressing the everyday man in everyday surroundings at all, and devoted himself completely to man in his unconscious or subconscious, man wholly in his interior workings, in his memories racial and personal. To do this he took over all the ideas of those who were in reaction against the methods of realism—the ideas of Rimbaud on the insignificance of everyday life and on the necessity of using words in many different meanings, the ideas of Verlaine that the musical sound of words and not their logical meanings were important, the ideas of Mallarmé that literature should not explain but suggest, that the theme in a piece of literature might have to be orchestrated as in music, that the logical development might have to be stopped in the middle of a sentence to take up some accessory theme, that a writer might even, to express all this, have to create his own vocabulary and his own language.

Every one of these ideas, plus the ideas and discoveries of the

psychologists, plus the ideas and discoveries of the philosophers and
philosophic historians, are in *Finnegans Wake*. Some of you who
have looked into this book may have thought it too cryptic for pe-
rusal, or even a hodgepodge that no one could understand, written
by a person who did not know what he was doing. But Joyce knew
exactly what he was doing, and his book is bound to have greater
and greater influence on writers, even though it can never have an
extensive popularity among ordinary readers. Now I am going to
open this cryptic book and quote a certain passage. It ought to be
read aloud, because the sound conveys part of the meaning. The
passage that I give here has but little to do with the objective world;
it describes the effect of twilight falling on a flowing river and on
its banks, the river in this case being the river Liffey in Dublin but
becoming the representative of all rivers and the symbol of all life.
Now I must ask you to allow your logical intelligence to remain
in abeyance, as in life it so often does, and allow your imagination, your emotions, your sense of the sounds of words to take in the
meaning:

Can't hear with the waters of. The chittering waters of. Flittering
bats, fieldmice bawk talk. Ho! are you not gone ahome? What, Thom Ma-
lone? Can't hear with bawk of bats, all thim liffeying waters of. Ho, talk
save us! My foos won't moos. I feel as old as yonder elm. A tale told of
Shaun or Shem? All Livia's daughter-sons. Dark hawks hear us. Night!
Night! my ho head halls. I feel as heavy as yonder stone. Tell me of John
or Shaun? Who were Shem and Shaun the living sons or daughtersof?
Night now! Tell me, tell me, tell me, elm! Night night! Telmetale of
stem or stone. Beside the rivering waters of, hitherandthithering waters
of. Night!

In the ending of the book the river, the symbol of life and history,
flows into the sea, in a passage about Death and Resurrection. There
passes through the group subconsciousness echoes of all that people
have heard of dying and resurrection, angels coming to take the soul
away, then the belief that some beloved person, father or mother,
husband or wife, son or daughter, comes at the moment of death
to greet the dying. Faint memories of childhood and of his past come
before the dying one. Then there comes the memories of stories of
the end of the world, of parables about the keys of heaven and the

twilight of the gods. The image of the river is always present, the river flowing on forever, flowing into the sea, always beginning again, so that the very first words in *Finnegans Wake* are a continuation of the very last words. All these ideas, feelings, and associations represent the effort on the part of literature to be an interpretation of life and not simply a record of everyday objective happenings and emotions.

The following passage from a recent poem by T. S. Eliot, *Little Gidding,* also treats of Death and Resurrection, in a way which shows a strong influence from *Finnegans Wake.*

> We shall not cease from exploration
> And the end of all our exploring
> Will be to arrive where we started
> And know the place for the first time.
> Through the unknown, remembered gate
> When the last of earth left to discover
> Is that which was the beginning;
> At the source of the longest river
> The voice of the hidden waterfall
> And the children in the apple-tree
> Not known, because not looked for
> But heard, half-heard, in the stillness
> Between two waves of the sea.
> Quick now, here, now, always—
> A condition of complete simplicity
> (Costing not less than everything)
> And all shall be well and
> All manner of thing shall be well
> When the tongues of flame are in-folded
> Into the crowned knot of fire
> And the fire and the rose are one.

A comparison of the end of *Finnegans Wake* and the end of *Little Gidding* with the lyrics in Yeats's remarkable play *Resurrection,* will be very revelatory of the concern of the most characteristic modern literature with Death and Resurrection, with the end of one civilization and the beginning of a new one.

In conclusion I feel that it is necessary to say that not all the real literature produced in any age belongs to the characteristic literature of the age. There is always an amount of great literature produced that has not the special characteristic of any age. But that is a very different thing from the stale continuation of a worn-out form. The writing I have discussed here as characteristic, as of the modern mode, is the special aesthetic expression of this age and could not be produced in any other age.

Popular and Unpopular Poetry in America

by LOUISE BOGAN

THIS SUBJECT, IT IS TO BE HOPED, WILL NOT BRING INTO MIND THE IDEA of "popular" in the sense of "successful" and "unpopular" in the sense of "unsuccessful." It is not a question of looking forward to a set of rules guaranteed to produce the kind of poetry that a great many people will read, although, as a matter of fact, one could formulate just such a set of rules. Rules of that kind, it can be demonstrated, are not worth learning, or worth putting into action once they have been learned. Here the words "popular" and "unpopular" will be used in a different sense: in the sense that came in with the great changes that occurred in Europe at the beginning of the nineteenth century, when the great Romantic and Industrial Revolution broke through the classic line that had endured for so long, and with so much seemingly unbreakable strength, in England as well as on the Continent.

To put the thought rather simply: What has happened to what was once called "folk song" or "folk poetry"? Into what has it been transformed, if it no longer appears before us in the colors it once wore, in the situation it once held? And then: What has happened to "formal" poetry? Why is it the subject of so much suspicion and even so much contempt? Why do some people seem to hate and fear it? Is it possible that formal poetry must disappear, or has it indeed already disappeared in America? Or is it possible to look forward to a development of formal poetry in America analogous to the past development of this art in Europe?

It is necessary to go back a little and go over familiar material, so familiar that, perhaps, it has been taken for granted. It is the historic background of the textbooks; but here it can be approached

173

from a slightly different angle in the hope that it can be rid of the opaque quality that everything taken for granted tends to assume.

In poetry the first thing to be noticed in the Romantic Revolution of the arts, with its background of actual revolution, is that formal poetry transformed itself by means of contact with folk song. The formal artists, in England and Scotland, with Wordsworth, Coleridge, and Robert Burns, and later, in France, with Victor Hugo, managed to re-connect their art with ordinary speech; managed to get back into their rhythms the hauntingly lovely, yet exquisitely simple, rhythms of the folk ballad; and managed, as well, to widen their field so that they could treat many subjects that had been for a long time closed to formal writing. New material techniques appeared almost immediately to aid the wide circulation of this new literature.

These techniques were those of the press (the newspaper), the new magazines and periodicals, and new methods of advertising and selling books. And not only lyric poetry, but dramatic poetry, the form hitherto encased in the most rigid tradition—that of the classic tragedy—began to break from the classic mold. Painting, too, turned away from the celebration of official occasions, either religious or secular, and the artist's canvas now had to compete with the lithographer's block, which, with Daumier as its master, was to bring in a whole new body of popular illustration. What was to become the most popular form of literature came into being almost overnight with Walter Scott's historical novels. The novel soon began to absorb creative energy on all sides. Poets, no matter how little vocation they possessed for the art of fiction, were by some obscure necessity compelled to write novels.

Dramatists, and even critics, tried their hand at this fresh and all-embracing, all-accommodating form. And in the truly miraculous way that Nature immediately supplies genius and supreme executants whenever a new form or a new apparatus appears—we think of the millions of years that mankind did without the pianoforte keyboard and the rush of great virtuosi, from Mozart through Chopin and Liszt, that promptly appeared directly it *was* invented—in this extraordinary fashion the novel was at once supplied with novelists of the most exuberant talent and unflagging energy: Scott, Balzac, Victor Hugo, Dickens.

While here it is a question of poetry, we see at once in the world rising out of the Romantic Revolution, that it is difficult to speak of poetry alone; many other arts come rushing in. And we see that even in its early phases, the world of the Romantic Revolution is already our world—so filled as it was with dynamic force, so eager as it was to break through old forms, so resourceful at pulling over from the past and at conjuring up from the future what it needed, without thought of breakage or without fear of making irreparable mistakes. It is a world we recognize as we do not recognize the eighteenth century, or the seventeenth, or the sixteenth. It becomes our world with incredible swiftness; and one of the strongest elements we recognize in the whole is the emergence of "popular art."

"Popular art": something quite different from the folk art of feudal times, or of any time preceding 1789, in Europe. The former folk art was based on the peasant; the new folk art was based on the citizen of the town. The evolving modern techniques began to feed this citizen all sorts of assorted amusement and information. The new daily gazettes, the new *romans-feuilletons,* the impressively thick works of fiction, the illustrated periodicals, shared this citizen's attention with the new and exciting popular theatrical performances, the new and exciting popular music. All sorts of influences began to shuttle back and forth, from England to France and through Europe in general. The world was made new again, artistically, politically, technically. The young and vigorous had ousted the rigid, lifeless, and outworn. There seemed no limit to the hopes that one could have for the future.

The early nineteenth century, then, lacked only the moving picture, the radio, and some forms of nationwide advertising to be the world filled with various pastimes for the citizen, almost exactly as we know it today. It is important to look at it in its full freshness. That freshness faded, became transformed. The last thing one wanted to do, early in the twentieth century, was to look back at these rather outmoded writers and artists and musicians. The great writers had been transformed, as it were, into crowds of bronze statues; avenues and streets and squares had been named after them. Other things had happened; later technical devices had rendered the earlier ones obsolete. But we look back upon these beginnings now because we are looking for some help in present bewilderment. Something was wrong in all that surging creativeness; something was left out; something was neglected. Some false emphasis was already pulling the pattern askew, even while it was forming. We know this now, because we are still living in what remains—and, as has been suggested, a good deal remains—of that world.

A new popular art had rushed into being. But what had happened to unpopular—formal, "high," classic—art? And what was this new thing that had inserted itself, without any outward show and insidiously, between the two: this poetry, criticism, fiction, painting, music of a kind never seen in quite this form at any previous time? This thin, sentimental—this cheap and raucous—or this heavy and pretentious—or this rather hypocritical, florid, and bedizened literature (poetry, drama, and prose), painting, and even music?— What it was, and what it is, was middle-class literature, painting, and music. It spread about and absorbed matters on all sides so quickly that, even at the outset, it was difficult to know where it ended, and where true literature (or painting or music) began. Had true popular art—the expression of the folk, urbanized or peasant— totally disappeared? Had formal art totally dissolved? Where was the line of demarcation between bourgeois letters and the crumbling façade of formal writing? In England not much attention was paid to the situation. But in France, in the generation following the first Romantic generation, two men appeared who analyzed the problem with the most bitter and caustic insight. Of these critics, Flaubert was the most uncompromising, the most clear-minded. And Sainte-Beuve, in an article written in 1838, "La Littérature industrielle," denounced the entry of industrial practices into literature. But let us leave the historical background for a moment.

II

Let us consider folk literature, especially American folk literature. What folk art have we? where can it be found and how can it be used? We know that creative aridity sets in at certain periods due to rules clamped down over a culture, or due to some spiritual or physical exhaustion. Then the fresh and strong touch of folk art, if a submerged folk art exists in the given culture, often brings about a new upsurge of energy, a new depth of emotion, a new lyrical awakening. We remember that the daffodil, that particularly fresh and simple "folk" flower, disappeared from English poetry for almost a hundred years; it went out with the late Restoration and came in again with Wordsworth. It seems to be a recurrent phenomenon, this turning away from nature for a period; and no one notices particularly, or sheds any tears about the matter, when the daffodil disappears. But what shouts of rejoicing are heard when the daffodil comes back!

Something magical has come to be associated with the pure powers of creation residing in the folk. Highly artificial cultures have tried to get back to simplicity by *playing* at simplicity, to touch this magic by imitating the surface manners of the folk tradition. But this play acting never really works; it results in some charming "pastoral" decoration, but in no profound art. A real break-through must be made. We remember that all sorts of revivals and collections of folk ballads began to appear in the exact center of the eighteenth century. Then came a period of enthusiasm for the medieval, then came forged "romantic" poetry and counterfeit ballads; these were mixed in with the authentic songs and ballads that were being disinterred and revived. It is important to remember this point: that during certain uncreative periods, the taste and the need for folk expression become so strong that people begin not only to *play-act* "folk," but to *manufacture* it artificially.

At present there exists in America a real desire to return to our more primitive art. There is a definite suspicion, in the minds and hearts of many Americans, that something we once had—something we once were—has disappeared. Some refreshment we could once draw upon has dried up. Folk art is always "romantic." And it is the kind of "romance" that can be trusted: it is based on real human anguish, and upon real human joy, and upon real human energy and passion. Our rural and primitive past, with all its richness of song and story and tall tale and picaresque narrative—it is so near us, and yet it is so difficult to conjure up, to tie in with our mechanized and urban present. It is so difficult to make it the basis for our creative work.

The turning toward the folk at the end of the eighteenth century was preindustrial as well as prerevolutionary. In our own times, two poets succeeded in getting back to a folk tradition in their respective countries: Yeats in Ireland and García Lorca in Spain. But in these two countries, these two poets were dealing with cultures that had escaped, in a large measure, any true industrial development. There was no rigid barrier of industralized attitudes to be broken through. Yeats in Ireland went back to the peasant songs and stories; Lorca went back to the *flamenco* tradition. Both of these poets received the experience of poetry *still attached to music* and still at an *improvisatory stage;* both were refreshed by the experience of an audience creatively involved (actual listeners and, at times, actual collaborators—not mere readers) in what these two men, as poets, produced.

We turn to examine our own folk tradition, and what variety and abundance we find! We can trace the line of the American folk songs through the ballads of English, Irish, Scotch, Welsh, and, sometimes, French and Spanish origin—broken away from their original background and variously transformed. Then come the work songs of all kinds—sea chanteys, songs of the plantation, the rivers, and the cattle range. Developing along beside these secular songs come the spirituals and hymns, elaborating out of a few basic tunes into countless variations.

Then the culmination and the turning point of American folk song appears in the person of Stephen Foster. This untrained and greatly gifted writer of popular songs managed to express fully the emotions common in a period of transition. On the one hand, through him, the loneliness as well as the rough gaiety of a primitive society found its voice. On the other, Foster gave expression to something quite new: to an emotion that was to become increasingly persistent in the American spirit—the emotion of profound nostalgia for an already disappearing rural way of life. The strong sentimentalization of Foster by his modern audience proceeds from the holdover of this crucial, though fairly well dissimulated, nostalgia into our own time. Clearly, Foster was the end of one kind of American folk, the point beyond which no pure development of his kind of material was possible.

We then begin to hear, after the hymns and marching songs of the Civil War, the beginning of what may be called *urbanized* folk music. The railroads building and having been built, we get the railroad songs. The cities once made, we get the hybrid genteel almost at once: the songs of the upright piano and the sheet-music era, along with songs a little nearer the bone of life, those of the minstrel show and vaudeville; and finally, the songs in which life shows up coarse, strong and wild and tragically clear—the songs of the cities' "underworld." Now it is becoming more and more difficult to get back to origins; the road back is falling into neglect. The Gilded Age is beginning—the influence of which persisted up to the time that we entered the war in 1917. After 1919 the earliest traditions began to possess interest once again. Interest in American folk began to be channeled into real research into Americana. The rural tradition in literature began to be of interest for novelists and poets again; it came back with the fashion for the earliest form of antiques.

People began to bring pine blanket chests and hooked rugs out of the attic or the dealer's showroom into their rooms, and collectors of folk song went into mountainous regions after folk ballads. In spite of the accusation recently made by certain American critics that Americans in the 1920's neglected and denied their own land and its folk art—that they chased after strange European gods and took no notice of anything that had ever occurred west of the Mississippi—the fact remains that the folk tales, the folk poetry, and the folk crafts of America received a great deal of attention in the 1920's. The songs and the literature were sung and read widely and made into anthologies. All this was brought over into urban life; it was incorporated into the industrialized culture of the time.

This last statement should be emphasized. Is it not true that our most primitive folk art has been pretty thoroughly absorbed into our middle-class mores, our bourgeois tradition? Is it not true that when we feel baffled by its elusiveness and uncomfortable about some of its translations into "formal" literature, we dimly realize that it has been carried into a region where the artist cannot get at it, into the middle region, where nothing living or nutritious for the artist's purposes exists? Has not this material been, so to speak, genteelized and sentimentalized so that at present it bears little relation to the rough, living stuff it once was? We can look at its forms, listen to its music, admire and imitate its sound, but can the artist, at present, call upon it to perform any important task? I, for one, feel that our early "folk" has been almost entirely absorbed into our industrial culture. Here we come up against that kind of industrial and commercial form of literature, that, let us call it, bourgeois form

of literature, against which both Flaubert and Sainte-Beuve fulmi-
nated when it first appeared more than a century ago. It is not necessary to hammer on this bourgeois form of art in a fanatical way. But
we can look at it without too much tension, consider it as a fact, try
to define it, try to trace its boundaries, try to understand where the
imitation leaves off and the real begins. We will get nowhere, as
writers, if we take to play-acting pastoral or imitating—counterfeiting
—folk.

III

Perhaps it is true that folk art can only be used by those artists
who are in themselves part and parcel of folk life, who have really
lived in its vigor and been part of its fabric. We think of Mark Twain
and of his direct use of his own experience as a boy and a young
man. If direct experience of folk life is necessary, where is the writer
to find that direct experience at the present time? Not, surely, by
going back to frontier days that have long been closed or by duplicat-
ing any form that has already been absorbed into a sentimental legend.

Where can the writer find a contemporary folk art? Well, we
are surrounded by folk vigor of all kinds. Because we cannot seem
accurately to ascertain just where or what it is, we must be all the
more searching in our analysis of the contemporary scene. The whole
trend, at the moment, is to take what surrounds us more or less for
granted; but this situation cannot last forever, and young writers
are the last people who should be taken in by the seeming opacity
of their surroundings. Young writers should be filled with both
vigor and curiosity, as well as with talent; and many of them have
instinctively and with enthusiasm picked out certain phenomena
that lie near the creative center of urbanized folk. Other young
people may be a little frightened of what they see and hear when they
look beyond their own safe and normal backgrounds. They cannot
be sure what is folk and what is mere cheapness and vulgarity. Many
people, other than the young, are not quite able to make up their
minds whether "swing" and "name bands" and "popular songs" are
folk art or merely manifestations of vulgar energy that quietly en-
lightened people have no relation to, no taste for, and, perhaps, should
have no dealings with.

We all have heard, perhaps with a certain amount of amusement, the claims of the extreme enthusiast who would have us abandon all music produced up to now and listen to nothing but his record collection: to his marvelous recordings of Louis Armstrong in his good period, to the subtleties of "boogie-woogie" piano playing, to the development of Duke Ellington or the nondevelopment of Bing Crosby, or whatever. This sort of enthusiasm is held with heat; it is filled with intolerance for people outside the magic circle; and, in many ways, it is all to the good. For these extremists have actually touched the center of the urbanized folk music and folk poetry by which we are surrounded on all sides. But we should not be extremists. And the problem remains complex. We should hold a steady interest, no matter what fashion or fashions sweep over the enthusiast, in finding and recognizing what is real folk and what is not. We listen to the radio, and hear the greatest mixture of genres that it is possible to imagine. We decide, perhaps, that the radio has its distressingly meek and namby-pamby side, even so far as popular music is concerned. We listen, then, to the juke-box favorites and sometimes we find that this repertory is quite different from what is being unfolded in the repertory of the radio at any given moment. The juke-box patrons know what they want and get what they like; the tone is at once rougher and more primitive—but more sentimental, too. Or, perhaps, we decide, tentatively, that anything "popular" must be folk song.

Stripped of its commercial coloring, and divorced in our minds from its Tin Pan Alley origin, perhaps every popular song, from the hillbilly tunes—or their imitations—through the sentimental ballads to the words and music of the "slick" revue, is authentic, is the material for which we search. But immediately we begin to cling to this notion, an expert tells us that we are completely mistaken. The brilliant and informed Mr. Virgil Thomson, music critic of the *New York Herald Tribune*, remarks, icily, in a critique: "Mr. X [a composer who had used 'popular' and 'commercial' usages in a formal composition] seems to think that the music called 'popular' is a style, a domain in itself like folk-lore, and hence material for art. He is wrong. It is the last stage of art-music's natural decomposition. It is all bromides and means nothing. There are musical raw materials among the folk, and hot jazz is one of them. But the commercialized 'popular' music that is Mr. X's world is not worth sympathetic re-working. Its stuff is worn too thin already."

How baffling the whole question becomes! For here we are confronted with a kind of "popular" music that perhaps we had overlooked: the broken-down high art form. I agree with Mr. Thomson that such a thing exists. That it has spread over all "popular" music —over all popular songs—I very much doubt. I could quote the names of a dozen popular songs that are indubitably tainted with this worst of all influences: the influence of high or formal art in deliquescence. But let us consider a moment longer commercialized, urbanized popular music as it exists today.—We are disturbed to find it more primitive than we expected. To a cultivated taste much of it is silly and maudlin; it is so repetitive in theme that very little of it can be listened to at one time. It is also repetitive in beat; the underlying rhythm does not change. The beat is the thing, and all the elaborate harmonic tricks serve only to embellish the beat. And it never gets much beyond the form, as someone has pointed out, of theme and variation.

Again, it is combination of words and music that leaves out whole areas of human emotion. The tragedy and lamenting and sense of death and dissolution—of violent death, of accident—never come into it. Violent people appear in it very seldom. Its roughness is oddly mixed with smoothness; its wildness keeps slipping over into something quite tame. It lacks, in spite of its range between nervous gaiety and a kind of dolorous "blue" quality, any real subtlety of joy, such as we find in the great art songs on the one hand, or any real tragic depth, such as once resided in truly primitive music. But—and this is the point to remember—the words are attached to music, are, rather, fused with the music, as in all primitive states of poetry and music.

We use here terms of music as well as of poetry because the material I have been dealing with is at that primitive stage when it is inextricably both. And if there is any doubt about the vigor of this folk art, witness the inexhaustible fertility of its inspiration, and witness as well its powers of improvisation. (Here we get into a purely musical phase of the matter, it is true, but how interesting it is to see pure spontaneous creation of this kind actually at work around us.) Granted that the line between the real and false is wavering and unclear. Surely we are surrounded nevertheless by a living folk poetry and music of extreme variety and vigor, compared to which the songs of the sheet-music era show up as awkward, saccharine, and devitalized. We are in a cultural period when folk is in a good creative era of *its own:* a period that should develop to the point where it can express anything, from simple to complex emotion, and express these things well.

Whether or not the formal artist can use folk in its present unmalleable stage and whether this folk art will ever manage to get completely clear from all sorts of commercial and middle-class influence that certainly cloud and hamper it at the moment, I do not know. Time must pass, and our formal art must clear itself of its myopic vision, its lack of insight, its shyness of self-analysis, and other weaknesses and defects, before the two lines of art that, perhaps, need to intersect before great literature can be expected, can meet.

IV

We now come to that most unpopular art at the moment in America: formal poetry. Formal writing in general receives little enough attention, but when we come to the two words "formal poetry," we come to a subject the discussion of which is dangerous in the extreme. For we have been confronted, for more than a decade, with the spectacle of writers defaming their own vehicle; insisting that it be put to some use; of men and women bringing to bear on the worth of their own talents, and the literary form in which those talents are expressed, all kinds of moral and even, one could say, evangelical disparagement. The incomprehensibility of modern formal poetry comes up frequently; the charge that it is unscientific also is heard. That we have been "betrayed" into one state of mind or another by our formal poets—even into a kind of treason against real American values—has been dinned into our ears for a considerable length of time.

This bitterness followed closely, let it be remembered, on a period in which Americans were delighted to discover not only the number of poets they were producing, but also the number of varieties of poets. Beginning around 1912, we had a "renaissance." We suddenly saw about us American satiric poets and American naturalists; American pastoral poets with a tragic sense of the past; bitter and witty elegiac poets; poets with a gift for sustained narrative; as well as men and women with poignant lyric gifts, and men and women with a talent for poetic drama. We produced, in some quantity, poets whose subtlety matched the subtlety of their French Symbolist masters; and in Eliot and Pound we realized that we had nurtured true virtuosi: men whose poetic influence affected a whole generation of English writers as well as a generation of Americans. For a time it seemed that we had managed to throw up a poetic generation that could compare with any recent creative generation in England or on the Continent.

What happened to this enthusiasm? Is it possible that economic and historical accidents and letdowns can wipe out, almost at one stroke, and in the short time of ten or fifteen years, the whole enthusiasm of a people for an art in which they, for a time, brilliantly excelled? Is it possible that moral pressures, which always appear in periods of material disorganization, can become so strong that they destroy the interest and the happiness of many people in what has been so vigorously created? If this revulsion on the part of Americans who admired formal poetry could come about with such a cutting effect of disowning one's own, of throwing the erring child out into the blinding snowstorm, what hope is there for formal poetry in America in the future? Have we not proved ourselves full of a kind of dislocated bigotry and, even, of ingratitude for our own gifts?

We must now face a fact that is a little irksome to face. We are a great nation, but we are a romantic nation. Victor Hugo, in the preface to *Hernani,* defined romanticism as the spirit of liberalism in literature. Fortunately, the spirit of liberalism in government has this same romantic base. The industrial pattern of our society, the commercial infiltrations into our culture, cannot change the fact that the Colonies became a nation during the Romantic period; and many Romantic faults, as well as many Romantic virtues, are fundamental in our nature. Being, at bottom, romantics, we like change. We tend to veer about. We are impatient; and we do not, so far, show any signs of ever wanting to go over into a rigid classicism or to subject ourselves to a series of canons and of rules.

The sharp criticism to which Flaubert subjected certain bourgeois tendencies of his day has been mentioned. His unfinished novel,

Bouvard et Pécuchet, has puzzled many people. To some, it has seemed a crushing indictment of middle-class foibles; to others, it represents a poisonous attack on mankind itself, somewhat in the manner of Swift. Or it can be considered a dissection of the Romantic temperament; or it can be considered a combination of all these things. "Flaubert's design," says Albert Thibaudet, "is not absolutely clear . . . but in the large, one can say that Flaubert wished to give a synthesis and a sum of all that pertains to automatism and to the grotesque, in the thought and life of the ordinary middle-class man—the man in the street—the conformist in society."

The main theme of *Bouvard et Pécuchet* is one of enthusiasms continually changed. These two well-meaning copyists are afflicted with a series of unparalleled manias. They rush into a passionate absorption of one thing after another. They rush into the collecting of antiques; then it is scientific farming; then the distilling of liqueurs; then chemistry, anatomy, medicine, geology, archaeology. Then comes a passionate interest in history, in historical novels, in grammar. Soon, urged on by contemporary events, they are fascinated by politics and social theory. A little later they are involved in gymnastics and physical culture, in magic, in spiritualism. All the while their lives become more and more absurd, farther and farther removed from normal realities. Everything natural and human they touch becomes mixed up in the most alarming way. Toward the end of the book they are violently seized by religion: religion of all kinds, including Buddhism. Then come educational theories, sketching, public speaking. And in Flaubert's notes we find that the two friends will try to work out a theory of the future of Humanity, of the future of literature, of the future of science. They will be interrupted from time to time by the arrival of outraged authorities, but they will keep on trying, until at the end they will have to acknowledge that the matters into which they have plunged themselves are a little beyond their full grasp. They had better go back to the job of copying from which they had emerged.

The most striking characteristic of these two figures is, of course, their lack of maturity. They are childish. They have no sense of proportion. Then again, they rush into things with complete single-mindedness, explore them to the point of satiety, and then reject them utterly, because they have lost so many traditional links with reality. They have no religion, no fixed material basis in life. They are floating men.

The point to make most strongly to young writers is that in some way, if one wishes to belong to a free and creative future, one must get outside this repetitive pattern of enthusiasm, satiation, repudiation, whether it be a fashion of thinking, of feeling, or of action. Let us call this tendency to reject only to embrace elsewhere, middle-class or Romantic or what you will; it is certainly not the approach of the artist. But, we have recently been told, the staying powers, the nervous organization, the quality of brains, in mere writers, cannot in any way compare with the same attributes in the man of action, the scientific investigator, the explorer. The 1920's were excited about literature; but how much of that literature can stand up against this, that, or the other exploit of men of action or scientific achievement? Do we hear Bouvard and Pécuchet speaking out of one of their enthusiasms when we hear this sort of statement?

v

I have read, as a reviewer, along with all the good poetry, practically all the bad poetry published in English since 1931. So that I can tell you exactly why the dullest poetry is dull; and I can trace for you the falling line down which bad, worse, and worst poetry sinks. Thoroughly poor verse, really "bad" poetry, is remarkable for two things. It is not a question of its being written to this rule or that, or in this fashion or that. It is a question, first, of its conformity to the middle and accepted view of things. It tends to pull every subject treated, from love to the starry heavens, comfortably and cozily into that view. The bad poet is not to be shaken from his smugness. Everything comes into his house, as it were, and puts on slippers and sits in his armchair and pats his dog. The winds, whether of nature or of doctrine, may howl as they will; he has everything quietly under control because he is on the side of the received idea, the conventional concept. It is remarkable how this middle tone can pervade the most diverse forms. I have seen imitation Elizabethan sonnets filled with it, as well as the most revolutionary calls to action.

The second sign of really bad poetry is its author's tendency to laugh things off—to transform tragedy into, if not exactly a joke, then at least into something that can be managed with sentiment rather than passion. The middle poet, like the middle painter and prose writer, tends to hush things up, smooth things over, transform the wild into the tame, the exact truth into the approximation, the terrible fact into the commodious fact. There is a kind of lulling rhythm, a peculiar turn of phrase, a refined and limp vocabulary that goes into this middle kind of expression. We laugh at the grave-yard verse of the eighteenth century and at the lame imitators of Pope. We think Felicia Hemans and her like delightfully "period" and definitely dead. Not at all; their kith and kin are around us on all sides. Because we are their contemporaries, it is difficult to hear their debased tone unless we are trained to hear it.

The young writer, then, must in some way stand outside middle-class art. Then, I feel that the time of experiment, as experiment, is over. There are no more stiff forms to break, and no more virtue in writing gibberish, and no more sense in "plumbing the depths of the subconscious" in a theatrical and artificial way. The depths of the subconscious appear in any work of art. Salvador Dali reports a remark made to him by Freud: "When I look at a formal work of art," Freud said, "I look for evidences of the subconscious. When I look at a surrealist work of art, I look for evidences of the conscious." How many tasks are waiting for the young writer—tasks that re-quire a sensitive, under-cutting perception, and a penetrating, in-formed wisdom! So much has had to be passed over or neglected. So many weights and tasks have been put upon literature that could not be put upon other forms of creative expression. Literature is the most useful carrier for ideas. And when materialists take it over for their own purposes, they must clear literature of much of its meaning; they must make literature's imaginative and spiritual resi-dues as small as possible, so that literature's useful side may function without too many hitches and jars.

The young writer should understand, at any given moment, at least some of these manipulations. He should be able to sense where creativeness ends and where pressure begins. He should be able to analyze any given work into its component parts, to see what is real and what is commercial, what is free to function as art and what is bound into various constricting patterns.

The more the times do not back him up, the more the young

writer should apply himself, with patience, to learning. The time is coming when it will be an accepted fact that writing cannot function either in a vacuum (without touching the human history of which it is a part) or in any kind of ideological strait jacket. The time has already come when we must read literature with a full knowledge of its reasons, both historical and psychological—of the backgrounds with which literature is interpenetrated. We can no longer run back and forth on the surface, from book to book, picking up a pretty little anecdote here or a piece of period costume there. So little has been done since inquiry into modern literature began, so much remains to do. Profoundly interesting linkages have been made between literature and the life literature must express, ennoble, and interpret. But how many remain to be made.

The young writer should be versed in the literature of the other arts. I have, many times, found ideas more to my purpose and hints as to the cause and direction of things, in the history of painting and engraving, or in the history of music, than in histories of literature. The new attitude toward literature as an indicator of life, the new re-valuation of writers with the use of new critical tools, are still fragmentary. One must look for clues, find ways from one piece of evidence to another. But the material is endless. It is waiting for the sincerity and enthusiasm of the writers and the scholars of the future.

Above all, the young writer must not become hardened and cynical, or sophisticated to the point of insensitiveness and glibness. He must remember that the notion that anyone, given a little good will and effort, can become an earth-shaking author is a rather unenlightened idea. And a culture should not be only *artist-deep;* it must be deep with thousands of appreciators, with a sincere and unaffected and wakeful audience. Therefore, if one has sensitiveness and still cannot manage to turn out a book that the world will not willingly let die, remember that there is a great need for sensitiveness—for steadfast sensitiveness. An unchanging, a non-venal, a detached, and anonymous group of appreciators; not showy, stocked with learning; humane, yet with a good set of arguments lined up to meet the most dogged and pretentious adversary—that is the audience I should like to see in America; ready to back up any glimmering-through of a new awakening of formal art.

Remember that our culture may not develop along the lines of former cultures; there is no reason why it should. We are a romantic people. Shall we be forced into that alternation of restraint and exuberance—classicism and romanticism—that for certain basic historic reasons marks most European cultures? Perhaps it will turn out that we shall resemble some culture where nothing of this sort happens; where, instead, a sparkling and vivid popular art bubbles up through art and life and literature, from source to summit. And our formal art—that tends toward sharpest satire, yet has a line of mysticism and transcendentalism that can be traced from Emerson and Thoreau to T. S. Eliot, that tends toward profound insight allied with elaborate form, as in our master of prose, Henry James—perhaps our formal art, too, will resemble the art of certain cultures somewhat outside the European pattern. Perhaps our ability to wisecrack will ripen into our ability to make profound *aperçus;* and, as Justice Holmes wrote to his friend Pollock: "The systems disappear, but the *aperçus* remain."

Remember, if you are a young poet, that you are endowed with emotion, that makes your work reverberate; with intellect, that gives your work form; and that you have another endowment as well: a spiritual ingredient that has not yet been isolated. It is this spiritual ingredient in which you must put your trust in barren times. It is the ingredient of your talent that the materialists will try to laugh off; but if you are really endowed, you will know that it is there and that it links you with whatever creative stream there is in nature. Stick to it; let it write *you;* allow its crotchets full play. If you hate the ocean, or can't abide the eighteenth century, write with these crotchets fully visible to your readers. Be yourself, to the top of your bent, as André Gide has counseled. "It takes great boldness to dare to be oneself," says Delacroix in his *Journal.* "In fact, the boldest of all things is to escape from the accepted and from habits." Remember that there have been innumerable barren periods in history, when the spirit and heart alike seemed dead. And remember that when the change-over into a creative time occurs, it begins, often, with something so small and simple and unpretentious that no one realizes that the new thing is there. Just one small cry, just one small hand-produced book called *Songs of Innocence and of Experience,* and the whole stiff façade of bad formal writing begins to show alarming fissures.

VI

In conclusion two passages may be quoted that have, it might seem, nothing to do with literature. The first is from an essay by the modern English painter, Walter Sickert. He said:

How is it that you do not know that a work of art is the extraction from natural objects of line, and light, and shade and colour, in themselves beautiful and delicate and precious? And the objects themselves may be *any* object. While the snobs of the brush labor to render the most expensive women and the richest fabrics cheap, the master-draughtsman shows us the wealth of beauty and consolation there is, in perceiving and following out the form of anything. *Anything!* That is the subject matter of modern art. There is the quarry, inexhaustible forever, from which draughtsmen and painters of the future will draw the endless line of masterpieces still to come. Of course there is an understood proviso to this *anything,* as important as the principle itself: namely, that the objects, whether men and women or still-life and landscape, shall be about their business in the world. Not the forms only, but the life within them, must be "significant." In other words, the mind must be drawn to sympathy with a life that is familiar, a life that never stands still, but which may sometimes hover trembling for a space, just long enough for the draughtsman to pin his game.

The second passage is a parable by Tolstoi, used at the end of Bruno Walter's reverent biography of his friend, the musician Gustave Mahler. It is a parable that would puzzle Bouvard and Pécuchet, and, I think, would send certain critics and writers of our day into fits of raucous laughter:

And that he [Mahler] kept on asking questions and wanted, ever again, to "learn" reminds one of Tolstoi's beautiful legend of the three devout old men whom the bishop visited on their island. They made him teach them the Lord's Prayer over and over again because they were unable to retain it. When he finally had succeeded [in his task] and his ship had long since left the island, they came to him one night, running over the waves, because, once more, they had forgotten it. But he said, deeply moved: "Why, you are walking on the waves—what further need is there for you to learn?"

And so it was with Mahler: he possessed and knew so much more than he asked, for in him was Music, in him was Love. And I think that, at the last, he will have found out that in the very fact of his faithful seeking lay the answer . . . .

The Unreality of Realism

by STRUTHERS BURT

IS THERE SUCH A THING AS REALISM IN WRITING, OR IN ANY OTHER KIND of art, and is realism in art possible? Is not the word "realism" in itself a contradiction in terms when applied to any form of art, to any form of conscious and controlled human expression? One can also say that the word is a contradiction in terms when applied even to such supposedly factual descriptions as a newspaper column or newspaper reporting. What is art? that is, conscious and controlled and directed human expression in all its myriad manifestations, high or low, moving or dull, worth-while or not worth-while, permanent or ephemeral? And what is realism?

This is a large question, for what we are asking is, what is life? And having decided this—which we can't—we are asking ourselves a second equally large question. What is the relationship of art to life? What is the connection? the umbilical cord? And why does art spring out of life? and almost at once? and inevitably? For nothing is clearer, or more proven by history and anthropology, than that man, almost the moment he began, exhibited an urge to express himself artistically. He was not satisfied with the shape of things as they were, but began to mold them or carve them crudely. After a while— in the comparatively small space of a few hundreds of thousands or millions of years—he became pretty good; he began to paint on walls, like the Cro-Magnon man, to carve intricate designs on tusks and bones.

The psychologists say that man has four basic hungers—food, thirst, sleep, and sex—the last two at times mutually antagonistic. To these, some, like Adler, and it seems to me very truthfully, add lust of power, and emphasize it as perhaps the most basic hunger of all. The emphasis, however, would seem to be doubtful, as there are certain primitive, or fairly primitive, tribes, such as the Zuñi, where power, or the desire for it, tells against a man. The lust for power would seem to be not so much one of the fundamental hungers as a later development. That it is powerful, as civilization develops, we know.

But on the other hand, the desire for self-expression, which, when conscious and controlled and directed, develops into some sort of art, does seem one of the basic hungers. H. G. Wells's description of the cave man is an answer to those who claim that war and conflict are fundamental with men, and so can never be eradicated. Wells says that we are led to believe that the cave man was a brutal and ferocious creature who killed on sight, whereas, so far as the only evidence we have concerning him goes, on the slightest provocation he would get up, rush over to the wall, and draw a picture of a buffalo.

It makes little difference, however, whether this impulse toward artistic self-expression is one of man's primal urges or not; we know that at all events it appeared early in man's existence and has continued unabated ever since. In every generation, with astonishing persistence, there are thousands of men and women who, forsaking all else, dedicate themselves to the painting of pictures, the making of music, and the making of books, and as a rule these desires, these directives, appear so early as to seem almost congenital. And even in the most primitive societies, in every generation appear men and women who, lacking the more sophisticated tools of civilization, nonetheless make music, paint pictures, and recite, if they do not also print, books.

Why? What makes them do it? That must be considered before coming to the various modes, and moods, of this expression, and hence to what we so carelessly and blithely, and glibly, call realism, or lack of it.

What is an artist—a writer, a painter, a composer? What makes them tick, and what started them ticking in the first place? And from now on we confine ourselves as much as possible to one type of artist, the writer: the man or woman who, with words and thoughts as tools, strives to gather from what has been up to the moment some small niche of silence, the materials—atmosphere, circumstances, human character, ideas, and thesis—which will outline a verbal picture other men can perceive, feel, understand, and, possibly, remember. What makes a writer? Although, of course, and once more, in asking that, we are asking what makes any kind of artist. For fundamentally all artists are the same. They merely use different mediums.

I cannot forbear a related story. I am, as possibly some of you know, a rancher as well as a writer, and have been for a great many years, although now I am pretty much retired and only keep a small ranch to live on during the summers and as a further place to write. In passing, and as a very practical hint to young writers, I will say that I first went ranching because I firmly believe, and so do most writers, that the best way to begin writing is to slowly creep up on it, as it were, by, at the start, earning your living in some other way. I will not go on with this, because it is a large subject in itself, but will merely add that since life itself is the material of writing, the best place to find it is somewhere else than in writing or editorial circles, and that it is a very thwarting thing to a young writer either to be so poor, as most of them are, that they have to depend on writing for their living, or, equally bad, so rich that they only write when the classic and mysterious effluvium, which does not exist, overpowers them.

To get on with my story.

The year before the first war, when I was running some big ranches, I had working for me a sort of cowboy-ranch-hand named Al—an excellent, honest and hardworking young man, but one of the most singularly innocent young men I have ever known. I remember that one day I was in the ranch meathouse, which had a screen door, and that Al, who had been delegated to kill as many flies as he could on the outside, suddenly paused, pressed his nose against the screen, and looked at me with wide and innocent blue eyes. "Mr. Burt," he drawled, "what makes flies?"

I was startled, taken aback. It was such a profound, direct, philosophical question that I had never thought of it before. Like most of us, I had taken flies for granted. There were just two possible answers, both equally direct, profound, and philosophical. One could either say, "Nature," or, if more religiously inclined, "God." The mystery, however, remained the same.

A year later Al was killed with the infantry in the Argonne. But in pondering the question of what makes writers—artists—as I have often done since, I invariably think of Al.

The fundamental mystery remains the same and is not to be solved, but the surface marks, the stigmata, of the writer, or any other artist, are fairly easy to recognize. Emerson says, "The conscious utterance of thought, by speech or action, to any end is Art." And that, it would seem, is correct, and is equivalent to the phrase already used—conscious and controlled and directed self-expression.

The artist, therefore, starts with the universal human desire for self-expression. But that is only the beginning, and in itself means little unless it is channeled by the will and by some clear and higher intention. Otherwise it takes itself out in a thousand varied and amorphous ways, from appreciation, which is a very fine thing, to the pure exhibitionism of jive-dancing or fainting in the presence of Frank Sinatra. Bad manners, zoot-suits, and Radcliffe overalls are also stigmata of the universal human desire for self-expression, as yet ignorantly channeled, or never to be channeled, for unfortunately this terrific hunger, this constant craving of the ego, in the majority of cases is never properly channeled at all, largely due to inertia, and so results in the frustration, serious or mild, we witness everywhere.

The longer you live, the more people you meet, especially if you happen to be a professional artist yourself, who labor under the delusion that if they only had a little more leisure they could write a great novel, paint a great picture, or compose a symphony. If this made them happy, it would be all right, but as a rule it doesn't, it merely makes them jealous and dissatisfied. And, incidentally, the most perfect specimen, perhaps, of this type is the average book reviewer. Here it is not a question of the real critic, such men as Sainte-Beuve, Sir Walter Raleigh, Ruskin, and so on. Real criticism, which is rare, is also an art and, like all art, is constructive. It is the book reviewer, the man who is supposed to read a book a day—an impossible task —and report upon it. Alfred Henry Lewis has said that a book reviewer is "a man who never buys a book, and never reads one." To this can be added, as a rule, someone who has written an unsuccessful novel, or is too lazy even to write a bad one.

So merely to mention the urge for self-expression in explanation of the artist, means nothing. It's like saying he has a stomach. He has to have one, and make no doubt about it, he has. But then, so has everyone else.

The artist thus has to have his urge toward self-expression definitely channeled, directed, and in constant motion toward an end; it has to run through a conduit, like water, and toward a destination. The force of what he says, or paints, or carves, or composes, is the result of the compression of channeling, or discipline, self-imposed or otherwise, with discipline's resulting knowledge of technique, all this headed toward an outlet. The same phenomenon is witnessed with electricity and its amperes.

In addition to this, the artist, it would seem, is distinguished by three things: observation, analysis, and discrimination. But, once more, a great many people have those qualities, all three, or one, or two. So one must add an adjective. And the adjective is—vigorous. Not only must the artist have the three qualities mentioned, and all three to a lesser or greater extent, but they must be *vigorous* observation, *vigorous* analysis, *vigorous* discrimination, and depending upon the vigor in each instance, depends whether he, or she, is a first-class artist, or even a great one. In other words, the artist is thoroughly alive, thoroughly aware, and completely interested. This is a *sine qua non,* and not to be contradicted.

One never meets a bored or unimpressionable artist, no matter how he, or she, may choose to face the world. Nor will we ever meet one. They may be irritable, furious, disagreeable, or sullen, but never bored. They live in a constant state of excitement, surprise, perception, and discovery, and that in a world where the majority walk with no appreciation that practically every encounter and view, every person and every horizon, is a novel, a story, a poem, a piece of music, a statue, or, at the worst, a newspaper column. And because the artist is interested, and to the exact degree of his interest, does he interest others. James Huneker, the critic, said in his essay on Chopin, "Scratch an artist and you surprise a child." Which, if it means something childlike, is correct, but if it means something childish, is not. I think Huneker meant the former, with a little bit of the latter thrown in. The best definition of the attitude of the artist is, possibly, that of C. E. Montague, the English novelist. He was not trying to define the artist, but fortunate people—spiritually fortunate people—as a whole. The description, however, fits the artist perfectly: "The lucky ones," he says, "seem to be always as if they just came into the world. . . . There is still in them something of Adam upon the first day; they reconnoitre, with shining eyes, the lay-out of the garden, and stare in admiration at such novel curiosities as the moon and stars."

Why is the artist this way? Does he become this way early in life, or is he born that way? Why is the artist marked by vigor and intensity? By the dogged will that directs his urge to self-expression? I do not know. Once more you get back to fundamental mysteries— to Al and the question about flies. You enter the realms of biology, metaphysics, aesthetics—all the more abstruse inquiries. It may even be glands, but the fact remains. To return to certainty, however, being what he is, and viewing the world as he does, the artist of necessity achieves a general, but at the same time especial, point of view, and all he does is directed and colored by it. By general, I mean a point of view common to all artists; by especial, I mean one not shared by the majority, who are not artists. You can call it the artistic viewpoint, if you wish. It is both constructive and critical, technical and philosophic, and, in the last capacity, persistently attacks what it thinks is wrong, disorderly, and ugly; and persistently, however subtly or evasively, attempts to show what is ordered, right, and comely.

Art is not life. We all know that. If it were merely life it would have no reason for existence. It would be merely a useless addition, an encumbrance, like a bustle. It would be merely the repetition of the tale of an idiot—nor is any pun intended. Art is selection, concentration, and direction on the part of a trained man, or woman, who to begin with is vigorously observant, vigorously analytical, and vigorously discriminating.

What does all this amount to? Now we can come to the gist and conclusion of this discussion, and to what so mistakenly and commonly is called realism.

The artist does behave like Adam in the Garden. And it is a garden in which he finds himself—this world. A garden in which there are extraordinary glimpses of beauty, goodness, grandeur, order, and symphony. But the snake has entered in, and so there is also a vast amount of horror, hideousness, wickedness, disorderliness, and unbelievable stupidity. Art is the enemy of these and always has been. The relentless and implacable enemy. And the artist lives in a constant knowledge of what could be, and a constant anger and pity at what is.

Go back of that statement, any who dare!

In other words, there is no such thing to the artist as the *status quo,* and the minute he accepts it, and some do—the weary, or the mercenary, or, sometimes, the too-successful—that moment he ceases to be an artist. Inevitably, in whatever he does, in whatever medium, and with whatever tools he is using, the artist is attempting to construct a world nearer to the heart's desire. This is not a phantasy, this desired and desirable world. It is not an ideal. A dream. A romance. A Utopia. It is something glimpsed at times, and so is something known and to be further known. And all but stupid or ignorant people know this to be a fact, and so all but the stupid or ignorant know what the artist is after and respect his quest, and so respect art, and seek to learn about one form of it, or better still, all.

The most bitter satirists in literature or any of the other arts, Dean Swift, Rabelais, Goya, Daumier—all the long, brilliant, and anguished list—have not been men superior to life, who scorned it, its essence, the fact of it. No great satirist has been a spiritual nihilist, a Hindu philosopher, regarding nothing as of value but Nirvana. To the contrary, to be a great satirist you must be so in love with life, and what it might so easily be if men only had the wit, the courage, and the heart, that you cannot abide what men, so stupidly, make life to be. Satirists are artists so thin-skinned that they lose their outer skin early in life and all the rest of their lives go around spiritually naked. Sinclair Lewis is an excellent example of this. John Marquand, in his own more restrained fashion, Thackeray, Dickens, Anatole France, Dostoevski—were all examples.

It was Anatole France who used the famous phrase "irony and pity" to describe the standpoint of the artist: irony, because men and things are what they are, pity, because they are not what they could be, and no men or women live up to their possibilities. "For pity runneth soon in gentle heart," said Chaucer, and all artists are born with gentle hearts, or they would not be artists. When they cease to have gentle hearts, it is a degeneration, not an achievement. It is not sophistication, but a return to ignorance.

Back of all great art has been a passionate desire for the good, and a passionate hatred of evil, and this has little to do with the actual behavior, weak or noble, of the artist himself. He hates the evil and the weakness in himself as much as he does in others. Art inevitably is on the side of the angels. And recently that has been proven again, and up to the hilt. Hardly a fine artist the world over but has fought Fascism and Nazism, and from the very beginning. They recognized intuitively the twin devils long before most people were aware.

So what, then, is the true function of art? Of painting? Of writing? Of music? To reproduce life as it is? To be a photograph? Well, we all know that isn't true. The ordinary photograph, unposed, unshaded, unselected, is not true. It is true neither to the subject nor to the moment in time of the taking. We also know that the so-called "candid camera" does not tell the truth, but is, in reality, a caricature. The good photographer, the imaginative one, thinks of himself as an artist. What does he mean? He means that he is aware that to approach, to approximate, the truth at all, the use of selection, of shading, of contrast is necessary, and that all these, and other factors, must be used within the frame of a composition. The artistic photographer has a design, a purpose, a thesis, a direction, just as has the portrait painter or the landscapist.

Art has to mean something. And it not only has to mean something to the artist, but to other people as well. It does not function in a mental, moral, spiritual, or physical vacuum. If it did, it would be not art but a maniac. An idiot.

All art, therefore, is essentially symbolic, like religion, like any of the higher functionings of man, for the moment you begin to select, compose, and direct, you leave the field of unassorted materials and enter the realms of symbolism. A house, a home, is, to begin with, a heap of stones, unassorted lumber, a bed of clay, depending upon the material from which you propose to build it—stone, boards, or bricks. But when you have selected and assembled and built these according to plan, you have performed a feat of symbolism.

The painter and the sculptor, dealing so directly as they do with their basic materials, have always recognized this much more clearly than the writer, the man or woman who deals in words, for the writer is likely to forget what he is actually doing in the pursuit of his idea or his story. He is likely to forget that every word he uses is a symbol, and that the carefully selected thoughts he is presenting, winnowed out from hundreds of others as best suited to his purposes, are also of their essence symbolic. They symbolize a thousand other thoughts not so adequate. This knowledge of the painter and sculptor, on the other hand, is so present in their minds that it leads to all kinds of absurd experiments, poses, schools, and chicanery, as we are witnessing all the time. But what the good painter is always trying to do is to bring into modern art the magnificent and deeply moving symbolism that motivated, let us say, Byzantine and Gothic art. He is attempting, consciously or unconsciously, to use modern symbols in the same fashion. He is not imitating these masterful periods. That would not be approaching the truth in any way. He is attempting to go forward, but with the same clear simplicity of vision and attitude. If we understand that, we understand better a great deal of the seeming confusion of modern painting and sculpture.

The thoughtful painter is always trying to live up to C. E. Montague's description of the Garden of Eden. Or rather, to put it better, he is not trying to live up to C. E. Montague's description. He is that way to begin with. He is that sort of person. He wishes to see life with the clear, unspoiled, unprejudiced eye of a child, backed by the reflective judgment of the mature man. And that, of course, is the exact description of the good writer, and even more obviously, because the writer is, of all artists, the one who deals primarily with ideas.

The evidence, where writers themselves have spoken through the ages, is practically unanimous. Goethe has summed this evidence up in his statement, "The highest problem of every art is, by means of appearances"—in other words, symbols—"to produce the illusion of a loftier reality." Once again, something—a loftier reality—that man can come near to obtaining and possessing if he so wills.

Back of all fine and lasting art, then, is an act of faith. Faith in life, no matter how horrible its temporary appearances may be. Faith in ordinary humanity, no matter how dreadfully at times it may behave, or how hopeless certain individuals may seem. Art, too, is "the substance of things hoped for; the evidence of things not seen."

Inevitably, therefore, the great artist, the great writer, is a democrat, whether he knows it or not. That goes almost without saying. Just as, inevitably, he is a radical, one, that is, who goes to the roots of things, waters them, fertilizes them, prunes them, or, if he thinks it necessary, cuts them away because they are rotten.

Aristotle was not a democrat. Neither was he a great artist. His political and social theories are formal and narrow. But he was a great critic, and his rules for art have not been improved upon. You remember his great rule of the unities? You also remember his great rule of catharsis? Actually, as you know, catharsis means a purge—a physical purge. It is the Greek word *katharsis,* which means pure. Hence, our modern word "cathartic." Aristotle, applying the word to literature, to art, meant that however tragic the subject, however sordid, the treatment of it must leave you elevated, purified, purged, with the sense that all this is part of a higher and better pattern, even if we cannot perceive what that pattern may be. In other words, great art moves the bowels of the spirit, and those who partake of it are purified. And in everything that Shakespeare wrote you find this. And in Goethe. And in all great poetry, and drama, and novels you find it. And in all great painting, and architecture, and sculpture. Not consciously—not deliberately. That cannot be repeated too often in order to make it clear. But, implicitly, it is there. It cannot help but be there.

The great writer, the great artist, is never a conscious moralist, a hagridden reformer. The more he becomes either of these, or both, the less he becomes an artist. Once more, he just is. He is born that way. As I have said, he is by instinct on the side of the angels. And I think this is because the good, or great, artist, the good, or great, writer is more sensitive than the ordinary run of people. More intuitional. More aware—always aware—that what we think we see, appearances, that is, are not reality at all. The intelligent artist distrusts the word "reality," just as he distrusts the word "practical," knowing that the former for the most part means merely an excuse for laziness of vision, the result of an inertia of belief and faith, and the latter, merely that myopic caution which results in penny cleverness and pound folly.

But actually the artist is the most practical and realistic of men, both adjectives, this time, written without quotation marks. Let me interpolate a conviction. The longer I live, the more convinced I am that the artist of every kind, in direct proportion to his ability and greatness, is one of the most realistic and practical men alive. Far more practical and realistic than most. He is that because he has vision and analysis; he is that because he knows how little realistic surface manifestations are. To make this point concrete, I have yet to meet a far-visioned businessman or politician who wasn't inherently an artist; I have yet to meet a far-visioned artist who wasn't by nature both a good businessman and politician. The ancient superstition that the artist is a careless, feckless person, a superstition existing even into this comparatively clear-eyed period, can be easily explained, although there is no time to do it now. Sufficient to say that the superstition is the refuge of the exhibitionist, young or old, who has vague artistic impulses, but never the persistence, the hardihood, or the vision to make these real. College campuses in every generation are filled with such "artists." Like the making of books, there is no end to them. Greenwich Village in New York, now largely a thing of the past, the Latin quarter in Paris, have been the home of young exhibitionists of this character, too interested in themselves to work, too interested in their personal rebellions to lose themselves, as the real artist does, in the great, perpetual, underlying rebellion of man's spirit, which has been going on ever since the world began.

And now what does the writer, the artist, who thinks of himself as "a realist" and, in certain periods, calls himself one, believe? Let us see what the so-called "schools of realism" have done, although the young American writer, being an American, never thinks of himself as belonging to "a school"; he merely admires some revolutionary or established trend and, instead of being himself, imitates it. The use of the term "school" is not recognized in this country as it is in France.

It would not be so bad if the so-called "Realists" throughout literary history had not chosen that word. It would have been better had they chosen no word at all, merely done what they wanted to do and kept quiet, for the word "realism," like all words of the kind —large and general—soon ceases to have any real meaning and becomes merely a worn and greasy cliché. A catchall like the present popular words "Fascist" and "Communist." Out where I live, for instance, and now spend half the year, anyone you don't like is a "Bolshevik." Last summer I heard a multimillionaire playboy cattleman, a fanatical reactionary, described as a "Bolshevik" by a rancher who didn't like him. I don't like him either, but I wouldn't call him a "Bolshevik."

The word "realism" is equally amorphous, equally Protean. It has been cut and fitted to what every period thought was realistic. It has no meaning at all, and it could not have, because each period, each generation, has a different notion of what is realistic, and because the whole theory is based on the gigantic error that realism consists of taking the world as it is and so describing it. The world is never as it is. Neither is man. Nor the universe. Everything is a becoming. Everything is the future, even as I speak.

Let us start with our Victorian forefathers. With Zola and his school in France, let us say, with George Gissing and the "Realistic School" in England; with both "schools" reflected in this country— the movement, a natural revolt from the somewhat shopworn romantic attitude of the Victorian period. From the amelioristic attitude that "God's in His Heaven" and that, if you just leave Him alone, there is a natural tendency toward improvement. A philosophy enthusiastically endorsed by the "practical men" of the period—the "practical" businessmen, statesmen, and scientists, who saw in science, the machine, and the Industrial Revolution, sure proofs of an almost constant upward curve. The real artist, Victorian or otherwise, has never thought so. I have only to refer to Samuel Butler and his *Erewhon*.

And what was "realism" at that time? To set things down exactly as you saw them. No nonsense. Just as you saw them. What you saw, naturally, seeing only with your physical eyes, was for the most part bad, ugly, and depressing. Up to the moment, if you painted a cow, you had painted, being under the influence of the Romantic School, an ideal cow, sleek, bovine-eyed, contented, grazing in a field of clover; and if every spot, shining and beautiful, was in place, you said, "How realistic!" Now, if you were one of the new "Realists," you painted a wretched cow, starved and degenerate; and your audience, if you had converted them, said, "How realistic!" Both the Romanticist and the Realist, you will notice, were speaking from the surface, since to speak from the surface was the Victorian way of speaking, save, as always, for the individual great artists, who have always known better. Hardly anyone said, "There is no such thing on the surface of the earth as a perfect cow, or even a thoroughly contented one. But, on the other hand, neither is a starved and degenerate cow typical, either. Why don't you paint a cow in such a way that the beholder is aware that whatever kind of cow you paint, there are other cows, and that in any event, in 'cowishness' there is something more than meets the eye?"

Meanwhile, the great painters, the great writers, went about their business as usual—working, making their own experiments, teaching themselves, being taught by life. The great Impressionists, the great novelists, the great poets.

Then along came the first war, gigantic and ferocious, and shocked everyone beyond measure, and upset or modified practically every idea we had. We saw man naked again, and we saw, as things still are, although not as clearly as we see this now, that even the good and gentle must at times commit murder—or war—in order to have any good at all. A strange and bloody paradox. At the same time two great and earth-shaking philosophical ideas entered the minds of men—psychoanalysis and the theory of relativity, the latter of which, in its philosophic application, comes pretty close to saying that there is no good or evil, but, as Shakespeare said, and as I have always thought, somewhat recklessly, to paraphrase him, "Only thinking makes it so."

As is always the case, both theories were eagerly adopted, and completely twisted, by almost everyone, especially those who wished at the moment some respectably high-sounding excuse for their own misbehavior, achieved or contemplated. There was no clear-cut good or evil act, it all depended upon the circumstances—it was all relative. And man was hardly responsible, anyhow. Back of him was a father, or mother, or grandmother—usually the entire family—who had conditioned him beyond his own control, and back of these were dim race impulses which made everything hopeless, anyhow.

Out of these circumstances arose the disillusioned writing of the twenties, the "School of the Lost Generation," the first practitioners of which were very fine artists, and still are. Nor do the survivors— the big ones—any longer think of themselves as a "lost generation." They have got over that. The imitators, and there were hundreds of them, fell by the wayside. We do not even remember their names. It was a rough school, as you recollect. Everyone spoke in short, sharp sentences, and no one exhibited any emotion, including the author. It has been spoken of by the irreverent as the "School of the False Hair on the Chest." But it did a great deal for American writing technically, and its innovators, especially Ernest Hemingway, were very fine, even great, artists. The critics, however, overused the word "realistic."

Was it realism in the sense that it was a perfect reproduction of life? Well, here is a very interesting and significant test. We remember how Hemingway's conversations in his novel *Farewell to Arms* were looked upon as perfect "realism." They were just the way certain people talked. Did they? The conversations were put to the acid test of the theater when the book was made into a play, and it was found that they were not realistic at all, in the sense implied. Of course not. Hemingway was too good a novelist for that. His conversations were selected and hence symbolic. They had the higher and universal realism.

With great truth, Samuel Butler has said, "The history of art is the history of revivals." And with that we come to the present. We are witnessing something interesting at present—just the beginning of it. How it will turn out, no one can predict. But there are faint signs of a new sincerity, a new unself-consciousness, a new desire to find the truth, but with an old sense, and technique, of gentleness and that much-maligned word, beauty.

Curious, isn't it?

This war, and all that is going on in the world, has had a different effect upon us than the first war. This war has been too gigantic, too much like a titanic struggle between Powers and Principalities for man to try to make head against it by the attitude of disillusionment. By the belief that everything is relative, and that there is no such thing as actual wrong. By the belief that realism is the unquestioning and unquestioned description of things just as we see them. Suddenly we have been confronted by evil so clear, so proven, so diabolic that we have been forced to take sides. And man has become humble again and searching. A sense of mystery has again come into men's lives.

Recently I have had an interesting experience. As one of the judges of this year's O. Henry Prize Stories, I read a number of short stories written by young, or comparatively young, authors. Technically, every one of them was excellent. For a long while now American writers have had little to learn technically. Many of the stories, and very fine they were, were a holdover of the latest popular school of story writing. For lack of a better term it can be called the *"New Yorker* School." Superb technique, selection of incident. Clear, sharp atmosphere. Superb, if one-sided, characterization. But utterly implicit. No comment, except what the reader makes for himself. No taking sides—a school, which, more sophisticated, is an outcome of the disillusioned school of the twenties. There was a time when I thought this a very fine way of writing. Now I know better. I know that it is merely brilliant reportage.

But amongst these stories there were some, written by the youngest of the writers, which were quite different. They had all the technique of the others, but something added. They also had emotion; they also took sides—definitely. They were on the side of the angels.

So maybe we were learning. Maybe we are learning again, relearning, that there is no such thing as "realism" except the realism of man's vision and aspiration.

Salvador de Madariaga says, "Art is the conveyance of spirit by means of matter." Santayana says, "Nothing is so poor and melancholy as art that is interested in itself and not in its subject." Browning says,

> What is art,
> But life upon a larger scale, the higher,
> When, graduating up in a spiral line
> Of still expanding and ascending gyres,
> It pushes toward the intense significance
> Of all things, hungry for the Infinite?

Towards American Cultural Maturity

by HARLAN HATCHER

W̲HY DO PEOPLE WRITE, OR WANT TO WRITE, OR READ WRITING? THE answers are already known, but we may profitably remind ourselves again of a few commonplaces about them. We shall skip the controversial points in the question: whether writers are queer misfits in conflict with their environment, whether they are hurt by the conditions of their living, or subconsciously protesting against their fathers, mothers, or older sisters, and other such theories that try to account for the lonely and trying occupation of writing. The basic impulse, surely, is the fierce urge to bring form and meaning into the bewildering chaos of life as it is lived on earth by human beings. That experience of living tends, for most people, evidently, to flow along on a dead level of repetition and monotony. Only the rare and exceptional moments are distinguished by being exalted into a memorable peak. Others might have been memorable if they had been differentiated and interpreted. Both are caught by the imagination of the poets, vivified, given life in words, and handed on to others who may share the experience through the reproducible magic of words. That which was unseen and unfelt, or seen through a glass darkly, then becomes luminous and intense. Browning put it in near final form in Fra Lippo Lippi, the young artist who was ablaze with wonder at the fair face of Florence, its river, its mountain round it, and, what is more, "the figures of man, woman, child, These are the frame to." Florentine citizens walked by with heads down and eyes dulled, seeing nothing, or seeing but little. Fra Lippo lifts a face from the multitude, draws it with charcoal, and the citizens who passed without notice now shake their heads in recognition and approval.

... we're made so that we love
First when we see them painted, things we have passed
Perhaps a hundred times nor cared to see;

. . . . .

... Art was given for that;
God uses us to help each other so,
Lending our minds out. Have you noticed, now,
Your cullion's hanging face? A bit of chalk,
And trust me but you should, though! How much more,
If I drew higher things with the same truth!

With pertinent modifications, the statement holds for all forms of writing. It is a process of ordering, selecting, and arranging. Everything cannot be reproduced in a work of art. Even if it were possible, which it isn't, the result would be a reproduction of the original meaningless appearance of chaos. This face and that mood, or this condition and that fact, must be singled out, re-created, and given new life in a form which bears the impact and conviction of truth. If this metamorphosis, which is Fra Lippo's miracle, can be wrought, we get good or great writing.

Let us for the moment assume Lippo's technical genius with the brush or the wood coal; the key to its use is form and selection. He saw instantly in the face of one of the knaves who had come to arrest him the model he needed for "the slave that holds John Baptist's head a-dangle by the hair With one hand . . . And his weapon in the other, yet unwiped!" For Lippo lived in the atmosphere of the Renaissance in Cosimo of the Medici's Florence. No one, seeing the same face, would select it for the same purpose—unless, perchance, he had decided to write another historical novel for a book-club distribution. He would more likely see the face with concern for the social situation which had produced its knavery.

That is to say, in any consideration of art, we quickly arrive at the nature and the quality of the culture which produces it. No artist, however supreme, can divorce himself from the culture of his time. He may attempt to see it whole under the eye of the absolute, but the preoccupations of his time and the culture of his age direct his scrutiny and move his pen. They determine in large part what he shall see, what he shall consider important, and the tone of his appraisal. If Homer, Dante, or Shakespeare were working today, endowed though they were with the genius which makes them our contemporaries, they would not produce the *Iliad,* the *Inferno,* or *Hamlet.* Their work might be equally great, but it would certainly be different. And one of the differentials would be the nature of the cultural environment and the preoccupations of the time.

We shall not attempt in this limited space to push the point further, or even to list what might be called the creases in the surface of the mirror which we hold up to nature, such as the psychology of Freud or the theories of Karl Marx. We shall limit ourselves to the status of American culture and its somewhat subtle, but no less profound, influence upon art.

Time has its own serene manner of slipping over us and registering its changes. It has been passing over Ohio and Michigan. You select your own category—the millennial rhythm of the glacial age or the hourly crises of a World War II. Still it passes and alterations occur. In the summer of 1945 we celebrated at Greenville the one-hundred-fiftieth anniversary of Wayne's treaty with the Indians which freed northern Ohio for white settlement and opened a road into Michigan. The transformation has been stupendous, and we should not lose sight of it: from a wilderness through which it was a grave risk for a man to pass, to a rich country of farms and fences, and much cattle; from a swamp where travelers perished in the muck, to a land of sugar beets and tomatoes, peach orchards and vineyards, and of towns and villages; from one-room country schoolhouses to great state universities. It was high adventure for our progenitors, but the transformation did not come without vision and hard work.

These ancestors of ours were conscious of their destiny, aware that they would not fully reap the rewards of their labors, but that their children and grandchildren would. It is inspiring to consider the work of Dr. Zina Pitcher of Detroit in founding a public-school system; of Peter White, a frontiersman without formal education, founding a library at Marquette. Even our prolific historical novelists have not done justice to the re-creation of these great men of the past century, and to the part they played in the building of America. They were laboring on a harsh frontier. By contrast with the old and established cultures of England and of France, the environment was indeed raw. Even Boston, New York, and Philadelphia were provincial to Vienna, Paris, and London. We imported much, we exported little. "Who reads an American book?" was more like a nineteenth-century English proverb than a clever quip. The answer was, "Almost nobody."

The American genius was not revealed by Henry James. It was better reflected in the erect vigor of Thoreau, Twain, and Whitman. Thoreau, of course, was trained at Harvard, and his culture was broad and classical. But the contribution for which the world honors him sprang from a hut and a bean patch in the woods at Walden Pond. Mark Twain was not of the cities nor of the universities. His productive roots were deep in the flood plains of the Mississippi River. He had the native quality of willows on the riverbank, of corn in the fields, of sand bars in the river bed. When he confronted the mature culture of Europe, he brought to it the naïve, humorous patronage of a steamboat captain and the man in homespun and shirt sleeves. Walt Whitman was magnificently unconfined, free as the blade of grass and the sweep of the expanding continent of which he sang. It is right that we should honor these men and sing their praise. It is significant that we should praise them for the virtues which contrast them most sharply with urban and with European cultures and with, shall we say, Spenser and Marlowe, Arnold and Housman.

The works of Thoreau, Twain, and Whitman point up a paradox in our theme. They have been honored, and rightly so, into an American tradition. Yet, though they have become a tradition, in an important sense they captured a phase of our growing culture which has passed and which we have outlived. And their work and its success have fostered a suspicion of the university atmosphere for writers at a time of maturing culture when universities have become more important in developing writers. It is still not uncommon to hear a prospective young writer advised to flee the university environment and ship as a deck hand on a cattle boat bound for Liverpool. Formal and directed studies in the physical and social sciences or in language and literature were supposed to stultify a writer, and the university atmosphere to seal him up in an ivory tower. The cattle boat was presumed to set him free and to teach him to understand life.

We need only to note this point, not to argue it. There are plenty of instances when the heavy hand of a sterile tradition has fallen upon universities, particularly in departments of English, and where spontaneous creativity has been smothered by a rank growth of historical scholarship and a barren concept of research. But the record of the Hopwood project at Michigan is a distinguished indication of what can be accomplished in the field of letters, and it speaks for itself. A certain amount of learning is not necessarily fatal to a writer. It is conceivable that he might actually profit by it. Neither is the atmosphere of leisure, nor the opportunity for mature advice and judgment, necessarily prejudicial to good writing. And the prize awards, though relatively handsome, are not necessarily corrupting. But nonetheless, historically, there has been this conflict between the homespun and the cultivated, between the grass roots and the library.

We are beginning, I believe, to resolve the conflict as our culture matures. It is somewhat like the process by which an awkward freshman becomes a more-assured senior. The days pass, the years advance, and, though the change is not perceptible from week to week, the leaven is at work, and one day parents, professors, and friends note that something gratifying has happened to the young man. Charles Dickens journeyed from Cincinnati to Cleveland in 1842. The distinguished novelist, who had come up from the London slums, was hard put to it to find the proper words to describe the primitive manners and feeding habits of the Ohio natives. He thought that their idea of the social use of leisure was to sit around a stove and spit. What he didn't see was the energy and vision of the citizens who were at that moment founding schools and colleges all over the state for the benefit of their children; nor did he foresee that a century later one would drive from Cincinnati to Cleveland over ribbon-smooth roads through some of the finest farm land on the planet without being at any time more than fifteen or twenty miles from a college or a university.

The Dickens mirror with its familiar creases has been held up to the American scene for a long time. It has had hard use in the very recent past. The generation of writers whose productivity fell primarily in the first third of this century viewed intensively in social picture in America. Many of them, we note, were college- and university-educated men and women; many of them born and reared and goaded into expression in the Middle West. Most of them wielded vigorous pens. They forced recognition in other lands. Their books were not only published and widely read in England, they were translated into the European languages and freely circulated on the continent of Europe. If you asked in the 1920's and 1930's, "Who reads an American book?" the answer was, "Almost everybody." In fact, the first Nobel prize award for literature given to an American went to Sinclair Lewis in 1930.

No nation had ever in history subjected itself to a more thorough-going self-criticism. One element in that criticism was the conviction that the American environment was inhospitable to artists. The conviction had actually become a tradition. The urge to write, to sculpture, or to paint was attended by the desire to escape. A long tradition was behind the urge. Sculptors, like Hiram Powers, who wished to attain repute, found it desirable to go to Rome or Florence to live and work. Painters with genius or with talent in the nineteenth century fled as a matter of course from their native American soil to take up residence in Düsseldorf and Venice, Munich or Paris. Writers were only a little less under this compulsion. Henry James preferred London to New York or Boston. Ezra Pound's soul could be nourished only in France and Italy, where the artistic spirit could flourish in freedom; we shall not pursue the point to its ultimate irony. William Dean Howells left Ohio for Venice and returned to Boston, and his first writing was about life in Italy, not about life in the Northwest Territory. Hamlin Garland escaped from the primitive Middle West to cultivated Boston. And so on through a long list.

We are not arguing that, under the circumstances, James should have lived in New England, that Howells should have remained in Ashtabula County, or that Garland should have stayed on an Iowa farm. We are only observing that they found insufficient reasons for doing so; the soil was too thin, the companionship of the native culture was too crude. In some instances, at least, one of the driving motives which sent writers into their trade was the opportunity it afforded to escape into a richer or a more sophisticated culture.

The writers of the 1920's not only escaped, but they painted a grim picture of what they had escaped from. I used to drop in from time to time on a course in American civilization at the Sorbonne in 1928. The source material was being taken from three novels by Sinclair Lewis: *Main Street, Babbitt,* and *Arrowsmith*—with a heavy reliance on *Main Street* and the first hundred pages of *Babbitt*. I had some difficulty in recognizing the culture of my native country as it was being interpreted out of these documents by young Frenchmen. I had the feeling that Europeans were not displeased to find that the provincial Americans who had invaded the Continent during World War I were indeed skilled and ingenious mechanics who could lay telephone wire and build railroads up to the Front with lightning speed, but their culture was, as had been suspected, crude and deadening. Across the great American continent, free and open and dedicated to liberty, stretched in dreary monotony the small grim towns of little souls. They were peopled, apparently, by crafty or empty-headed, raucous businessmen and by their thwarted and gossiping wives. They were frightened of nonconformity, and they bolstered their egos by waving the flag of one-hundred-per-cent isolated Americanism and shouting for bigness.

You are all familiar with that picture. It does not require further amplification. It was so characteristic of its period that it became a part of the temper of the time. Joseph Wood Krutch made an analysis of the period in 1929 which he called *The Modern Temper.* The outlook did not at the time seem too hopeful. The period is a nice example of how certain characteristic rhythms can affect writers and pull them into an orbit. Even so assured and conscientious an artist as Willa Cather felt the pressures. Her Pulitzer-prize novel, *One of Ours,* and her *A Lost Lady* are cases in point, and are to be contrasted with *My Ántonia* and with *Death Comes for the Archbishop* and *Shadows on the Rock. A Lost Lady* is not a bad symbol of the period. Mrs. Forrester was unable to retain her refinements when transferred from a wealthy urban background to exposure to the vulgarity of small-town pressures. Conceivably, of course, she might have been lost in any environment because of fundamental weaknesses in her character; the point is that the loss occurred in a small Midwestern town. It was fatal to get caught in Winesburg, Ohio. To avoid the destructive virus and to save your soul, it was compulsory to escape. Few writers of the period were to be found in their home towns, or even on their regional soil.

A few years ago the editor of the *Saturday Review of Literature* asked the late Ted Robinson of the *Cleveland Plain Dealer* to write an article about Ohio authors. The request surprised him. It took him ten minutes to think of more than three. After considerable reflection and research he was able to set down thirteen names. He observed that they were scattered about the world and that they had, so far as he could discover, no "greatest common denominator." If any of them had ever met personally, he surmised that the meeting took place in New York or in Paris.

These were the two spots where in our particular period authors were most likely to congregate. Greenwich Village was a symbolic oasis in the great American cultural desert, an American substitute for the Left Bank. The standard by which the small towns and the countryside were measured was the idealized cultivation of Vienna, Paris, and London. It personified gaiety, charm, and amusement; it contrasted with the depressing and monotonous ugliness of Gopher Prairie, with Dave Dyer imitating the Norwegian catching a hen and old Rauskukle with his filth and his dollars. Carol Kennicott, product of a state university, and somewhat spoiled thereby, is represented as longing for the swifter and more sophisticated style of living in the East. She is quite unfitted for her role as wife of a doctor in Gopher Prairie. As a matter of fact, Ántonia Shimerda is the only heroine of the period in my recollection who has serenity and poise, who is not in conflict with her environment, who draws any strength from the soil or deep satisfaction from motherhood. She was unspoiled by a university education.

The significant point, of which these observations are illustrative, is that the typically American environment, whether in small town or countryside, was oppressive and stultifying to writers. They escaped from it, they looked back upon it from a distance, and they wrote critically and satirically of it in poetry, essay, and fiction. A few words and phrases from that era are embedded in the language, like glacial boulders, to remind us of its temper: Main Street and Babbitt, the Bible Belt and the Booboisie.

The American landscape itself was viewed generally through the same lens. It tended to fare badly, and it aroused only a mild interest in our writers. The Mississippi River was a muddy stream subject to disastrous floods. The Rocky Mountains lacked the glamour of the Alps. Hot winds blew over the Dust Bowl. Kansas wheat fields and Iowa hogs were a bit vulgar. If small-town life was wretched, farm life was unbearable. We had but a meager sense of history and of tradition. It was not uncommon to meet Ohio citizens who knew all the stones and the solar orientation of Stonehenge from personal inspection, but had never visited Fort Ancient or inspected the ceremonial mounds at Newark or the Serpent Mound, even though they lived within a few minutes' drive of those monuments. There were detailed guidebooks to all the hill towns of Italy with the names of the obscure artists who had painted the altar pieces and the dates when the churches had been destroyed by fire and rebuilt. There was no such documentation for the United States. It was too new and too raw to excite the interest or to justify the trouble.

But time, as we observed earlier, has a way of passing over us and altering our point of view. I suspect that, when things settle down a little more and a perspective shapes up more firmly, the decade just passed, during which we began to think of One World, may be appropriately designated as the period of Rediscovery of the Homeland. If I read the times rightly, this spirit of rediscovery is the most characteristic and salutary thing about them. I don't mean to imply that a sense of appreciation of what we were building on this continent was ever entirely lacking; I only say that it was obscured and was not a dominant part of the preceding period, that it has now risen to almost symphonic proportions, though the necessary background of critical spirit is not by any means lacking.

The evidence is all about us, and you may cite your own preferred examples. I shall select a few which impress me. If Ted Robinson were writing his article in 1946, his difficulties would be lighter. I imagine that he could actually bring together within a few hours at least half of the authors whose names he would set down. They are not so widely scattered as they were a few years ago; new ones have emerged; and many of them are on the home soil. The same truth would hold for other states. There is a strong disposition on the part of authors at the present time to live and do their work in their own region; less urge to flee to some better or faraway place. This is neither provincialism nor sentimentality. It is growth toward cultural maturity. It is not even Thoreau's concept of ignoring the big world to travel much about Concord. It is a recognition of the compatibility of concern for the interdependence of the nations of the world with a deeply rooted interest in the local parish.

There have been many causes, no doubt, for this shift of mood and outlook, but two of them are of particular concern to us. One is the spiritual collapse of Europe and the destruction of its culture.

Many of the great Continental cities are rubble, the universities and art galleries are in ruins, the lands are laid waste, the people have moved through depression into war and on into starvation and disease. It is a most melancholy scene. Under the rule of Hitler and Mussolini, the fair lands of Germany and Italy became dangerous not only to the spirit but to the persons of unapproved writers. They were intolerable with a ghastliness never dreamed of by American authors in their own country. They spread their blight over the Continent as their armies brought nation after nation under subjection. America again became the land of the free. It was the harbor of refuge for those who could manage to escape to its shores. One of the masterpieces of reporting during the invasion of Germany was the account of the American searching party in one of the salt caves of Germany coming upon an aged custodian trying to keep together deep in the bowels of the earth a few relics of art rescued from the maniacal fury sweeping into destruction on the surface of the earth what was left of a civilization. It was Spenserian in its symbolism.

By contrast, if not by intrinsic worth and growth, the expanding American cities and villages, the long fields of ripening grain, the feeding pens and the silos, the cattle ranges, and the sense of fundamental strength made America appear to be very desirable. And simultaneously we got a shock of realization that we had built here something very precious to ourselves, and to the world, and that this possession was being challenged for the first time in history by a hostile power which might be able to destroy it. We also realized that we could not merely take it for granted and inherit it, but must cherish it and keep re-creating it.

We were already moving toward a more mature understanding of ourselves and of our culture before the catastrophic events of Hitler's war accelerated it and opened wide our eyes. Consider, for example, our sudden and widespread interest in America as a place with a history. The spirit of rediscovery during the past decade has produced a library and reached the proportions of a movement. Almost every phase of our history and of our culture has been restudied and re-created in historical novels. The reading public has supported them enthusiastically and has kept them near the top of the best-seller lists since 1930. The American Guide Series revealed an almost forgotten America. Many of the states of the nation have had special books written about them to show by what process, by what human toil and vision, and with what rapidity these states have been built from a wilderness into their present preëminence. Again we must note that the tone is not sentimental or provincial, but of greater maturity and understanding. The Rivers of America Series and the American Lakes Series are another indication of the growing interest in regional America. The chances are that they would not have been attempted twenty-five years ago.

The rediscovery, or perhaps we should now say the discovery, is not confined to our own citizens. During the war, while the paper shortage in England was most acute and books went unpublished, the English set aside each month enough of their meager supply to publish fifty thousand copies of the magazine *Transatlantic*. It was written and edited to interpret America to Britons, and each issue featured a description and an analysis of some distinctive region of the United States. The articles were in boldest contrast to the reports sent back a century ago by Mrs. Trollope, Mrs. Jameson, Harriet Martineau, and Charles Dickens.

The tide has reversed itself and is flowing again westward across the Atlantic. Louis Bromfield is back at home on his Ohio acres, and he is spreading with missionary zeal his conviction that the good life is to be found on the farm near a fine city like Mansfield. He has brought to his farm a passion for soil improvement, for conservation, for bringing back the fertility of the land and the stalwart virtues of good citizenship. Pleasant Valley has supplanted Main Street as the signature of the times. Jesse Stuart has never left his home in W-Hollow, except to serve his country during the war. If he had published his *Man with a Bull-Tongue Plow* in 1919, the chances are good that he would have moved to Paris. He is at ease on his native soil, and his roots are deep.

I take these things which I have touched upon so briefly as signs of basic health in a time of epidemic sickness on a world-wide scale. I have not dwelt upon the procession of crises through which we have passed and which we are still confronting. We are beginning to learn how to live in a state of almost continuous crisis without losing our courage or our faith, and without accepting defeat or despair as the ultimate answer. And I certainly have not said that the world is without pressing problems, or that their solution is clear and easy. But I do firmly hold that we are a more mature nation than we were a quarter of a century ago, that we have acquired some understanding of our heritage and our purpose, and that it is not impossible that we shall come through in spite of all the apparent grounds for pessimism and bleak despair.

Nothing is more certain than our need for understanding. We need, like Joseph and Isaiah, the supplemental strength that derives from the spiritual power of faith and a great tradition to overcome the shattering effect of a fragmented civilization in conflict. We need the fullest possible knowledge of the nature of the physical world which can produce radar, proximity fuses, jet propulsion, and atomic bombs. We need more urgently a better knowledge of men and of the social institutions through which men must function in order to continue to live at all. We need wider understanding of the long and troublesome history of human relationships and of the high adventure of personal living and satisfaction in the masterpieces of literature. And we need writers who have that understanding coupled with Lippo's technical genius to make the cullion's face live and to draw the higher things.

The material for American writers has hardly been touched. It lies about us on every hand ready for the writer with imagination to see it, feel it, and interpret it. The environment of a great state university is the proper place to foster a healthy American culture and to train artists to draw strength from it and in turn to make their contribution to it.

The Themes of Robert Frost

by ROBERT PENN WARREN

A FAIRLY LARGE BODY OF CRITICISM HAS BEEN WRITTEN ON THE POETRY of Robert Frost, and we know the labels which have been used: nature poet, New England Yankee, symbolist, humanist, skeptic, synecdochist, anti-Platonist, and many others. These labels have their utility, true or half true as they may be. They point to something in our author. But the important thing about a poet is never what kind of label he wears. It is what kind of poetry he writes. We are not interested primarily in his "truth" as such—as label, as sampler work—but in the degree in which it is an organizing and vitalizing principle in his poem. For only in so far as it operates as such a principle—in so far as the poem becomes truly expressive—does the truth have meaning at all. Truths are very cheap and meaningless. But truths operative are neither cheap nor meaningless.

In any case I do not want to begin by quarreling with the particular labels. Instead, I want to begin with some poems and try to see how their particular truths are operative within the poems themselves. I know perfectly well that there are some readers of poetry who object to this process. They say that it is a profanation, that they simply want to enjoy the poem. Now my experience with such people is that very frequently they do not want to enjoy the poem; they want to enjoy themselves. Such a person is like a big overripe grape, ready to ooze or spurt juice at any pressure or pinprick, and any pressure or pinprick or poem will do to start the delicious flow.

But this is not quite fair to say, for after all everyone wants to enjoy the poem and we ought to take such people at their word without reference to the kind of people they are or the motive of the word. True, we all want to enjoy the poem. And we can be com-

218

forted by the fact that the poem, if it is a true poem, will, like the baby's poor kitty-cat, survive all the pinching and prodding and squeezing which love will lavish upon it. It will have nine lives, too. Further, and more importantly, the perfect intuitive and immediate grasp of a poem in the totality of its meaning and structure—the thing we desire—may come late rather than early—on the fiftieth reading rather than on the first. Perhaps we must be able to look forward as well as back as we move through the poem—be able to sense the complex of relationships and implications—before we can truly have that immediate grasp.

But we know that the poets sometimes seem to give aid and comfort to the ripe-grape kind of reader. First, this is because the poet is in the end probably more afraid of the dogmatist who wants to extract the message from the poem and throw the poem away than he is of the sentimentalist who says, "Oh, just let me enjoy the poem—it gives me such beautiful feelings!" At least the sentimentalist does not want to throw the poem away. That is something, anyhow.

Frost himself has been especially shy of the dogmatists and has not shown too much sympathy with a reader who, to quote him, "stands at the end of a poem ready in waiting to catch you by both hands with enthusiasm and drag you off your balance over the last punctuation mark into more than you meant to say." Or we have the case of Coleridge and poor old Mrs. Barbauld, who objected that there was no moral in *The Ancient Mariner*. "Madam," he replied, "the moral obtrudes far too openly."

Or we have the case of Yeats. An admirer sent Yeats an interpretation of one of his poems and asked if it was right. Yeats replied, grudgingly, that it was, but added that he did not think poets ought to interpret their own poems, or give the green light to the interpretations of other people, for this would serve to limit the poems.

But this does not imply that a poem is a stimulus to which any response, so long as it is intense, is acceptable. It does not mean that the poem is merely a body of material which the reader may fancifully reorder according to his whim. But it does imply that, though the poem is a controlled focus of experience, within the terms of that control many transliterations are possible as variants of the root attitude expressed. (There are many ways to state the theme of a poem.)

To turn to the poems: The poets may make their protests and reservations, but discussions will continue. As a starting point I am taking one of Frost's best-known and most widely anthologized pieces, *Stopping by Woods on a Snowy Evening*.[1] But we shall not be content to dwell exclusively on this poem, attractive as it is, for it will quite naturally lead us into some other poems. It will lead us to the other poems because it represents but one manifestation of an impulse very common in Frost's poetry. Here is the poem:

> Whose woods these are I think I know.
> His house is in the village though;
> He will not see me stopping here
> To watch his woods fill up with snow.
>
> My little horse must think it queer
> To stop without a farmhouse near
> Between the woods and frozen lake
> The darkest evening of the year.
>
> He gives his harness bells a shake
> To ask if there is some mistake.
> The only other sound's the sweep
> Of easy wind and downy flake.
>
> The woods are lovely, dark and deep.
> But I have promises to keep,
> And miles to go before I sleep,
> And miles to go before I sleep.

Now, the poem we are dealing with may be said to be simple— that is, the event presented is, in itself, simple and the poet says, quite simply, what the event presumably means. But this does not mean that the implications of the event are not complex; the area of experience touched upon by the poem is "suggestive" or "haunting." And all good poems, even the simplest, work, it seems to me, in exactly that way. They drop a stone into the pool of our being, and the ripples spread.

Well, we have been away from the poem too long. Let us go back to it. It does look simple. A man driving by a dark woods stops to

[1] This and subsequent quotations in this lecture are from *Complete Poems of Robert Frost*. Copyright, 1930, 1949, by Henry Holt and Company, Inc. Copyright, 1936, 1942, 1945, by Robert Frost. Used by permission of the publishers.

admire the scene, to watch the snow falling into the special darkness. He remembers the name of the man who owns the woods and knows that the man would not begrudge him a look. He is not trespassing. The little horse is restive and shakes the harness bells. The man decides to drive on, because, as he says, he has promises to keep—he has to get home to deliver the groceries for supper—and he has miles to go before he can afford to stop, before he can sleep.

At the literal level that is all the poem has to say. But if we read it at that level, we shall say, and quite rightly, that it is the silliest stuff we ever saw. That is what the Amazon queen in Shakespeare's *Midsummer Night's Dream* said to her husband as she watched the play Bottom and his fellows were giving in honor of her marriage. But Theseus, her husband, replied: "The best in this kind are but shadows; and the worst are no worse, if imagination amend them." We shall try to be a little less literal-minded than the Amazon queen and shall try to see what reality our little poem is a shadow of.

> Whose woods these are I think I know.
> His house is in the village though;
> He will not see me stopping here
> To watch his woods fill up with snow.

With that first stanza we have a simple contrast, the contrast between the man in the village, snug at his hearthside, and the man who stops by the woods. The sane, practical man has shut himself up against the weather; certainly he would not stop in the middle of the weather for no reason at all. But, being a practical man, he does not mind if some fool stops by his woods so long as the fool merely looks and does not do any practical damage, does not steal firewood or break down fences. With this stanza we seem to have a contrast between the sensitive and the insensitive man, the man who uses the world and the man who contemplates the world. And the contrast seems to be in favor of the gazer and not the owner— for the purposes of the poem at least. In fact, we may even have the question: Who is the owner—the man who is miles away or the man who can really see the woods?

With the second stanza another contrast emerges:

> My little horse must think it queer
> To stop without a farmhouse near

Between the woods and frozen lake
The darkest evening of the year.

Here we have the horse-man contrast. The horse is practical, too. He can see no good reason for stopping, not a farmhouse near, no oats available. The horse becomes an extension, as it were, of the man in the village—both at the practical level, the level of the beast which cannot understand why a man would stop, on the darkest evening of the year, to stare into the darker darkness of the snowy woods. In other words, the act of stopping is the specially human act, the thing that differentiates the man from the beast. The same contrast is continued into the third stanza—the contrast between the impatient shake of the harness bells and the soothing whish of easy wind and downy flake.

To this point we would have a poem all right, but not much of a poem. It would set up the essential contrast between, shall we say, action and contemplation, but it would not be very satisfying because it would fail to indicate much concerning the implications of the contrast. It would be a rather too complacent poem, too much at ease in the Zion of contemplation.

But the fourth and last stanza in the poem as we have it brings a very definite turn, a refusal to accept either term of the contrast developed to this point.

The woods are lovely, dark and deep.
But I have promises to keep,
And miles to go before I sleep,
And miles to go before I sleep.

The first line proclaims the beauty, the attraction of the scene—a line lingering and retarded in its rhythm. But with this statement concerning the attraction—the statement merely gives us what we have already dramatically arrived at by the fact of the stopping—we find the repudiation of the attraction. The beauty, the peace, is a sinister beauty, a sinister peace. It is the beauty and peace of surrender—the repudiation of action and obligation. The darkness of the woods is delicious—but treacherous. The beauty which cuts itself off from action is sterile; the peace which is a peace of escape is a meaningless and, therefore, a suicidal peace. There will be beauty and peace at the end of the journey, in the terms of the fulfillment of the promises, but that will be an earned beauty stemming from action.

In other words we have a new contrast here. The fact of the capacity to stop by the roadside and contemplate the woods sets man off from the beast, but in so far as such contemplation involves a repudiation of the world of action and obligation it cancels the definition of man which it had seemed to establish. So the poem leaves us with that paradox, and that problem. We can accept neither term of the original contrast, the poem seems to say; we must find a dialectic which will accommodate both terms. We must find a definition of our humanity which will transcend both terms.

This theme is one which appears over and over in Frost's poems —the relation, to state the issue a little differently, between the fact and the dream. In another poem, *Mowing,* he puts it this way: "The fact is the sweetest dream that labor knows." That is, the action and the reward cannot be defined separately; man must fulfill himself, in action, and the dream must not violate the real. But the solution is not to sink into the brute—to act like the little horse who knows that the farmhouses mean oats—to sink into nature, into appetite. But, at the same time, to accept the other term of the original contrast in our poem, to surrender to the pull of the delicious blackness of the woods, is to forfeit the human definition, to sink into nature by another way, a dangerous way which only the human can achieve. So our poem, which is supposed to celebrate nature, may really be a poem about man defining himself by resisting the pull into nature. There are many poems on this subject in Frost's work. In fact, the first poem in his first book is on this subject and uses the same image of the dark wood with its lethal beauty. It is called *Into My Own:*

> One of my wishes is that those dark trees,
> So old and firm they scarcely show the breeze,
> Were not, as 'twere, the merest mask of gloom,
> But stretched away unto the edge of doom.
>
> I should not be withheld but that some day
> Into their vastness I should steal away,
> Fearless of ever finding open land,
> Or highway where the slow wheel pours the sand.

I do not see why I should e'er turn back,
Or those should not set forth upon my track
To overtake me, who should miss me here
And long to know if still I held them dear.

They would not find me changed from him they knew—
Only more sure of all I thought was true.

Here the man enters the dark wood but manages to carry his humanity with him; he remains more sure of all he had thought was true. And thus the poem becomes a kind of parable of the position of the artist, the man who is greatly concerned with the flux of things, with the texture of the world, with, even, the dark "natural" places of man's soul. He is greatly concerned with those things, but he manages to carry over, in terms of those things, the specifically human.

From *Into My Own* let us turn to a late poem, which again gives us the man and the dark wood and the invitation to come into the lethal beauty. This one is called *Come In:*

As I came to the edge of the woods,
Thrush music—hark!
Now if it was dusk outside,
Inside it was dark.

Too dark in the woods for a bird
By sleight of wing
To better its perch for the night,
Though it still could sing.

The last of the light of the sun
That had died in the west
Still lived for one song more
In a thrush's breast.

Far in the pillared dark
Thrush music went—
Almost like a call to come in
To the dark and lament.

But no, I was out for stars:
I would not come in.
I meant not even if asked,
And I hadn't been.

In this woods, too, there is beauty, and an invitation for the man to come in. And, as before, he declines the invitation. But let us develop the implications of the contrast a little more fully. The thrush in the woods cannot now do anything to alter its position. Practical achievement is at an end—the sleight of wing (a fine phrase) can do no good. But it still can sing. That is, the darkness can still be conquered in the very lament. In other words, the poet is prepared to grant here that a kind of satisfaction, a kind of conquest, is possible by the expression, for the expression is, in itself, a manifestation of the light which has been withdrawn. Even in terms of the lament, in terms of the surrender to the delicious blackness, a kind of ideal resolution—and one theory of art, for that matter—is possible. (We remember that it was a thing for a man to do and not for a horse to do, to stop by the other dark woods.)

But here the man, as before, does not go into the woods. He will not make those terms with his destiny, not, in any case, unless forced to do so. (The thrush cannot do otherwise, but a man can, perhaps, and if he can do otherwise he more fully defines himself as man.) No, the man is out for stars, as he says. Which seems to say that man, by his nature (as distinguished from bird), is not dependent upon the day; he can find in the night other symbols for his aspiration. He will not lament the passing of the day, but will go out for stars.

> I would not come in.
> I meant not even if asked,
> And I hadn't been.

What are we to take as the significance of this last little turn? Is it merely a kind of coyness, a little ironical, wry turn, without content, a mere mannerism? (And I think that in some of Frost's poems we do have the mere mannerism, a kind of self-imitation.) Why had not the man been asked to come in? The thrush's song had seemed to be an invitation. But it had not been an invitation after all. First, because the invitation does not fit the man; his object is different and the invitation to surrender, to lament, is not for him. Second, and more importantly it seems, we have the implication that the bird cannot speak to the man. It has not the language of man. It can only speak in terms of its own world, the world of nature and the dark woods, and not in terms of the man who is waiting for the darkness to define the brilliance of the stars. So here we have again the man–nature contrast (but we must remember that nature is in man, too), the contrast between the two kinds of beauty, and the idea that the reward, the dream, the ideal, stems from action and not from surrender of action.

Let us leave the dark-wood symbol and turn to a poem which, with other materials, treats Frost's basic theme. This is *After Apple-Picking,* the poem which I am inclined to think is Frost's masterpiece, it is so poised, so subtle, so poetically coherent in detail.

> My long two-pointed ladder's sticking through a tree
> Toward heaven still,
> And there's a barrel that I didn't fill
> Beside it, and there may be two or three
> Apples I didn't pick upon some bough.
> But I am done with apple-picking now.
> Essence of winter sleep is on the night,
> The scent of apples: I am drowsing off.
> I cannot rub the strangeness from my sight
> I got from looking through a pane of glass
> I skimmed this morning from the drinking trough
> And held against the world of hoary grass.
> It melted, and I let it fall and break.
> But I was well
> Upon my way to sleep before it fell,
> And I could tell
> What form my dreaming was about to take.
> Magnified apples appear and disappear,
> Stem end and blossom end,
> And every fleck of russet showing clear.
> My instep arch not only keeps the ache,
> It keeps the pressure of a ladder-round.
> I feel the ladder sway as the boughs bend.
> And I keep hearing from the cellar bin
> The rumbling sound
> Of load on load of apples coming in.
> For I have had too much
> Of apple-picking: I am overtired
> Of the great harvest I myself desired.
> There were ten thousand thousand fruit to touch,

Cherish in hand, lift down, and not let fall.
For all
That struck the earth,
No matter if not bruised or spiked with stubble.
Went surely to the cider-apple heap
As of no worth.
One can see what will trouble
This sleep of mine, whatever sleep it is.
Were he not gone,
The woodchuck could say whether it's like his
Long sleep, as I describe its coming on,
Or just some human sleep.

The items here—ladder in apple tree, the orchard, drinking trough, pane of ice, woodchuck—all have their perfectly literal meanings—the echo of their meaning in actuality. And the poem, for a while anyway, seems to be commenting on that actual existence those items have. Now some poems make a pretense of living only in terms of that actuality. For instance, *Stopping by Woods on a Snowy Evening* is perfectly consistent at the level of actuality—a man stops by the woods, looks into the woods, which he finds lovely, dark and deep, and then goes on, for he has promises to keep. It can be left at that level, if we happen to be that literal-minded, and it will make a sort of sense. Some poems are consistent at that literal level.

However, *After Apple-Picking* is scarcely consistent at that level. It starts off with a kind of consistency, but something happens. The hero of the poem says that he is drowsing off—and in broad daylight, too. He says that he has a strangeness in his sight which he drew from the drinking trough. So the literal world dissolves into a kind of dreamworld—the literal world and the dreamworld overlapping, as it were, like the two sets of elements in a super-imposed photograph. What is the nature of this dreamworld? And what is its relation to the literal world, the world of real apples and the aching instep arch and the real woodchuck?

The poem opens with a few lines which seem to apply wholeheartedly to the literal world:

> My long two-pointed ladder's sticking through a tree
> Toward heaven still,

And there's a barrel that I didn't fill
Beside it, and there may be two or three
Apples I didn't pick upon some bough.

It is all literal enough. We even observe the very literal down-to-earth word "sticking" and the casualness of the tone of the whole passage. In fact, it would be hard to say this more simply than it is said. Even the rhymes are unobtrusive, and their unobtrusiveness is rendered greater by the fact that all of the lines except one are run-on lines, so that we do not linger on the rhyme word. But let us, in the light of the rest of the poem, look more closely. The ladder, we observe, has been left sticking "toward heaven still." That is, as we have said, casual and commonplace enough, but we suddenly realize it isn't merely that, when we remember the poem is about the kind of heaven the poet wants, the kind of dream-after-labor he wants—and expects.

So we have, to break the matter down into crude statement and destroy the quality of the suggestive-in-the-commonplace, a kind of preliminary appearance of the theme which concerns the relation of labor and reward, earth and heaven. With our knowledge of the total poem, we can look back, too, at the next several lines and re-read them: Maybe I missed something in my life, in my labor, the poet says, but not much, for I tried quite conscientiously to handle carefully every item of my harvest of experience, to touch with proper appreciation everything that came to hand. Maybe I did miss a few things, he seems to say, but I did the best I could, and on the whole did pretty well.

But now the harvest is over, he says, and the "Essence of winter sleep is on the night, The scent of apples." He is aware of the conclusion, the successful conclusion of his effort, and in that awareness there is a strangeness in his sight. He is now looking not into the world of effort but the world of dream, of the renewal. It is misty and strange, as seen through the pane of ice, but still it has the familiar objects of the old world of effort, but the objects now become strange in their very familiarity. He is poised here on the frontier between the two worlds, puzzling about their relationship. But he can already tell, he says, what will be the content of the dreamworld, the world of reward for labor now accomplished.

And I could tell
What form my dreaming was about to take.
Magnified apples appear and disappear,
Stem end and blossom end,
And every fleck of russet showing clear.

The dream will relive the world of effort, even to the ache of the instep arch where the ladder rung was pressed. But is this a cause for regret or for self-congratulation? Is it a good dream or a bad dream? The answer is not to be found in statement, for as far as the statement goes he says:

For I have had too much
Of apple-picking: I am overtired
Of the great harvest I myself desired.

No, we must look for the answer in the temper of the description he gives of the dream—the apples, stem end and blossom end, and every fleck of russet showing clear. The richness and beauty of the harvest—magnified now—is what is dwelt upon. In the dream-world every detail is bigger than life, and richer, and can be contemplated in its fullness. And the accent here is on the word "contemplated." Further, even as the apple picker recalls the details of labor which made him overtired, he does so in a way which denies the very statement that the recapitulation in dream will "trouble" him. For instance, we have the delicious rhythm of the line, "I feel the ladder sway as the boughs bend."

It is not the rhythm of nightmare, but of the good dream. Or we find the same temper in the next few lines, in which the poet returns to the fact that he, in the real world, the world of effort, had carefully handled and cherished each fruit, and "cherished" is not the word to use if the labor is mere labor, the brutal act. So even though we find the poet saying that his sleep will be troubled, the word "troubled" comes to us colored by the whole temper of the passage, ironically qualified by that temper. For he would not have it otherwise than troubled, in this sense.

To quote again:

One can see what will trouble
This sleep of mine, whatever sleep it is.

Were he not gone,
The woodchuck could say whether it's like his
Long sleep, as I describe its coming on,
Or just some human sleep.

Well, what does the woodchuck have to do with it? How does he enter the poem, and with what credentials? His sleep is contrasted with "just some human sleep." The contrast, we see, is on the basis of the dream. The woodchuck's sleep will be dreamless and untroubled. The woodchuck is simply in the nature from which man is set apart. The animal's sleep is the sleep of oblivion. But man has a dream which distinguishes him from the woodchuck. But how is this dream related to the literal world, the world of the woodchuck and apple harvests and daily experience? It is not a dream which is cut off from that literal world of effort—a heaven of ease and perpetual rewards in the sense of rewards as coming after and in consequence of effort. No, the dream, the heaven, will simply be a reliving of the effort—magnified apples, stem end and blossom end, and every fleck, every aspect of experience, showing clear.

Now, we have been considering the literal world and the dream-world as distinct, for that is the mechanism of the poem, the little myth of the poem. But here it may be well to ask ourselves if the poet is really talking about immortality and heaven—if he is really trying to define the heaven he wants and expects after this mortal life. No, he is only using that as an image for his meaning, a way to define his attitude. And that attitude is an attitude toward the here and now, toward man's conduct of his life in the literal world. So we must make another transliteration.

This attitude has many implications. And this leads us to a rather important point about poetry. When we read a poem merely in terms of a particular application of the attitude involved in it, we almost always read it as a kind of cramped and mechanical allegory. A poem defines an attitude, a basic view, which can have many applications. It defines, if it is a good poem, a sort of strategic point for the spirit from which experience of all sorts may be freshly viewed.

But to return to this poem: What would be some of the implied applications? First, let us take it in reference to the question of any sort of ideal which man sets up for himself, in reference to his dream.

By this application the valid ideal would be that which stems from and involves the literal world, which is arrived at in terms of the literal world and not by violation of man's nature as an inhabitant of that literal world. Second, let us take it in reference to man's reward in this literal world. By this application we would arrive at a statement like this: Man must seek his reward in his fulfillment through effort, and must not expect reward as something coming at the end of effort, like the oats for the dray horse, in the trough at the end of the day's pull. He must cherish each thing in his hand. Third, let us take it in reference to poetry, or the arts. By this application, which is really a variant of the first, we would find that art must stem from the literal world, from the common body of experience, and must be a magnified "dream" of that experience as it has achieved meaning, and not a thing set apart, a mere decoration.

These examples, chosen almost at random, are intended merely to point us back into the poem—to the central impulse of the poem itself. But they are all summed up in this line from *Mowing,* another of Frost's poems: "The fact is the sweetest dream that labor knows." However, we can step outside of the poems a moment and find a direct statement from the anti-Platonic Frost. He is comparing himself with E. A. Robinson, but we can see the application to the thematic line which has been emerging in the poems we have been considering:

I am not the Platonist Robinson was. By Platonist I mean one who believes what we have here is an imperfect copy of what is in heaven. The woman you have is an imperfect copy of some woman in heaven or in someone else's bed. Many of the world's greatest—maybe all of them —have been ranged on that romantic side. I am philosophically opposed to having one Iseult for my vocation and another for my avocation. . . . Let me not sound the least bit smug. I define a difference with proper humility. A truly gallant Platonist will remain a bachelor as Robinson did from unwillingness to reduce any woman to the condition of being used without being idealized.

Smug or not—and perhaps the poet doth protest his humility a little too much here—the passage does give us a pretty clear indication of Frost's position. And the contrast between "vocation" and "avocation" which he uses leads us to another poem in which the theme appears, *Two Tramps in Mud Time.* The last stanza is talking about the relation of "love" and "need" as related to an activity—which may be transliterated into "dream" and "fact" if we wish:

> But yield who will to their separation,
> My object in living is to unite
> My avocation and my vocation
> As my two eyes make one in sight.
> Only where love and need are one,
> And the work is play for mortal stakes,
> Is the deed ever really done
> For Heaven and the future's sakes.

And we may notice that we have, in line with our earlier poems on the theme, the apparently contrasting terms "mortal stakes" and "Heaven."

If there were space, I could offer fuller documentation from the poems. But in any case I may cite *Desert Places,* which is a late and more bleakly stoical version of *Stopping by Woods on a Snowy Evening,* and *Birches,* which is almost a variant of *After Apple-Picking.* I shall remind you of the ending:

> So was I once myself a swinger of birches.
> And so I dream of going back to be.
> It's when I'm weary of considerations,
> And life is too much like a pathless wood
> Where your face burns and tickles with the cobwebs
> Broken across it, and one eye is weeping
> From a twig's having lashed across it open.
> I'd like to get away from earth awhile
> And then come back to it and begin over.
> May no fate willfully misunderstand me
> And half grant what I wish and snatch me away
> Not to return. Earth's the right place for love:
> I don't know where it's likely to go better.
> I'd like to go by climbing a birch tree,
> And climb black branches up a snow-white trunk
> *Toward* heaven, till the tree could bear no more,
> But dipped its top and set me down again.
> That would be good both going and coming back.
> One could do worse than be a swinger of birches.

For the meaning, in so far as it is abstractly paraphrasable as to theme: Man is set off from nature by the fact that he is capable of the dream, but he is also of nature, and his best dream is the dream of the fact, and the fact is his position of labor and fate in nature though not of her. For the method: The poet has undertaken to define for us both the distinction between and the interpenetration of two worlds, the world of nature and the world of the ideal, the heaven and the earth, the human and the nonhuman (oppositions which appear in various relationships), by developing images gradually from the literal descriptive level of reference to the symbolic level of reference.

It may be said quite truly in one sense that this interpenetration, this fusion, of the two worlds is inherent in the nature of poetry—that whenever we use a metaphor, even in ordinary conversation, we remark on the interpenetration in so far as our metaphor functions beyond the level of mere mechanical illustration. But the difference between the general fact and these poems is that the interpenetration of the two worlds, in varying ranges of significance, is itself the theme of the poems. We can whimsically say that this does not prove very much. Even the most vindictive Platonist could not do very differently, for in so far as he was bound to state his Platonic theme in words, which belong to our world of fact and contingency, he would be unwittingly celebrating the un-Platonic interpenetration of the two worlds.

But there is a practical difference if not an ultimate one. We might get at it this way: The process the poet has employed in all of these poems, but most fully and subtly I think in *After Apple-Picking,* is to order his literal materials so that, in looking back upon them as the poem proceeds, the reader suddenly realizes that they have been transmuted. When Shakespeare begins a sonnet with the question, "Shall I compare thee to a summer's day?" and proceeds to develop the comparison, "Thou art more lovely and more temperate," he is assuming the fact of the transmutation, of the interpenetration of the worlds, from the very start. But in these poems, Frost is trying to indicate, as it were, the very process of the transmutation, of the interpenetration. That, and what that implies as an attitude toward all our activities, is the very center of these two poems, and of many others among his work.

The Writer's Responsibility

by J. Donald Adams

Perhaps there never was a time in which the writer, and particularly the young writer, faced so many challenges as he does today. Merely to live in this disordered world of ours, to carry on a day-to-day existence that makes sense and seems geared to some worthwhile purpose, is in itself a challenge to our sense of proportion, to our sense of perspective. How much more, then, is it so in the case of those who undertake to reflect and interpret this world we live in, those who feel they have something to say to us, and who would like, if possible, to bring some illumination to the life we are living.

These challenges are of two kinds. There are the basic ones, which concern the writer as an individual, just as they concern us all at this moment in the world's history, but which necessarily have their effect upon his work. And in addition to these, there are the problems which are his specific concern as an artist—the problems that are peculiar to his craft at this particular moment.

In what may be called the basic group, he is confronted first of all by the predominant character of the time in which we live. Contemporary writers have defined it in phrases which, although varied, rest upon a common base. They have called it the age of perplexity, the century of fear, the age of anxiety. That these are apt designations we are all aware. Men today are apprehensive to a degree which they have never been in all our history. And the fears by which they are surrounded are not imaginary; they are very real. There is no need to specify them; we are all made painfully conscious of them as we turn to our newspapers every morning. We know that surrender to them would be fatal, as surrender to fear always is, and that what we have most to fear is fear itself. And so the first challenge to the writer is to his courage, to his capacity for hope and determination.

There is another aspect of our age which, while it affects us all, has a particular significance for the writer. It is the submergence of the individual life. Never before has the race been so acutely conscious of mankind in the mass; never has our belief in the importance of the individual life been so sorely tried. And that is a condition which strikes at the core of the novelist's art and which threatens the very stuff of which poetry is made. As the English writer Storm Jameson remarked several years ago, the novelist today "sees that there are moments in the history of the human race when what is personal in a man is less important than the fears and hopes, the impulses he shares with a great many of his fellows. He suspects that this is such a moment. And perhaps he despairs. He thinks: If I am to write about this movement, this change, it will dwarf any men and women I can conceive. It will depersonalize them."

It is true, of course, that there are times when what is personal in a man should or must be subordinated to a welfare that is larger than his own; it is true not only for masses of men in certain crises, it is true for every individual life, in whatever time it is lived. Yet the novelist cannot lose sight of personal values, of individual desires and problems. He cannot, if he is to be effective, write abstractly. Our understanding of how men live, of what life means to them, can be deepened only by studying the individual relationships of one man, one woman, to another, or that individual's relationship to his family, his social group, his country, or whatever aggregate you may choose to name. Out of these relationships issue conflicts and adjustments of various kinds, and it is in these that the novelist finds his richest material. But to present these conflicts and adjustments effectively, he must individualize them. Thus, we have another challenge to the writer imposed upon him by the character of his time: in this case a challenge to his ability to keep in balance his awareness of the tremendous currents which affect us all and his sense of the individual's importance.

There is a third condition of our period with which the writer must deal both as an individual and as an artist. It is what the Swiss writer Picard has referred to as the disjointedness of our time. His thesis is that modern man, whose inner world is chaotic, is constantly

facing an equally chaotic outer world, where momentary impressions
are rained upon him in quick succession, without connection or order
of any kind. As typical manifestations of this condition he instances
the radio, with its interminable abrupt transitions, and the increasingly scattered character of our magazines, especially those on the
lower intelligence level, which seem to devote less and less space to
more and more topics. The newsreel, which shuttles us back and
forth between tragedy and comedy and heaven knows what else in
a matter of seconds, is perhaps an even more striking instance. Our
modern interest in man's unconscious has served to intensify the
disjointedness by which we are surrounded, for chaos reigns in the
unconscious. Because so much of our world presents itself to us in
this fragmentary fashion, like the unrelated objects in a surrealist
painting, it becomes increasingly hard for us to see life steadily and
see it whole.

These, then, are some of the conditions of our time which not
only have a direct bearing on our daily lives as human beings, but
create as well the atmosphere in which the writer must conceive
and carry on his work. But he is subject also, as I have already remarked, to various conditions which are peculiar to him in his role
as artist. He has, for one thing, been living through a period in which
intense experimentation has been characteristic of all the arts. This
ferment has been most active in painting and sculpture, in music and
poetry, but it has been at work in the novel and in other literary forms
as well.

These periods are of course necessary to the continuous flow of
vitality in art. But during them there occurs both a widening and a
narrowing of horizons—a widening in the sense of new techniques
and new approaches being opened up, and a narrowing due to a
contraction in the size of the audience addressed. For it seems inevitable when this process of change is at work that the writer or
other artist should address himself more and more to his fellow
craftsmen, to that small group whose ideas he shares and whose
objectives are common to his own. There is a stoppage of that "fluid"
which Victor Hugo described as running between the writer and
his reader, in a stream from which they both draw strength. There
comes a point at which that stoppage must be removed, so that the
relationship between writer and reader may be once more vitalized.

In literary, as in political revolutions, there are inevitably excesses in the direction of change and an indiscriminate discarding of the traditional in our literature. It would be unreasonable to insist that nothing constructive had been accomplished by the revolution which T. S. Eliot and others wrought in poetry, as it would be blindness to deny that some of the forces which they set in motion have been harmful to poetry in that they have produced too great obstructions to that vital stream between writer and reader to which I have referred. The same may be said of the influence which James Joyce and Virginia Woolf exerted upon the craft of fiction. They deepened our conception of the subjective method in fiction, but they deflected us from concern with the narrative function of the novel.

It seems to me that the time has now come, in all the arts, for the work of consolidation. The artist today is faced by the need to take whatever of positive value has been gained by the work of the experimenters and to fuse it with whatever in the traditional has been too often neglected or discarded. It is essential to all living things that there be an interplay between the old and the new, for it is in that fashion that all true progress is made.

In that interesting book by Alice Marriott about the tribal life of the Kiowa Indians, *The Ten Grandmothers,* there is a passage which delighted me by its homely but vivid statement of this ancient truth. Two Kiowa young men are talking. Eagle Plume's father has just died, and by tribal tradition his horse should be killed where he was buried. It happened that the Kiowas were going through a difficult time, and Eagle Plume's friend, Wood Fire, remonstrates. "This is a good horse," he says. "People will need good horses." But Eagle Plume replies, "This is what my father would want," and cuts the horse's throat. Afterward, as they sit by the fire, Wood Fire remarks, "That is the end of one kind of living. I think all the old things will be dead soon." They begin to argue about the unwillingness of some people to give the old things up, and the right of others to get new things started. Eagle Plume felt very old as he said to his friend, "You have to have new things. You have to have new springs to make the grass grow. But grass grows out of the old earth. You have to have old things for new things to have roots in. That's why some people have to keep old things going and some people have to push new things along. It's right for both of them. It's what they have to do." "And," he might have added, "some of us can do both."

There, reduced to the simplest terms, you have the age-old conflict between tradition and innovation. Eagle Plume, taking his analogy from the earth, direct from Nature as an Indian would, is saying precisely the same thing that André Gide reports himself as once thinking: "It suddenly seemed clear to me that if there were no names in the history of art except those belonging to the creators of new forms there would be no culture; the very word implied a continuity, and therefore it called for disciples, imitators and followers to make a living chain: in other words, a tradition."

Or, as John Buchan once put it: "[If a man regards the past] as the matrix of present and future, whose potency takes many forms but is not diminished, then he will cherish it scrupulously and labour to read its lessons, and shun the heady short-cuts which end only in blank walls. He will realise that in the cycle to which we belong we can see only a fraction of the curve, and that properly to appraise the curve and therefore to look ahead, we may have to look back a few centuries to its beginning."

In all departments of human activity there must be this shuttling, this backward and forward motion, this interplay of forces. So far as literature and the other arts are concerned, it is when we have absolute intolerance of the representatives of one force for the other that we get the dry rot of sterile repetition or the gross exaggerations, the absurd extremes by which the intolerant innovator proclaims his absolute freedom from tradition. There is no more absolute freedom in art than there is in human liberty. Our own time, being a period of violent experimentation in all fields of activity, has seen a great deal of condescension toward those who have worked with one eye on the curve of which John Buchan reminds us. It might make a profitable half hour to sit down and compile a list of those whom we think of as the acknowledged great in literature, in painting and music, and to find how many of them could not properly be classed as belonging among the innovators—at least, not in the sense of those whose aim was to break completely from the curve of tradition.

It is to be hoped, however, that these statements do not leave the impression that what is asked for is a cessation of experimental writing. Nothing could be further from my intention, for some amount of it is an essential to the healthy condition of any art. But it is suggested that the need for it is not now as great as it was, and that what is more urgent is the more necessary work of consolidation. Already, particularly in poetry, there are signs of a growing awareness of this need among young writers. There is evident in the work of some of them a recognition of the fact that the lines of communication between writer and reader, especially in poetry, require strengthening. They are writing more directly, more simply, with less dependence upon private imagery.

There is another challenge to the contemporary writer as a craftsman about which so much has recently been written that I shall touch upon it only briefly. It is composed of the various threats to his integrity which have been created by the growing commercializing influences to which the literary career has been subjected. I am not referring to the siren song of Hollywood alone. It is a time when opportunism is in the literary air. There are publishers who are the best friends that a writer could have in relation to his work; there are others who can be his worst enemies, those who urge him into production, after a first success, before he is ready. There are agents who are helpful in many ways besides the matter of marketing, and there are those with whom their commission is the prime consideration. Nor is it an easy matter these days for the young writer of a first success to keep his head; that requires an unusual sense of balance and proportion.

One evening, during a discussion of what writers are thinking about today, I heard the publicity director of one of our large publishing houses, in a confessional mood, say that she regarded the job she performs as one of the heaviest handicaps against which the young writer has to contend. She had watched too many egos disastrously inflate as a result of the promotion that had been considered necessary. The writer today lives in a world of increasing ballyhoo, and heaven help him if he lacks a sense of humor about himself.

The scarcity of a sound and responsible criticism is of course another factor. But if these conditions constitute a challenge to the writer—the temptation to trim his sails for financial advantage, to go on repeating the pattern of a first success, the impact of absurd claims regarding his importance—it is good to remember that there are writers who meet that challenge and surmount it. No better ex-

ample can be suggested than Thornton Wilder, who has never allowed himself to be deflected from his course. At every step in his
career he has written the book that it interested him at that time to
write, and for no other reason.

Perhaps a little more should be said about the part that reviewing
and criticism play in our writing at this time. There is good reason
to believe that it could be much more effective than it is. Too much
of our reviewing is insufficiently based on standards which have more
permanence than those crude substitutes supplied by the prevailing
mode of the moment. Too much of what is dignified by the name of
criticism is written in an intellectual vacuum, divorced from life, and
phrased in a scientific or pseudoscientific jargon which is an exaspera-
tion to read.

Reviewing and criticism have two functions. The first, and the
one that is more satisfactorily performed than the other, is to supply
information and, in varying degrees, guidance, to the reading public.
The other, which is very imperfectly performed, is indeed, a potential
rather than an actual service. It is to give values and direction to
contemporary writing. This is a function commonly regarded as
reserved for criticism, but reviewing on its best level can also contribute something to that end. At this point someone may mutter
and say, "Bosh! Every writer worth his salt must find his own values
and his own direction; let the critics and reviewers mind their own
business." There is a measure of truth in that protest, but it is not
the whole truth by any means. Reviewing and criticism *can* be creative, as Mary Colum has ably demonstrated in her book *From These
Roots: The Ideas That Have Made Modern Literature.*

Of course every writer of consequence must find and hold to
values by which to do his work, and that work is likely to benefit by
the fact that he knows where he is going and why. But, important
as self-expression of the individual is, he is necessarily not only a
writer of particular gifts and abilities, but, like any other man, in
John Donne's phrase, "a peece of the Continent, a part of the maine."
And as coral islands are made by the deposits left by innumerable
small creatures, and as continents are molded by various natural
forces, so is the writer subject to many influences, and he is a solemn
ass if he thinks that his contribution to literature is entirely one of
his own making.

Intelligent, creative criticism can contribute much to molding the character of a period's writing. Would the course of English poetry have been the same had Wordsworth never written the Preface to the *Lyrical Ballads?* Who is there to say that if as gifted but rudderless a writer as the young Scott Fitzgerald had encountered sound and constructive criticism of his talents at the time it was most needed, he would not have greatly profited thereby? For he had sufficient humility of spirit and enough consecration to his craft to have recognized its value. That is not true, of course, of all writers, even able ones; some of them must find their way by their own efforts alone.

Enough has been said about the conditions under which the contemporary writer carries on his work—both those which arise from the general character of the time in which he lives and those which have their origin in the atmosphere peculiar to his craft. The writer's responsibility stems in part from some of the conditions which have been discussed, and its nature must to some degree be already apparent. It is a responsibility that has more than one aspect: there is the writer's responsibility to himself, to his craft, and to the reading public. And it is the third of these which should be emphasized, because while the others have always had the same importance, it would seem that the writer's responsibility to the public is today greater than it has ever been.

It is not necessary to point out that a deep hunger of the spirit stirs in every thinking man and woman today. It was not accident that made a book called *Peace of Mind* the first choice for so long a time of readers the country over. We live in a world that is in desperate need of reassurance, which desires above all else to recapture its belief in the dignity of man, and in his capacity to deal justly and generously with his fellows. The last thing we need at this moment, it seems to me, is the emergence of a twentieth-century Dean Swift; we know the worst there is to know about ourselves, and the events of the past few years have made us painfully conscious of the degradations of man's spirit to which we can descend. Keep them in mind we must, and I am not suggesting that the writer omit from his picture of the world in which he lives the contemptible depths of which man is capable; merely that he remind us also that aspiration still dwells with him.

One is reminded here of some words of Van Wyck Brooks, writ-

ten during the days when he was formulating some of the most penetrating criticism that we have had in America. He said:

> The writer, whose office it was in more primitive times to glorify
> the deeds of the man of action, finds himself now in a world that is
> eager for nothing so much as the record of his own spiritual processes.
> And that is perhaps natural. Thanks to the universal blocking and check-
> ing of instinct that modern industrialism implies for the run of men
> and even women, the type of life that still, at whatever cost, affords scope
> for the creative impulses is haloed with an immense desirability. In our
> age in which everything tends towards a regimentation of character,
> the average man, presented with no ideal but that of success, finds him-
> self almost obliged to yield up one by one the attributes of a generous
> humanity. No wonder the artist has come to be the lodestone of so many
> wishes. He alone seems able to keep open the human right of way, to
> test and explore the possibilities of life.

It has been interesting to observe the recent revival of Victorian
reputations. Most of us are aware how marked a phenomenon this
has been. Something like a note of envy, of rather unwilling admiration, has crept into contemporary references to that period. Partly
this change of attitude stems from acute awareness of our own bewilderment, our consciousness of the lack of firm ground beneath
our feet. We cannot escape a somewhat grudging recognition of
their sturdy stance in life, even though we may question the solidity
of the foundations which supplied it. But this explanation does not,
I think, account for the popularity which Victorian novelists are
enjoying. There is something else back of the renewed interest in
Henry James, in the fact that Dickens is recapturing an audience,
and that the public libraries cannot keep sufficiently stocked with the
novels of Anthony Trollope.

The answer, perhaps, lies in the Victorian's consuming interest
in character. It was Mr. Brooks also who has suggested that our
age of psychology is not an age of interest in human nature. That
statement would seem at first thought to be almost paradoxical, but
the distinction rests on the idea that psychology turns our attention
to the causes of things, to the reasons for our behavior in a certain
set of circumstances, whereas what really matters is the significance
of our actions. The modern, he contended, has lost the feeling for
character, and he quoted in support of that belief T. S. Eliot's remark

that "Nothing seems more odd about the Victorian age than the respect which its eminent people felt for one another." What is odd, Mr. Brooks asked, about respect for character?

There is no doubt that the Victorians had an excited wonder over human nature, and this excitement, this sympathetic interest, found its way into their fiction. The Victorian novelist cared, deeply and vividly, about his characters, and was consequently able to make his readers care. He allowed himself to live their emotions instead of striving, in the modern manner, to keep himself as detached from his characters as possible. Too often the contemporary novelist approaches his desk as if he were a scientist entering his laboratory. He doesn't put himself inside his characters; he examines them.

To recover some of this human warmth, to free ourselves more often from the clinical atmosphere in which too much of contemporary fiction is written, seems to me an objective worth striving for. It was in part its effort in this direction which distinguished John Hersey's *A Bell for Adano* and which was notably present in Gerald Brace's *The Garretson Chronicle*.

Do not misunderstand. A retreat from a realistic attitude is not suggested, rather the adoption of a broader and deeper realism, one that takes into account the positive as well as the negative aspects of human character. What rests in one's mind is an honest effort toward balance in regarding the complexities of the human being—the kind of balance that was too often lacking in the facile cynicism that fattened in our books during the period between the wars. Facile, that is, though some of it was honest and deeply induced, because too much of it was merely the product of a fashionable attitude. It was a period, as Charles Morgan has pointed out, when too many writers made a deliberate refusal to choose, maintain, and accept responsibility for a point of view. Today it would seem we are all more keenly aware of our individual responsibility: writers will be less easily herded into coteries than during recent years.

We are all as much the creators of our time as we are the products of it. Our writers can play a tremendous part in fixing the mood and temper of the period in which they live. We had, after the last war, a generation which surrendered to its fears. Let us not have another.

The Responsibilities of the Critic

by F. O. Matthiessen

My deliberately grave title is in the tradition from matthew Arnold, my first critical enthusiasm as an undergraduate thirty years ago. But at that very time a new critical movement was rising, the critical movement in which we are living today. T. S. Eliot's first important essay, *Tradition and the Individual Talent,* was written in 1917, when he was twenty-nine; and I. A. Richards' first independent and most influential book, *The Principles of Literary Criticism,* came out in 1924, when he was in his early thirties. The talents and principles of those two then young men have been the most pervasive forces upon the criticism of the past quarter century.

We know now what a revolution they instigated, if one may use such a violent word as "revolution" in the field of the arts, where all victories fortunately are bloodless, and where what was overthrown remains undestroyed and capable of being rediscovered at the next turn of the wheel of taste. When Eliot was growing up, the tastes and standards of Arnold were still prevailing; and Eliot found himself wholly dissatisfied with Arnold's preoccupation with the spirit of poetry rather than with its form. The form of Eliot's own first poems was deceptively radical, since he was really rejecting the easily flowing forms of the romantics and the Elizabethans for the more intricately weighted forms of the symbolists and the metaphysicals.

When Richards, as a psychologist who believed in the basic importance of the words with which men try to fathom their meanings, began to read Eliot's poems, he encountered the kind of language that proved most compelling to readers just after the First World War. The immense loosening of speech that had accompanied the rapid expansions in mass education and mass communication had reached the point where, if the artist was again to communicate the richness and denseness of real experience, he must use a language that compelled the reader to slow down, to be concerned once more with the trip rather than with the arrival. As the young English critic T. E. Hulme had been arguing, before he was killed in battle in 1917, poetry must always endeavor thus "to arrest you . . . to make you continuously see a physical thing, to prevent you gliding through an abstract process."

What resulted from the joint influence of Eliot and Richards was a criticism that aimed to give the closest possible attention to the text at hand, to both the structure and texture of the language. You are all familiar with the names of its practitioners, who, if we confine ourselves to America alone, have already produced a more serious and exacting body of work than we had previously witnessed in this country. To be sure, Richards' most gifted follower was one of his own students at Cambridge, England. William Empson, in his precocious *Seven Types of Ambiguity* (1929), begun when he was still an undergraduate, pushed to its subtle extreme Richards' kind of linguistic analysis. Empson in turn has had a particular vogue here among the critics whom we now associate with the newly founded Kenyon School of Criticism, most notably with John Crowe Ransom, Robert Penn Warren, and Cleanth Brooks. Others whose names are linked with that school, Kenneth Burke, R. P. Blackmur, Allen Tate, Austin Warren, and Yvor Winters, however divergent their methods and emphases, reveal throughout their work how they have had to reckon with Eliot and Richards, whether in concord or belligerence.

The effect of this new movement upon the study of literature in our universities has been by now considerable. Although opposed by both the old guards of philologists and literary historians, most of the critics I have mentioned now hold academic appointments, which may or may not have been good for their work. But their work has thereby become instrumental in the revolt against concentrating exclusively on the past, and against concentrating on literary history instead of on literature. As a result both teachers and students are more capable of close analysis and lively appreciation than they were a generation ago.

But by now we have reached the stage where revolt has begotten its own set of conventions, to use the terms of one of Harvard's great former teachers, John Livingston Lowes. As we watch our own generation producing whole anthologies of criticism devoted to single contemporary authors and more and more detailed books of criticism of criticism, we should realize that we have come to the unnatural point where textual analysis seems to be an end in itself. The so-called little magazines have been essential and valiant outposts of revolt in our time when the magazines of wide circulation, in decline from their standards in the nineteenth century, have abandoned serious discussion of literature almost entirely.

But the little magazines seem now to be giving rise to the conventions and vocabulary of a new scholasticism and to be not always distinguishable from the philological journals which they abhor. The names of the authors may be modern, but the smell is old. The trouble is that the terms of the new criticism, its devices and strategies and semantic exercises, can become as pedantic as any other set of terms if they are handled not as the means to fresh discoveries but as counters in a stale game. In too many recent articles literature seems to be regarded merely as a puzzle to be solved.

This is not to underestimate the great and continuing service performed by the few quarterlies devoted to criticism, or by those even littler magazines that often last only long enough to introduce one or two new talents in poetry or fiction. The important experimental work of our time has again and again been able to secure its first publication only through their pages. This is one of the consequences of what F. R. Leavis, the editor of *Scrutiny,* has called the split between "mass civilization" and "minority culture." But to recognize that phenomenon in our democracy should only be to combat it.

There is potentially a much greater audience in America for the art of literature than the blurb writers, who often pass for reviewers in the Sunday supplements, would seem to suspect. The effectiveness of the critics in the little magazines in having by now prepared a wider public for, say, Joyce or Kafka or Eliot, amply testifies to that. But the dilemma for the serious critic in our dangerously split society is that, feeling isolated, he will become serious in the wrong sense, aloof and finally taking an inverted superiority in his isolation. At that point criticism becomes a kind of closed garden.

My views are based on the conviction that the land beyond the garden's walls is more fertile, and that the responsibilities of the critic lie in making renewed contact with that soil. William James used to insist that the first duty of any thinker is to know as much as possible about life in his own time. Such an exhortation may seem too general to be of much use, but it can be grasped more concretely if we envisage the particular responsibilities of the critic in a whole series of awarenesses. These awarenesses may encompass some of the breadth and comprehensiveness which James assumed to be the thinker's goal, and some of the feeling of being drenched with actual life, which he believed to be the thinker's best reward. Much of the ground that we will traverse was also implied to be within the critic's scope by the early work of Eliot and Richards, though some of it has been lost sight of by their followers.

The first awareness for the critic should be of the works of art of our own time. This applies even if he is not primarily a critic of modern literature. One of Eliot's observations which has proved most salutary is that of the inescapable interplay between past and present: that the past is not what is dead, but what is already living; and that the present is continually modifying the past, as the past conditions the present. If one avails himself of the full resources latent in that perception, one is aware that it is not possible to be a good critic of Goethe today without knowing Mann, or of Stendhal or Balzac without knowing Proust, or of Donne or Dryden without knowing Eliot.

The converse is equally true, if less necessary to be argued in the academy. But once outside, particularly in the rapid and rootless life of our cities, the tendency even for practitioners in the arts is to be immersed wholly in the immediate. This is not what James foresaw, since he took for granted the constant meeting point between what was already known and what was still to be known. But today we can take no tradition for granted, we must keep repossessing the past for ourselves if we are not to lose it altogether. The value in this urgency is that what we manage to retain will really belong to us, and not on authority at second hand. The proper balance, even for the critic who considers his field to be the present, is to bring to the elucidation of that field as much of the art of the past as he can command.

A recently dead critic, Paul Rosenfeld, was a heartening example of this balance. Prolonging in this country the rich cultural life of his

German-Jewish forebears, he moved naturally among the arts, and it would never have occurred to him that a critic of contemporary music would try to speak without having all the great composers of the past at his finger tips. But he regarded the work of the present, especially in America, as his particular province, and often said that if our younger composers were to have a sense of possessing any audience, someone must make it his function to listen to them all. In complete modesty and selflessness he took that task upon himself. As his friends knew, Paul Rosenfeld gave himself away to his generation, a very unusual act in our fiercely competitive world, where even our intellectual life seems so often to become poisoned by the habits of our business civilization.

I have cited Rosenfeld because his generous openness to all the arts and his devoted impressions of what he found now seem so foreign to the grimly thin-lipped disciples of a more rigorous analysis. Indeed, one of them, writing currently in the *Hudson Review,* has declared that the recent volume of tribute by Rosenfeld's contemporaries from the twenties and thirties praised him for a "thoroughly degraded function." Such total lack of comprehension is a devastating illustration of what Auden meant by saying that one of the worst symptoms of sterility in our present culture is that of "intellectuals without love."

No incapacity could be less fruitful in the presence of the arts. Its recent frequency may be another unhappy by-product of the sort of specialization that leaves the student knowing only his own field. Such self-enclosed knowledge may often mean that he really knows nothing at all. At least it is hard to conceive of a good critic of literature who does not have an alert curiosity about other fields and techniques. Anyone understands his own subject and discipline better if he is aware of some other subject and discipline. To what extent this awareness should lead to mastery will vary greatly with individual aptitude. It does not seem profitable to insist that any given critic should also be expert in linguistic theory or mathematical logic or Marx or Freud, but I can hardly think of a critic today being indifferent to the access of power his mind could gain from a close study of one or more of these.

This does not mean that the misapplication of theory from one field to another is not as big a pitfall as it always was, or that fads don't often outrun facts. But as one instance of valuable cross-fertilization between fields there is cultural anthropology. Utilizing the disciplines of history and sociology, it has proved a particularly stimulating ally to the study of literature in a period when literature itself, in the hands of Joyce and Mann, has been rediscovering the vitality of primitive myth. Through our renewed awareness of folk patterns we now realize that the fertility rites which solemnize the death and rebirth of the year are equally germane to our understanding of *The Waste Land* or *The Winter's Tale* or *The Peace* of Aristophanes or the *Bacchae* of Euripides.

Another awareness which our split society makes it hard for us to keep in the right proportion is that of the popular arts of our technological age. The consequences for all our lives of the mass media of communication become ever more insistent, so that we must either channel them to socially valuable ends or be engulfed by them. The first results of our new discoveries are often as discouraging as when Thoreau scorned the transatlantic cable on the grounds that the initial news that would "leak through into the broad, flapping American ear" would be that the Princess Adelaide had the whooping cough.

The first results of television would appear to be that it has made conversation impossible in one of its few remaining American strongholds, the barroom, and is debauching the customers with entertainment that is a long throwback to the juvenile days of the penny arcade. But then one recalls how the radio, despite its intolerable deal of soap, has during the past twenty-five years built up a taste for the best symphony music among millions of listeners who would not otherwise have ever heard it. The chief art form of our age, the moving picture, is the compelling reminder of our immense potentialities and continual corruptions. Even now when, in its postwar doldrums, Hollywood seems again to have forgotten that standardization through mass production is more suitable for soup than for art, the great new Italian films are demonstrating the important access of social truth that the art of the film can gain by utilizing some of the solid techniques of the documentary.

I have mentioned these disparate examples of good and bad as a way of enforcing my conviction that we in the universities cannot afford to turn our backs upon them or upon the world from which they come. The proper place for the thinker, as William James con-

ceived it, was at the central point where a battle is being fought. It is
impossible for us to take that metaphor with the lightness that he
could. Everywhere we turn in these few fateful years since the first
atom bomb dropped on Hiroshima we seem menaced by such
vast forces that we may well feel that we advance at our peril. But
even greater peril would threaten us if those whose prime responsibility as critics is to keep open the life-giving communications between art and society should waver in their obligations to provide
ever fresh thought for our own society.

In using metaphors of battle here and now, I am not thinking in
an academic void. If we believe that freedom of thought and of speech
are the distinguishing features of the culture of a true democracy,
we must realize by what a thin margin they now survive in this
country. Within the past year there have been the most serious viola-
tions of academic freedom, caused, ironically, by officials who are
determined to prove that the United States is so much better than
any other country that it is above criticism. We must recognize the
full gravity of these casualties of the cold war, for they are a product
of the very kind of blind suppression that their instigators declare
exists only behind what they denounce as "the iron curtain."

The most flagrant recent case of national importance has nothing
to do with the issue of communism, and thus furnishes a concrete
demonstration of how, once official opinion embarks on the course
of stamping out dangerous views, every shade of dissent becomes
dangerous. Olivet College, as you all here know, was founded in the
great pioneering period of our education, when Americans were
expanding the frontiers of their thought as well as of their territory.
Its recent career, particularly in the period between two world wars,
added a notable chapter to our experiments with education by tutorial
work and group discussion. When members of its faculty of such
national distinction as a Pulitzer-prize winner for biography and the
candidate for vice-president on the Socialist ticket are dismissed,
none of us can stand aloof or feel that we are not implicated.

If what I have just been saying seems an unwarranted digression
from the responsibilities of the critic of the arts, I want to correct
that impression. The series of awarenesses which I believe the critic
must possess lead ineluctably from literature to life, and I do not

see how the responsible intellectual in our time can avoid being concerned with politics. It is at this point that my divergence becomes most complete from the formalists who have followed in the wake of Eliot, as well as from Eliot himself, whose reverence for the institutions of monarchy and aristocracy seems virtually meaningless for life in America.

I would like to recall the atmosphere of the early 1930's, of the first years of the last depression, when the critical pendulum had swung to the opposite pole, from the formalists to the Marxists. I am not a Marxist myself but a Christian, and I have no desire to repeat the absurdities of the moment when literary men, quite oblivious theretofore of economics, were finding sudden salvation in a dogma that became more rigid the less they had assimilated it. But I believe the instinct of that moment was right, as our greatest recent cultural historian, Vernon Parrington's instinct was right, in insisting upon the primacy of economic factors in society. Most artists and students of literature remain amateurs in the field of economics, but that does not prevent them from utilizing some of the basic and elementary truths which economists have made available for our culture.

Emerson held that a principle is an eye to see with, and despite all the excesses and exaggerated claims of the Marxists of the thirties, I still believe that the principles of Marxism—so much under fire now—can have an immense value in helping us to see and comprehend our literature. Marx and Engels were revolutionary in many senses of that word. They were pioneers in grasping the fact that the industrial revolution had brought about—and would continue to bring about—revolutionary changes in the whole structure of society. By cutting through political assumptions to economic realities, they revolutionized the way in which thinking men regarded the modern state. By their rigorous insistence upon the economic foundations underlying any cultural superstructure, they drove, and still drive, home the fact that unless the problems rising from the economic inequalities in our own modern industrialized society are better solved, we cannot continue to build democracy. Thus the principles of Marxism remain at the base of much of the best social and cultural thought of our century. No educated American can afford to be ignorant of them, or to be delinquent in realizing that there is much common ground between these principles and any healthily dynamic America.

This is not to say that Marxism gives what I consider an adequate view of the nature of man, or that it or any other economic theory can provide a substitute for the critic's essential painstaking discipline in the interplay between form and content in concrete works of art. But a concern with economics can surely quicken and enlarge the questions that a critic asks about the content of any new work of art with which he is faced, about the fullness to which it measures and reveals the forces that have produced both it and its author. Walt Whitman might have said, in *Democratic Vistas:* "Man becomes free, not by realizing himself in opposition to society, but by realizing himself through society." That sentence was actually written by Christopher Caudwell, a young English Marxist who was killed fighting for the Loyalists in Spain. His book *Illusion and Reality,* published in 1937, has recently been reissued, and is having a renewed vogue now with younger writers and students. Their enthusiasm for it, I gather, springs from the fact that Caudwell, despite the sweeping immaturity of many of his judgments, keeps asking the big questions about man in society that the school of close textual analysis has tended to ignore.

I do not mean for a moment to underestimate the value of that school. It has taught us in particular how to read poetry with an alertness and resilience of attention that were in danger of being altogether lost through the habits set up by an age of quick journalism. All I would suggest is that analysis itself can run to seed unless the analyzing mind is also absorbed in a wider context than the text before it.

Mention of Caudwell's name has brought me to the last of the awarenesses that I would urge upon the critic: that of the wide gap which still exists between America and Europe. Henry James discovered long ago his leading theme in the contrast between American innocence and European experience. Although the world that he contemplated has been altered beyond recognition, that theme is still peculiarly urgent when we are faced with the difference between a Europe which has undergone fascism and destructive war at first hand and an America which has come out of the war richer and more powerful than ever before. Stephen Spender has noticed the difference in reading Randall Jarrell's book of poems called *Losses*. For the American, as Spender observes, even when the losses are those of our own fliers, they are something that happens far away on distant continents, they are not yet immediately overhead and inescapable. Allen Tate has described the kind of false superiority that can be engendered by such special isolation:

> The American people fully armed
> With assurance policies, righteous and harmed,
> Battle the world of which they're not at all.

How do Americans become part of that greater world? Not by pretending to be something they are not, nor by being either proud or ashamed of their vast special fortune. It does no good, for example, to adopt the vocabulary of the Paris existentialists in order to emulate the crisis of occupation which we have not passed through. The ironic lines of Tate's *Sonnet at Christmas* suggest a more mature way of meeting experience. None of us can escape what we are, but by recognizing our limitations, and comprehending them, we can transcend them by the span of that knowledge.

Here is the area where breadth of concern becomes most rewarding for the critic. By perceiving what his country is and is not in comparison with other countries, he can help contribute, in this time of fierce national tensions, to the international understanding without which civilization will not survive. He will also find that he has come to know his own country better.

The art of a country always becomes richer by being open to stimulus from outside, and criticism can find a particularly fertile field in observing the results of that interchange. For one fascinating instance, how much we can learn about both Europe and America from the high estimation that French writers are now giving to the novels of Faulkner. At a period when the French have felt a debilitation in their own tradition, they have turned to the new world for an access of vitality. But what has seemed to them most real in America is not our surface of optimism, but the terrible underlying violence that has possessed the imaginations of nearly all our naturalistic novelists. It may seem a strange paradox that America, spared so far the worst violences of fascism and war, has imagined violence in a way that impresses men who have experienced the savage brutality of both.

But as we look back at America through French eyes, we become more conscious of what the preponderantly genteel reviewers for our organs of mass circulation have done their best to obscure: that Faulkner is not a writer of meaningless sensationalism, but one who has seized upon basic forces in our history, particularly upon the tensions resulting from our initial injustice to the Negro. Faulkner may often overwrite and use some of the cheap devices of melodrama, but we should not allow these to deflect us from the truth of his record. If we prefer a more smiling version of ourselves, we are liable to the peculiarly American dilemma of passing from innocence to corruption without ever having grasped maturity. By which I mean the maturity that comes from the knowledge of both good and evil.

In proposing an ever widening range of interests for the ideal critic, I have moved from his central responsibility to the text before him out to an awareness of some of the world-wide struggles of our age. We must come back to where we started, to the critic's primary function. He must judge the work of art as work of art. But knowing form and content to be inseparable, he will recognize his duty to both. Judgment of art is unavoidably both an aesthetic and a social act, and the critic's sense of social responsibility gives him a deeper thirst for meaning.

This is not a narrow question of the wrong right or right left politics. The *locus classicus* on this matter was furnished by Marx's judgment of Balzac, who as a monarchist and Catholic reactionary supported the very forces to which Marx was most opposed. Yet Marx could perceive that, no matter what this novelist's views, his vision of the deep corruption of French society by money made him the most searching historian of his time. Engels proceeded to evolve the principle inherent in this judgment: "The father of tragedy, Aeschylus, and the father of comedy, Aristophanes, were both very clearly poets with a thesis. . . . But I believe that the thesis must inhere in the situation and the action, without being explicitly formulated; and it is not the poet's duty to supply the reader in advance with the future historical solution of the conflict he describes."

A poet describes many other things besides conflict, yet without some sense of conflict there is no drama to engage us. The way in which the artist implies social judgments and entices the critic to meditate upon them may be elucidated by a pair of examples. Wallace Stevens' second book, *Ideas of Order,* appeared in 1935. Until then he had been known by his richly musical *Harmonium,* by what he himself had called "the essential gaudiness of poetry." The besetting weakness of criticism, when faced with a new writer, is to define his work too narrowly, and then to keep applying that definition like a label. Stevens had been bracketed as "a dandy of poetry," as an epicurean relisher of "sea surfaces full of clouds," as one who had found his role in discovering "thirteen ways of looking at a blackbird," as identical with his own Crispin in his relish of "good, fat, guzzly fruit."

He was, to be sure, all these enchanting things. But no one seemed to have been prepared for the fact that his imagination was so fecund and robust that it would compel him to launch forth, in his midfifties, upon the new territory indicated by his explicitly philosophical title. He was also making his own response to the vast disequilibrium that every sensitive mind had to feel at the pit of the depression. He had come to recognize that "a violent order is disorder." Or, as Horace Gregory put it more explicitly, Stevens' new poems were demonstrating that he was not merely a connoisseur of nuances, but—not unlike Henry James—a shrewdly trained observer of "the decadence that follows upon the rapid acquisition of wealth and power."

Stevens' kind of symbolist poetry never makes the explicit approach. So far as he has any political or social views, they would appear to be conservative. Yet in *Sad Strains of a Gay Waltz,* the second poem in *Ideas of Order,* he gave to a then young radical like myself a sudden clarification of the clouded time in which we are living. It is this kind of "momentary stay against confusion," as Robert Frost has said, that a poem is designed to give, and that becomes one of the measures of its authenticity.

In listening to almost any poem by Stevens, the first thing that strikes you is his past-masterly command of rhetoric, a reminder that, unlike the poets of the imagist movement, he is still rooted in the older tradition that leads from Bridges back to Milton. In this poem his rhetoric is formed into three-lined unrhymed stanzas of a basically iambic pentameter pattern, but with many irregular line lengths which quicken but do not break that pattern. The conflict that constitutes his theme is between an age that is dying and a hazardous potential new birth. He adumbrates this by offsetting a character whom he calls Hoon, a lover of solitude like Thoreau, against the rising masses of men in a still formless society. But his controlling symbols are more oblique, they are "waltzes" and "shadows." Music that has become played out seems to its listeners to be "empty of shadows," and by a very effective repetition of the phrase, "Too many waltzes have ended," Stevens sets up his counter-poise for a new, more dynamic music that will again be full of shadows:

> The truth is that there comes a time
> When we can mourn no more over music
> That is so much motionless sound.
>
> There comes a time when the waltz
> Is no longer a mode of desire, a mode
> Of revealing desire and is empty of shadows.
>
> Too many waltzes have ended. And then
> There's that mountain-minded Hoon,
> For whom desire was never that of the waltz,
>
> Who found all form and order in solitude,
> For whom the shapes were never the figures of men.
> Now, for him, his forms have vanished.
>
> There is order in neither sea nor sun.
> The shapes have lost their glistening.
> There are these sudden mobs of men,
>
> These sudden clouds of faces and arms,
> An immense suppression, freed,
> These voices crying without knowing for what,
>
> Except to be happy, without knowing how,
> Imposing forms they cannot describe,
> Requiring order beyond their speech.
>
> Too many waltzes have ended. Yet the shapes
> For which the voices cry, these, too, may be
> Modes of desire, modes of revealing desire.

Too many waltzes—The epic of disbelief
Blares oftener and soon, will soon be constant.
Some harmonious skeptic soon in a skeptical music

Will unite these figures of men and their shapes
Will glisten again with motion, the music
Will be motion and full of shadows.

The extension of our sense of living by compelling us to contemplate a broader world is the chief gift that literature holds out to us. This sense is never limited to our own place or time. What makes the art of the past still so full of undiscovered wealth is that each age inevitably turns to the past for what it most wants, and thereby tends to remake the past in its own image. The cardinal example is Shakespeare. What the nineteenth century saw in Hamlet was what Coleridge saw, the figure of a transcendental philosopher absorbed in himself. What we see is a man inextricably involved with his own society, as may be suggested in brief by one of the scenes which nineteenth-century producers usually cut. This is the scene in the fourth act where Hamlet, on his way to England, encounters a Captain from Fortinbras' army. The Captain is bitter at what his orders are compelling him to do:

Truly to speak, and with no addition,
We go to gain a little patch of ground
That hath in it no profit but the name.
To pay five ducats, five, I would not farm it.

The effect of this speech upon Hamlet is to heighten his awareness of the difference between the Captain's situation and his own, of how he, Hamlet, has every reason for action and yet cannot bring himself to act:

Examples gross as earth exhort me;
Witness this army of such mass and charge
Led by a delicate and tender prince,
Whose spirit with divine ambition puff'd
Makes mouths at the invisible event,
Exposing what is mortal and unsure
To all that fortune, death, and danger dare,
Even for an egg-shell. Rightly to be great
Is not to stir without great argument,

But greatly to find quarrel in a straw
When honour's at the stake. How stand I then,
That have a father kill'd, a mother stain'd,
Excitements of my reason and my blood,
And let all sleep, while to my shame I see
The imminent death of twenty thousand men,
That for a fantasy and trick of fame
Go to their graves like beds, fight for a plot
Whereon the numbers cannot try the cause,
Which is not tomb enough and continent
To hide the slain?

As John Gielgud speaks these lines, we feel what Shakespeare meant his audience to feel, the necessity for Hamlet's revenge. But we also bring to the passage our own sense of vast insecurity, our need of being engaged in the public issues of our menaced time, and yet the need of making sure that the seeming issues are the true issues, that we are not betrayed into engagements that are merely "th'imposthume of much wealth and peace."

There is a basic distinction between bringing everything in your life to what you read and reading into a play of the past issues that are not there. All I am suggesting is the extent to which our awareness of ourselves as social beings is summoned by the greatest art. That is the root of my reason for believing that the good critic becomes fully equipped for his task by as wide a range of interests as he can master. The great temptation for the young writer at the present moment is to think that because the age is bad, the artist should escape from it and, as a superior being, become a law simply to himself. Some memorable romantic poetry has been written on that assumption, but not the great forms of drama or epic, nor the comparable great forms in prose. However, the critic should freely grant that the artist writes as he must. But for his own work the critic has to be both involved in his age and detached from it. This double quality of experiencing our own time to the full and yet being able to weigh it in relation to other times is what the critic must strive for, if he is to be able to discern and demand the works of art that we need most. The most mature function of the critic lies finally in that demand.

In Defense of a Writing Career

by NORMAN COUSINS

A FEW WEEKS AGO A JOURNALISM SENIOR AT COLUMBIA UNIVERSITY
visited the offices of the *Saturday Review* in New York. He was looking for an editorial job. He was hardly seated when he began to express serious doubts about the career he had selected and for which
he had invested so many years of study.

"I like to write," he said. "My idea of heaven is a big back porch
in the country overlooking a green valley, where I can squat in
front of a typewriter and poke away till the end of time. Next to that
I'd like a job on a magazine or in a book-publishing house. But it's
no use. Either as a writer or editor the chance of breaking in is so
slight that there's hardly any point trying. And I haven't got enough
of that folding green paper to endow myself with my own back
porch and let the rest of the world go hang."

This was a new twist. Generally, the journalism seniors stride
into the *Saturday Review of Literature's* offices in the spring with
more bounce and spirit than the second act of *La Bohème*. They may
be rebuffed, they may be detoured, they may be diverted, but they
won't be discouraged and they won't be dismayed. They know exactly what they want to do and where they want to go. They may
not have the foggiest idea how they're going to get there, but trying
to hold them back is as futile as putting your hand over the spouting
nozzle of a fire hose. Yet here was a young man with a brand new
script, saying he was sorry he had ever persuaded himself to make
writing a career. He meant it, too. His face couldn't have been more
liberated from enthusiasm than if he had been dreaming of flying
to Paris in a Constellation only to wake up and discover that all the

259

time he was in a subway car stalled under the Hudson River in the tubes to Hoboken.

I was anxious to find out more about both the dream and the awakening. Why did he decide to take up journalism in the first place, and what suddenly soured him? Why so great a gap between the original vision and the present disillusion?

In the next forty minutes he answered those questions fully and frankly. I'd like to summarize what he said because I suspect that his viewpoint and the experience on which it was based may be of some interest to new writers. For almost two months he had devoted nearly every hour of his spare time to visiting magazine and publishing offices, canvassing the possibilities of employment. He had also spoken to a number of prominent writers, soliciting their advice about the glories and perils of free-lance writing. He was especially anxious to find out from these successful writers how he ought to go about persuading a book publisher to give him a juicy advance to sustain him while he wrote the great American novel—no doubt on that big back porch overlooking the green valley.

First of all, he said, the only job opening in a magazine or publishing house he had been able to detect was as assistant to the associate editor of a master-plumber's trade journal. None of the national magazines wanted him, though he was quite sure that at least a few of them really needed him. And, judging from what he observed, even if he could crack open a spot for himself at *Life* or *Time* or *Newsweek* or *Collier's* or the *Atlantic* or *Harper's,* he wasn't sure that it would be a wise thing to do. No possibility for advancement. The good jobs were all sewed up and would be for years to come. Most of the magazines were edited by a few men, who, despite the ulcers and anxiety neuroses of their calling, would probably live forever. Men like Mr. Luce, Mr. Hibbs, Mr. Weeks, and Mr. Allen quite obviously weren't going to step down—at least not during the second half of the twentieth century, and those on the next echelon were all braced to resist any replacements or reinforcements for perhaps even longer.

On the news magazines, he said, the most you could hope for was perhaps breaking out of the open arena of the researchers, where men engage facts like toreadors do bulls, into the well-populated pen of the assistant editors. Here the facts are digested—sometimes passing into the blood stream of the magazine without leaving a trace. Salaries of the assistant editors are adequate though not spectacular. Above everyone, however, is the iron ceiling of anonymity. In such a job one's writing is as shorn of individuality and personality as toothpicks being processed out of a plank of wood. When the mountain labored, it at least brought forth a live mouse; here you labor over your typewriter for a week and produce half of a dead, overset galley—unsigned, of course.

Newspapers were out of the question, my young friend continued. All right, perhaps, as an opening gambit, just to get it out of your system so you could say you were a newspaperman once. A nice thing to have in your past, but not in your future. True, you meet such interesting people, or so they say, but there's not much creative inspiration in the written material or the weekly pay check. Of course, my friend said, it is a different proposition if you are lucky enough to become a syndicated columnist, conjuring up your own assignments in various corners of the world. But it's obvious, he said, that heavy-pay jobs such as this are all filled.

What my friend wanted most of all to do, of course, was to write a novel. He had spoken to a number of prominent writers and had made something of a survey of the creative-writing field—all of which had convinced him that the way was practically barred to all but a few fortunate newcomers. He said he was certain that the un-solicited-manuscript department of the average publishing house was actually the uninvited-manuscript department. He proceeded to give me the results of his investigation, which showed that Norman Mailer's *The Naked and the Dead,* for example, had been rejected by almost a dozen publishers. And Betty Smith's *A Tree Grows in Brooklyn* turned down by about ten. Or Gertrude Diament's *Days of Ophelia* spurned by six. Or Mildred Jordan's *One Red Rose Forever* thumbed-down by twenty-two. Or Mike Woltari's *The Egyptian* ignored by eleven.

Let us suppose, he said, that a young author sending in his first manuscript relied on a single publisher's judgment. Suppose he received a rejection slip the first time out. Wouldn't he be justified in thinking that the publisher knew more about writing than he did, and in deciding to give up his writing career right then and there? And even if he preserved his confidence in his own work, submitting his book to publisher after publisher, what was he to do if he received rejection slips from them all? Does anyone know how many Norman Mailers or Betty Smiths there might be whose manuscripts were spurned by all the publishers?

No, said my young friend, shaking his head sadly, he didn't believe that even if he did write the great American novel, there was any chance that it could get by the unsolicited-manuscript department. The publishers didn't want to risk either their judgment or their capital on untried talent, and most of them string along with the big names. Some of them even dangled bait before the roving eyes of famous authors who belonged to competitors.

Putting all this together, the journalism senior concluded that he had made a serious error six years earlier when he had decided, on the basis of his editorship of the high-school paper, that he had a natural talent for a professional career as writer.

It was a bleak picture, but, I am afraid, an incomplete one. There are some facts worth considering—facts, I contend, which would justify the choice of writing or editing as a career for anyone with a reasonable amount of talent in that direction. I agree it's a difficult field to break into, but then again, what profession isn't? Anyone who has applied for admission to a medical school recently might have some underscoring he'd like to do on that point. Or, to underscore the underscoring, talk to a graduate of a medical school looking for an internship. Or a law-school graduate looking for an apprenticeship. Or a young artist trying to get his works exhibited, to say nothing of the business of finding a cash customer. Sisyphus rolling a stone up-hill was on a cakewalk compared to this.

Another conspicuous omission in my young friend's jeremiad concerned his own faulty approach to the problem of finding a job. In talking to him about the magazine and publishing offices he had canvassed, for example, it became apparent that he had failed to apply any imagination to the problem before him. All he had done was to write for an appointment with a key person, and then go in to present his credentials.

"What else was there to do?" he asked.

One thing he might have done, I replied, was to recognize that he had arranged a dead-end tour for himself. What reason was there to believe that his own cold application for employment would stand out in bold relief above the hundreds upon hundreds of other applications—most of them from qualified young people? A job applicant should familiarize himself with each magazine or publishing house the way a surgeon examines the X rays before going into the operating room. Anyone who marches into a publishing office looking for a job ought to know the history of that publication; he ought to know a great deal about its format and editorial content; about the particular audience it is trying to reach and what the problems seem to be in reaching it; about editorial features tried and discarded; about the people who work on the staff, their fields of special interest, and their functions on the magazine.

This is pay-dirt knowledge. It's not easy to come by, but it's worth trying to get, for it can give an applicant a toe hold on an interview. It's axiomatic in human relations that if you expect someone to be interested in your problems, you ought to know something about his. Don't wait for a job opening. Most good jobs don't open up; they are created. You create a job by presenting not only yourself but an idea that can fit into an editorial formula; an idea that reveals your own knowledge of the publication and your understanding of its audience and its needs. My friend had failed to recognize that the best way to sell himself into a publishing job was to sell his ideas. And these should not have been merely random ideas, but ideas carefully tailored to fit the particular needs of a particular periodical or publishing house.

The same theory operates with respect to advancement. Naturally, it's somewhat difficult to offer every young man who goes into publishing a money-back guarantee that he can have the boss's job within five years, but ideas plus the ability to carry them out go a long way. If this sounds like a cross between Horatio Alger and Dale Carnegie, I'd be glad to quote names, places, and dates.

Next, for the newspaper business. First of all, let's modify the Hollywood stereotype somewhat. It isn't true that every newspaperman is comprehensively slouched—slouched hat, slouched shoulders, slouched smile, and a slouched psyche. My recollections of my own newspaper experience and my impressions in traveling around America and meeting many newspapermen in many cities are that most American newspapermen are far ahead of their papers. I've met some hard-bitten cynics, to be sure, but I've also met them in politics or teaching, for that matter. The pay doesn't begin to compare with that, say, of the corporation lawyer, but I've known a number of newspapermen who did fairly well by their families by using their spare time to good advantage in free-lance writing. Offhand, I know of at least six newspapermen now writing novels and perhaps three more writing nonfiction books, and, despite the high mortality of the average unsolicited manuscript, I'd be willing to bet that the majority of them will have their works accepted and published. Yes, the newspaper field is a tough one—tough to get into, in some cases even tougher to get out of. But it's excellent proving grounds for disciplined writing. After a while, of course, the discipline can be replaced by routine, and the routine by rote. But, so far as I know, there's no law preventing anyone from moving on to more fertile pastures if he finds he's been squatting too long near a dry well.

This brings us to the final problem surveyed by my journalism-senior friend—in particular, writing a new book and getting it published. I can agree with him readily that the orphan of the publishing industry is the unsolicited-manuscript department. I believe it to be a fact that no branch of a publisher's organization is as understaffed—qualitatively as well as quantitatively—as the unsolicited-manuscript department. The pay for first readers in many houses isn't much higher than for bookkeeper assistants or even for shipping clerks. Many publishers, on those infrequent occasions when they take their hair down, will confess that they have virtually written off their unsolicited-manuscript department as expendable, returning submitted works on the basis of a cursory examination by a forty-dollar-a-week reader.

A publisher will spend thousands of dollars in sending one of his editors on a tour around America, beating the brush for concealed literary talent, but seems reluctant to spend more than a few dollars to appraise fully and competently such talent as may be found in his own mailbag. It has occasionally happened that an editor on tour will make the discovery of an exciting new manuscript which only the week before had been routinely shipped back with a form letter by his own firm. Apparently, there is no shame in the matter. Indeed, one publisher, on the occasion of his firm's twentieth anniversary, blandly announced in an advertisement that with only a single exception, he had never accepted an unsolicited manuscript.

It would have been interesting to get a box score on some of the important books that he happened to miss because they were apparently not worth a careful reading.

My friend was quite right when he listed the names of outstanding books turned down in the unsolicited-manuscript departments of many publishing houses. It's even worse than he supposed. Copies of the two opening chapters of *War and Peace,* and an outline covering the rest of the book, by general consent a fairly acceptable novel, were recently sent to ten publishers in order to test the competence of the unsolicited-manuscript departments. Only four of them spotted the material for what it was. The others sent back routine rejection slips.

It may be asked, Where then do most of the accepted books come from? They represent books written to order or on contract—books by name-writers for whom space is regularly reserved on a publisher's list.

I am not completely unaware of the publisher's problem. When hundreds of book-length manuscripts are received each week—many of them looking more like tied-up bundles of leftover leaves from last fall—it would put a publisher out of business if he had to maintain a highly qualified staff of readers who gave thorough consideration to every single manuscript. What has happened is that a sort of literary Gresham's law has been in operation for many years, the bad manuscripts driving out the good.

At one time not so long ago in the history of book publishing, the chief business of the publisher when he arrived at his office in the morning was to inspect personally all the manuscripts in the morning mail. In the memoirs of the publishers of forty or sixty years ago, it is not uncommon to find reference to this daily stint as the most delightful aspect of publishing. The biggest joy in a publisher's life was represented by the thrill of discovery in chancing across an unsolicited manuscript that heralded a new talent. But that was back in the days when a publisher's mail could fit on top of his own desk instead of requiring something on the order of a coal bin, as happens today. And that was before so much of the publisher's time was taken up with arrangements for reprint rights, motion-picture negotiations, contests for bookstores, and the care and spoon-feeding of authors.

A few publishers have recognized this problem and their own responsibility in meeting it. Their experience is worth citing. These publishers have worked out a triple-platoon system whereby the first shock wave of manuscripts is absorbed by a corps of readers who have authority to reject only the blatantly inadequate. All the others are passed along to somewhat more specialized readers, who make no final decisions themselves but who winnow out the worth-while books for the editors, who constitute the third platoon. It is an expensive system, if done by competent and well-paid people all along the line, but it does succeed in filtering out in many cases the really deserving books, which, so far as the general public is concerned, would seem to be the main function of book publishing.

Meanwhile, the new novelist would do well to stay out of the bottomless pit that is the unsolicited-manuscript department. That is, to stay out if he can. At the very least, no manuscript ought to be submitted without the benefit of an advance letter to the publisher attempting to establish some contact on a responsible level and seeking some genuine expression of interest. The reply to such a letter is not, of course, conclusive, but its tone and responsiveness may offer some encouragement. It is sound policy, moreover, to write to firms whose lists over the years reveal no prejudice against beginners.

It would be even better, of course, if the young novelist were able to obtain the enthusiastic backing of a recognized third party—perhaps a book reviewer or a teacher or another author who might be sufficiently interested to write to a publisher, expressing his high opinion of a particular manuscript. Strategically, this puts the young author in the happy position—if the plan works—of being courted by a publisher. Of all the consummations in a writer's heaven most devoutly to be wished, none can quite compare with the postal ecstasy of opening a letter from an established publisher which begins: "Dear Mr. Smith: It has come to my attention that you have just written a book . . ." etc., etc.

Perhaps the most meaningful and fruitful way of all to fashion a key to the literary kingdom is through such writing and study units as exist at the University of Michigan—though I doubt that there are more than a dozen really first-rate writing courses at the university level in the country. The men and women who head these workshops are known and respected in the publishing offices and are constantly pursued by publishers for promising names. These magistrates of writing talent have built up over the years a position of respect among publishers and editors.

Finally, there are the various literary awards, of which the Avery Hopwood awards in creative writing occupy such an important place. There are fifty-three local, regional, and national writing prizes and distinctions of one sort or another—many of which lead to publication. The value of these contests, however, is represented not only by the prizes themselves, but by the fact that a manuscript generally receives a much more careful and competent reading than in the ordinary course of submission through the unsolicited-manuscript channels. Leading national publishers, such as Harpers, or Dodd, Mead, or Houghton Mifflin, or Farrar, Straus, accept many manuscripts for publication out of their prize-contest hoppers in addition to the ones that receive the top awards.

All in all, I told my young friend that anyone with ability who selects writing as a career today—whatever the particular branch may be—need not fear that all the doors are shut or that once inside there is no place to go. The difficulties are real, but they are not insuperable, so long as there is a reasonable degree of familiarity with what not to do, a fair amount of ingenuity in mapping and pursuing alternatives, and, most important, patience of the order usually associated only with camel drivers.

Writing as a career offers a good life and a rewarding one. It represents a continuing challenge. Each writing project is like a difficult battle, requiring a skilled combination of strategy and tactics to accomplish a specific objective. It demands a mobilization of concentration —and concentration is or should be one of the higher gifts of human mental activity. It is agonizingly difficult work at times, and you almost feel in need of a drip pan to catch the droplets of cerebral sweat, but, as John Mason Brown recently said about creative writing, it is the sweetest agony known to man. This is the one fatigue that produces inspiration, an exhaustion that exhilarates. Double-teaming the faculties of imagination and reasoning and keeping them coördinated and balanced is a tiring process, but you've got something to show for your efforts if you succeed. I suppose that was why Socrates liked to refer to himself as a literary midwife—someone who helped to bring ideas to birth out of laboring minds. As a master of cerebral obstetrics,

Socrates also knew and respected the conditions necessary for the conception of ideas and recognized the need for a proper period of germinating reflection.

With all these delights of the creative process it may seem extraneous and crass to mention the tangible inducements, but it may be said for the record that most people in the writing profession eat very well. Some authors even make as much money as their publishers, and a few of them a great deal more. True, there is what you might call the law of the dominant fraction these days by which the government can obtain the larger part of an author's royalties, but retention of capital has always been the prime problem of authors anyway, with or without respect to taxes. A not-inconsiderable advantage is also afforded by the fact that this is one profession in which you can take a trip to Paris or Switzerland or the Riviera or the Antarctic, for that matter, for the purpose of obtaining material and vital repose for your next book, and be able to charge all the costs of this soul-stretching safari up to deductible business expenses.

Apart from all these reasons—biological, philosophical, materialistic—in favor of a writing career, there is yet another reason as significant as it is compelling. That prime reason is that there is great need in America today for new writers. I am not thinking here of a technical shortage of supply, for production is still several light-years ahead of consumption. The need for new writers I am thinking of has to do with the type of book and voice America is hungering for today. That type of book will not be afraid to deal with great themes and great ideas. It will not be afraid to concern itself with the larger visions of which man in general and America in particular are capable, for America today is living far under its moral capacity as a nation. It will not be afraid to break away from the so-called hard-boiled school of writing which has made a counterfeit of realism by ignoring the deeper and more meaningful aspects of human existence.

This need of which I speak has come about because too many writers have been writing out of their egos instead of their consciences; because too many of them have been preoccupied with human neuroses to the virtual exclusion of human nobility; because too many of them, in their desire to avoid sentimentality, have divorced themselves from honest sentiment and honest emotion. Indeed, we have been passing through what later historians may regard as the

Dry-Eyed Period of American literature. Beneath the hard and shiny surface of the school of the supersophisticates there is no blood or bones, merely a slice of life too thin to have meaning. Instead of reaching for the grand themes that can give literature the epic quality it deserves, too many writers have been trying to cut the novel down to the size of psychiatric case histories.

Beyond this there is need for writers who can restore to writing its powerful tradition of leadership in crisis. Most of the great tests in human history have produced great writers who acknowledged a special responsibility to the community at large. They have defined the issues, recognized the values at stake, and dramatized the nature of the challenge. Today, in the absence of vital moral leadership on the official world level, it is more important than ever that writers see themselves as representatives of humanity at large. For the central issue facing the world today is not the state of this nation or that nation, but the condition of man. That higher level needs champions as it never did before. There is no more essential and nobler task for writers—established writers, new writers, aspiring writers—than to regard themselves as spokesmen for human destiny.

The Possible Importance of Poetry

by MARK VAN DOREN

POETRY DESIRES TO BE INTERESTING; OR IT SHOULD. BY TRADITION IT HAS a great right to this desire, for there have been times when nothing was more interesting than poetry. If this is not such a time, the reason may be simply that we have lost our desire; or if not so, that we have lost touch with tradition. The present fact would seem to be that people do not consider poetry either interesting or important—two words for the same thing; and the people are the judge. So have they always been, in spite of every appeal to something beyond or above or beneath them. There is no appeal. It is to people that poetry must be interesting.

When they do not find it so, the fault conceivably is theirs: they have forgotten how to read. It is they, and not the poets, who have lost touch with tradition. But it is dangerous for poets at any time to make such a charge. In our time it is a plausible charge, for we can suspect, and indeed we are often told, that universal literacy has depressed literature. When the only aim is that everybody should be able to read something, no matter what, and when mass production of printed words has become the business of cynics who despise the very audience by which they profit, the outlook for distinguished thoughts and feelings would appear on the face of it to be poor. The contemporary poet, however, cannot afford to rest here. His job is what the job of poets has always been: to think and feel as deeply as he can, and to assume the existence of persons who will be glad that he has done so. And he had better assume that these are more than a few—ideally, he had better assume that they are all of us. He had better not count the number, at least beforehand; for if he does, he will end by limiting himself. "I am always made uneasy," Emerson wrote in his Journal, "when the conversation turns in my presence upon popular ignorance and the duty of adapting our public harangues and writings to the mind of the people. 'Tis all pedantry and ignorance. The people know as much and reason as well as we do. None so quick as they to discern brilliant genius or solid parts. And I observe that all those who use this cant most, are such as do not rise above mediocrity of understanding. . . . Remember that the hunger of people for truth is immense. The reason why they yawn is because you have it not."

If Emerson sounds optimistic, one should remember his reputation in his time. It was a popular reputation, not incompatible with the fact that Matthew Arnold and other young aristocrats of the mind in Oxford of the 1840's thought they heard nowhere else so high and fine a voice as this of the American prophet who assumed that everybody could understand him. It was a remarkable time, that generation before our Civil War. Lewis Mumford has called it the Golden Day, and F. O. Matthiessen called it a Renaissance. It was full of writers who said great things and sang great songs, and they wanted multitudes to hear them. Walt Whitman, who had no illusions about the average American, addressed himself nevertheless to the normal American for whom no subject was too noble. The subject, for instance, of death. A great people, he decided, would have great poems of death; and he proceeded to write some—proceeded, and all of his life continued, so that his two masterpieces, *Out of the Cradle Endlessly Rocking* and *When Lilacs Last in the Dooryard Bloom'd,* have that for their subject without which life cannot be comprehended to its depth. I have never heard that Whitman believed he would not be understood by more than a few friends and fellow poets. His faith was simpler and broader than that; and it has been vindicated.

Whenever poetry has been good, it has had good subject matter—good for anybody, and it has not agonized about numbers. Today, I think, we do not hear enough about the subject matter of poetry. Criticism tends to ignore the question altogether. Poets are damned or praised for their way with language, as if language were the aim and end of all their art. Language is a lovely thing, and only human beings have it; but they have it, presumably, for something better still, and the greatest poets are those who have best understood this. There is no lord of language like Shakespeare; he could and did do everything with it; but what finally moves us as we read him or watch his plays is the knowledge he has of us, on a level deeper than words. We adore Shakespeare because he is wise, and because the world of men is given its right value in his works. It was for the same reason that the Greeks all but worshiped Homer, whom they knew by heart even though they knew nothing about the world of which he had written. The truth was, of course, that they did know his most important world, for it was the human world, and as such it was not different from theirs. Again they had in him a lord of language, but they noticed this less than they noticed how well he understood the passions, the ideas, and the absurdities of men. They watched Achilles learning what honor means; they watched Odysseus coming home; and they saw the soul of Hector reflected in the love of those around him—his family, his comrades, and his friends among the gods. By the same token, what is it that in modern times convinces a true reader of Dante that his reputation is deserved? His verbal cunning, and the peculiar fitness of his rhymes, his syntax? These of course; but at last it is the knowledge of the man, and the pity; the power of his feelings, the unwearied work of his thought, and the deep lake of his heart. Without these he would merely be ingenious, as without them Homer would be sound and fury, and Shakespeare nothing but incessant bustling in the scenery.

But those three are the greatest poets, one of you may say—the very greatest; and what can we learn from them? They are too far removed, they are monsters of perfection, they are studied more than they are read, they are statues whose pedestals only may be approached. I do not doubt at all that one at least of you is saying these things now. And nothing could be more mistaken. Yet it is the custom of our time. We do not believe that we can learn from the greatest things. They are not for us. Which is why so few discussions of poetry today, even among those who ought to know better, even mention the names of Shakespeare, Homer, and Dante; and why the poet is defined in terms that exclude those masters; and why the impression is abroad that it is somehow bad taste for poetry to be interesting to people. Subject matter is itself an embarrassing subject, from which quick refuge is sought in the techniques of rhythm and image, of caesura and ambiguity. Those things all have their fascination, but it is secondary to the further fascination of the art when ultimate demands are made upon it. The ultimate demand is that it be faithful to its ancient trust; that it treat of human truth, and more wisely and movingly than most men treat it even when they know, as ideally all men know, the content of such truth.

Poetry today means lyric poetry; it means the short poem; and that too can be a great thing, but it is not the greatest. It is as great as it can be when its author has wisdom and passion, and when it is clear that if there were an occasion he could convey his understanding in the more complex forms of narrative and drama. The Greeks never forgot that lyric poetry is but a third of poetry itself, and perhaps the least third. The big things are done in narrative and drama, for poetry's chief business is the business of story—of mankind in motion. Philosophy and science give us knowledge of men in the aggregate, or in essence; poetry commits individuals to action, and follows them through careers. It conceives beginnings, middles, and ends, and is perhaps the only thing that can conceive them. Nature does not, and neither may philosophy or science; but poetry must. And it is the test of any poet—that is, of any storyteller—whether or not he can finish the story he has started. The beginning is fairly easy, as any young writer knows; even the middle sometimes charts its own course; but the end—for that, alas, experience and penetration are required. And in addition to those, a familiarity with the forms in which all human conduct finally manifests itself, the two forms of tragedy and comedy.

Tragedy and comedy are forms, not statements; or it may be that they are forms of statement. But any statement which they make is as far from platitude as the most sophisticated poet could desire. Poetry today despises platitude, and it is right in that. The pompous homilies, the "affirmations" and hymns of self-praise that pass in times like these as the sort of thing we ought to love in preference to the dim poetry we do on the whole have—I for one will take the dim poetry, since at least it is not hollow. But it must be clear that I would rather have something better than either of these. I would rather have story, and I would like to see it well grounded in the tragic and the comic visions which embrace all the knowledge we have yet accumulated concerning the significance of man's life.

Man's life is never good enough, and only men can know what this means. It means more than that the world of any given moment is a poor thing for even the best persons in it. Contemporary literature spends too much time, perhaps, and certainly too much effort, in proving by documentation that the twentieth century is not what some people thought it was going to be. What did they think it was going to be? An earthly paradise? Heaven itself? But if they thought this they were children, and poetry is not for children. Neither can it be written by children. It is the product of long seasoning and of bittersweet experience, neither of which things we have any right to expect in the very young. We do not think of Homer as very young; or Dante, or Shakespeare, of Sophocles, or Milton, or Hardy, or Yeats. Or Chaucer—who sounds in every verse he wrote as if he had been born with quizzical old eyes, and perhaps the small beard we cannot think of him without. The great poet knows the world, and how to live in it—also, how not to live in it. He is not surprised because it has failed at being heaven, or because most people in it fall grotesquely short of being angels. He seems to have expected this, and to have been prepared. The current notion of the poet as young, ignorant, helpless, and complaining is more recent than many of us think. Through most of human time the poet has been thought of in terms that suggest the old man of the tribe— the one who has lived longest and seen most, and whose voice nevertheless has retained its original sweetness. Even in our day we have been witness to examples of this: Thomas Hardy, beginning to write poetry at fifty-five and ceasing only with his death at eighty-eight; William Butler Yeats, turning at middle age into the great poet he was at last to be; Robert Frost, unheard of by the world until he was nearing forty, and proceeding after that to become better with every advancing decade. We have these examples, and still we go on thinking of the poet as knowing less than we do—less, not more, which immemorially has been the assumption.

The poet knows how to live in the world and how not to live in it. That is to say, he locates the good life where it actually is—in the mind that can imagine and believe it. The mind of man not only sees worlds but creates them; and the worlds it creates are not here. This does not mean that they are illusory worlds, made up for solace and thin comfort. They are more substantial than the one we move through every day; but they are not here, and they cannot be verified by those who think this is the only world there is. Those who think that are either deceived or disillusioned, and chronically so. The poet is not deceived, for he has sharp eyes. But neither is he disillusioned, for in one very important sense he has never suffered from illusion. He has not thought that heaven was in cities—or in the country, either, if that is what you think I mean. It is where it is, and only the mind can travel there. Shakespeare must have known contemporary England very well, but his mind traveled elsewhere in search of persons, stories, tragedies, comedies. It traveled to that region where all men's minds are at home, and it brought back news that made this world seem somehow a foreign place, as indeed it must always seem to the uncompromising imagination. It is the only place where we have addresses, but it is not where we chiefly live. Nor need we hate it because this is true. Dante, traveling also into heaven and hell, took his memories with him and used them there. Homer, dropping back several centuries in time, found heroes—which was what he wanted, and he knew he should not look for them in his next-door neighbors; whom nevertheless he did not despise. They had not disappointed him, because he had never counted on them for more than they could deliver.

Poetry, in other words, takes it for granted that the world is not good enough for its best men. But all it can do with these men is to make them tragic or comic heroes—to show them as defeated by the very world to which they are superior. What if they succeeded? Poetry asks this question; asks it again and again; and at last decides that the answer is for no man to give. The poet is a man, too, laughing and crying with other men. He certainly is not God. So he does not know the answer. But he knows the question, which he asks over and over in such a way as to suggest the extreme distinction of man's predicament. Man wants to change the world and cannot do so. The world will punish him if he tries, just as gravity will operate upon his body no matter how light he thinks it is. Hamlet is inconceivably brilliant, but he must die like any other man, and for the commonest reason—he has not survived his crisis. Don Quixote is the greatest gentleman we know, but the world cannot tolerate one who tries to teach it to be other than it is. The world is indeed a tough place. But what man could make it tender? No man, says poetry, no man at all; and sacrifices King Lear on the altar of the unchangeable. He learned, but learned too late. There is no appeal from the ways of the world, which must continue on its own terms or take us all down with it into chaos and confusion. Which does not mean that we should think it a nice thing. It is a terrible thing; or if not terrible, absurd. So tragedy and comedy say; and salvage out of the wreck the best ideas we have, the ideas that certain men could become heroes by expressing, even though they failed.

What if they had succeeded? The question is meaningless; or rather, we cannot imagine what it means, nor does the poet try. What if Socrates had succeeded in making all Athenians think well? What if Jesus had succeeded in making all Jerusalem over into the image of his Father? What if Don Quixote had persuaded all of Spain that knights were more real than merchants and monks? What if Hamlet had cleansed Denmark of its sin? What if Oedipus' finding of the truth had made him free? For one thing we should not now have the books of which these persons are the heroes. Or if we did have them, we could not believe them. We believe them as it is because they falsify nothing in their report of the world. Their report of the human spirit—well, that is another matter. Neither do they falsify that by minimizing the dangers it must undergo, or by denying the supreme courage it inspires in those who properly possess it. The world is what it is, and the human spirit is what it is. And somehow they live together: ill-sorted companions, but the only companions there are for poetry to watch disappearing down the long perspective of life. The final distinction of the author of *Don Quixote* is that he both put them in perspective and personified them as two men.

The possible importance of poetry is immense at any time. And why not now? I would make no exception of our time, though there are those who do. They are the ones who persist in identifying poetry with short poems, and who even then do not remember how great a short poem can be—for it can be dramatic, too, and somehow narrative; it can imply careers, for ideas and for men. The short poem is better in those ages when the long poem is better; or, at the minimum, when it exists. The forms of literature reinforce one another, as tragedy and comedy do, which are the forms of thought. When fiction is good, then poetry can be good; and vice versa. Fiction indeed *is* poetry; or as I have put it here, poetry is story. This is not my idea, as you very well know; it is at least as old as Aristotle, and it has prevailed whenever poetry has been important to people.

But when I say fiction do I mean merely narratives or dramas in verse? Not necessarily. The ancient categories of lyric, epic, and dramatic poetry were not conceived in terms of verse alone, and it is fatal for us to suppose so. What we call prose fiction today is in fact the most interesting poetry we have; Aristotle would think so if he were alive, and he would be justified by the interest we show. Our movies, our westerns, our detective tales—he would wonder, perhaps, why so many of us failed to recognize those things too as contributions, however bad or good, to the poetry of this age. I have already spoken of Cervantes as if I thought he was the great poet of his age, along with Shakespeare his contemporary. That is exactly how I regard him, and I am not prevented from doing so by the fact that he wrote his greatest work in prose. He was a versifier too, but as such he does not interest us; whereas his vast poem called *Don Quixote* is among the glories of the world. Shakespeare wrote both verse and prose—sometimes, it would seem, indifferently, as if convenience alone dictated his choice; and his prose, unlike the verse of Cervantes, was itself a great thing, there being no better prose I think in English. But the question does not greatly matter. The vision was the thing in either case: the vision, and the knowledge that backed it up. The wisdom of these men is what makes them poets, as it is the wisdom of Tolstoi and Dostoevski and Chekhov that makes us think of them, when we are serious, as Russia's poets. Is Dickens not a poet? Consider his passion and his joy as he contemplates humanity and sets it moving. He is among the very great, and we are missing more than we know if we think of him merely as one of six hundred English novelists. The possible importance of poetry includes the chance that such men as these should continue to appear, and that we should have the generosity to recognize them as belonging to the highest class.

That we do not do so is perhaps the fault of our education, which keeps first things separate from one another. We study literature as if it were a thing by itself, and not only literature but English literature—even American literature, God save the mark. When American literature is good it is *literature,* as English or Greek literature is. And when *literature* is good it is a part of all we know. Not the only part, or even the best part, but certainly a part; and it is well that we should remember this. It is more likely to excel when the society that produces it considers neither it, nor science, nor mathematics, nor philosophy, nor theology, nor medicine, nor law, nor mechanics, nor politics, nor economics, nor history as the central subject matter of its thought. The central subject matter for any great age is life and truth; or perhaps it is justice and mercy. At any rate it is something that all arts and studies serve, and serve, we may suppose, equally. The Greeks were at one and the same time supreme in poetry, in philosophy, in science, and in mathematics. But this was not a coincidence, I suspect. They were great in each of these things because they were great in all the others, and because they thought that each of them but testified to a vision which itself was the central thing. Their education, that is to say, was not specialized. All arts for them were finally one art, and the name of it was living well. Nor did they set the fine arts of poetry, painting, music, and sculpture above the practical arts and the intellectual (we should say liberal) arts. There was no hierarchy of importance among them, because there was none of them with which serious men could dispense. The carpenter made a house, the logician made a syllogism, and the poet made a poem. Each was doing what he could and therefore should, and nobody doubted the benefit.

We specialize, with the paradoxical result that no one knows for sure what it is that he is doing. Where there is no connection there can be no comparison. What is the difference, for instance, between the poet and the philosopher, or between the poet and the scientist? We do not state it well, because we do not think of all three men as artists. If they had that much resemblance in our minds, then they might have differences, too, and we could measure these. We tend to assume that the differences are absolute; but this means in the end that they are absolutely small; or that the men themselves are. We often talk, as I have said, as if the poet were very small. He might grow larger if he knew, or if we knew, what sphere he works in as distinguished from any other man; and if we thought of him as working in that sphere for our benefit; and if we thought of all men in their spheres as working in them for our good—our knowledge, our happiness, and our wisdom.

The poet has his subject matter as well as his skill; and his skill increases as he realizes what his subject matter is. If poetry has made any advances in our time—in, that is to say, the twentieth century— we should wonder what new subject matter it has found. I for one think it has made advances; but I am not in sympathy with those who say that these are merely technical. The concern, the conscious concern, has often been with devices of language and principles of diction. So was it in 1798, when Wordsworth called for poetry to adopt the language that men use. But Wordsworth had something to say in his new language; he needed the language, in fact, so that he *could* say what he thought and felt. The situation is no different now. With the new style of 1912—if that is the year from which we date a certain renaissance—there came new stuff; and I think the stuff explains the style. Wherever we look in that time we discover poets who themselves have discovered, or rediscovered, something worth saying in human speech. Irony returned, and the sense of tragedy; the sense of comedy, too, and even the sense of sin. Edgar Lee Masters dug up the Greek Anthology; Ezra Pound ransacked the older poetries of Europe and Asia; and E. A. Robinson attempted again the difficult art of story. T. S. Eliot experimented, to be sure, with stanzas and free verse; it is quite important that he did so; but it is still more important that he restored to poetry the stuff of theology, long absent and all but lost. What explains the peculiar interest of his verse plays? Their verse? I do not think so. I think it is rather the serious concern he has been able to manifest with some of the oldest and deepest ideas that men have had—ideas of martyrdom and salvation. What he has done with these ideas is another question, not especially relevant here. The relevant point is that he deals with them at all, and thereby makes poetry once more interesting to people. They may say that they do not know what his poems mean, but they do not talk as if they were about nothing. They are about something indeed, as poetry at any time had better be.

Robert Frost, if he has done nothing else, has rediscovered Job, whose wife says in *A Masque of Reason:*

> Job says there's no such things as Earth's becoming
> An easier place for man to save his soul in.
> Except as a hard place to save his soul in,

A trial ground where he can try himself
And find out whether he is any good,
It would be meaningless. It might as well
Be Heaven at once and have it over with.

There we have the accent of great poetry, and it is inseparable from the subject Frost has found. He found it where it waited for him, as the world waits for any man to recognize it. For any man, and for any poet. For there is nothing more important about a poet than that he is a man. He may not know more at last than all men do, but what he does know he knows well, and perfects himself in the art of expressing. What he knows, and what we know, is that the world is a hard place to live in at any cost, but that the cost is prohibitive only for those who make the mistake of thinking it is heaven— or should have been.

Dramatic Art in Poetry

by Horace Gregory

As I prepared the subject of the lecture I am to give you this afternoon, there was a temptation to turn it into the kind of talk that is usually given on the campus of an educational institution at this time of year. It is the end of the college year; the campus is beautiful, the air is warm; classes are dismissed and the younger generation sits at the feet of the visiting lecturer. Madness fills the mind of the visiting lecturer; perhaps it is better to call it a passion rather than madness, but the impulse behind it is not altogether sane; it is a mellow yet overpowering desire to give advice—to be rhetorical and to talk of world affairs. This is talk that often takes the form, so familiar to all of us, of the commencement address, the didactic poem in prose in which all of us are eagerly, fearfully, told of the mistakes that have been made and how the younger generation is to avoid them in the future. I shall warn you now that I have resisted this temptation; I shall not speak of "the wheels of progress," nor of how to keep them turning, nor shall I remind you that "life is a motion picture" that so closely resembles "the march of time." My subject is not concerned with didactic utterance, but with a dramatic element that enters poetry.

Perhaps what I have to say is slightly out of season with a particular time and place. I rather hope it is. Any discussion of the poetry that we care to read more than once is always both in and out of season; it is both in and behind and beyond the moment at which we read it. And my subject, dramatic art in poetry, though it may be as suitable to a winter's evening as it is to an afternoon in May, is not entirely inappropriate to a Hopwood lecture. Avery Hopwood was a playwright who had no pretensions of being a dramatist; but

281

he did write enormously successful plays. He held to one attribute of dramatic art: he avoided dullness; he chose the mystery melodrama as the object of his craftsmanship. Rarely enough—and this is rare among writers of all description—he founded an institution for the benefit of succeeding generations of younger writers, writers of plays, of poems, of fiction, of criticism, and all other forms of prose.

Nor is my subject entirely out of keeping with current revivals in poetic drama; fifty years ago the possibility of a contemporary poetic drama seemed remote; today it exists. Even the plays of W. B. Yeats (though he received a Nobel prize for the writing of them) are not the kind of failures they once seemed to be. But my subject is not a survey of poetic drama, its actual performances, its progress through the last fifty years, the details of its achievements, its hopes, its failures.

A good poem abhors dullness as much as nature abhors a vacuum or wit abhors a vacant mind. Even the "good bad" poems that George Orwell mentions in his essay on Rudyard Kipling avoid dullness memorably. The "good bad" poems of Kipling, which he called verse, have remained in the memory of at least two generations; how long they will endure I do not know. Behind the verses existed the presence of a vigorous intelligence and mind as well as a perception into the realities of material existence; these are qualities that are not to be lightly set aside. He had wit; surely his phrase, "It's pretty, but is it art?" is more than clever. In his lines on *The Gods of the Copybook Headings* he provided a title for Aldous Huxley's novel *Brave New World* with an irony that had more force than any of Huxley's writings. His verses had the melodramatic art of shocking his readers into attention. He compressed a violent and memorable short story (a story, by the way, that anticipated the economy of Ernest Hemingway's prose) in the four short stanzas of *Danny Deever,* and even now there is some probability that Hemingway will be remembered as an American Kipling.

Kipling's verses were an assault upon all the so-called finer feelings and sensibilities of his day. It was his conception of masculine heroism that made it possible for Winston Churchill during World War II to coin the phrase, "blood, toil, tears, and sweat." Kipling was an archconservative who appointed himself the first critic of conservative Britain. Rereading his verses today, one finds a deliberately antiartistic master of a craft, one who is excellently trained to recite his piece and then have done with it. (His family had Pre-Raphaelite associations; at an early age Kipling was unusually sophisticated in matters of artistic shoptalk.) His art, let us say, was artfully concealed; he had sudden, unforced revelations of literal, brutal reality as it existed in a power-driven world; he believed in power, he believed in the righteousness of the British Empire, and he could not resist the dramatic act of showing the sources of its power—in war and in the sacrifice of human life. His revelations were not unlike those who write of crime—the mystery-story novelist, the writer of "thrillers"— and a kind of romantic blood relationship exists between the author of Sherlock Holmes and Kipling. For his pains he did not receive the poet laureateship; his rewards were those of a generous income from his writings.

So much then for the element of melodrama as it has entered the "good bad" poetry that so few of us take pride in remembering at all and many have found difficult to forget. But what of dramatic art in poetry of another order? I assume that we know how deeply that art affected the poetry of the Elizabethans, even when the lines were not spoken from the stage; we know well how many Shakespearean sonnets suspend their resolutions, their judgments, their paradoxes, their conceits, until we reach the couplet which is the last of fourteen lines. The clearest possible remark that could be made of Shakespeare—and there have been many clouded, speculative commentaries on him and his writings—is that elements of his dramatic art are readily found within his lyrical verse. As a number of his sonnets near their end, we are waiting for the knife to fall, or rather the fall of the curtain of the fifth act. We also know that Shakespeare set the stage, as it were, for a great deal of the poetry that was to be written after him. I shall not labor this point concerning Shakespeare, for one can prove almost anything by his example, and on this occasion I have no intention to add another chapter to the formidable body of Shakespearean analysis which fills such a large corner in our university libraries. My intention is far more modest and is directed to a different end; I mention him only because the evidence he presents is obvious and because so many of us can remember lines of his sonnets that are examples of dramatic art.

I could go on to say that Donne's metaphysical wit has forceful dramatic elements in it; that an epic and moral poet such as Milton wrote *Samson Agonistes;* and that Pope, who was essentially a didactic poet, and who also possessed an extraordinarily delicate eye and ear, wrote his *Epistle to Dr. Arbuthnot*—that remarkable autobiography in verse—with considerable dramatic skill. But I shall not go into these particular examples that are relevant to my subject; I shall speak of a little less familiar ground—familiar, that is, to those who have made their lifework a study of English poetry.

I shall have to ask your indulgence for my particular interest in the subject, which I shall approach from two separate points of view. One is from the poetry of a philosophic poet who was unable to write a producible play. To gratify his dramatic intentions, he wrote an epic drama called *The Dynasts;* he did not deceive himself into thinking it could be produced in Shaftsbury Avenue or in the Haymarket or on Broadway. He wrote it to be read. The other approach shall be from a vantage point that is not far from the scene of the mystery story, and will show how its dramatic elements have left their traces in contemporary poetry.

II

I do not know how widely the poetry of Thomas Hardy is being read today. I suspect that it holds a position of prestige; he is rather more of a poet's poet than a critic's poet, and he is probably difficult for readers who do not share the depth of his historical perspective. In much of current criticism the use of an historical imagination has dropped out of fashion, but we need have no fear that it will return again, and as one fashion changes into another, we are often startled by the arrival of an unexpected guest, which is the past wearing a mask that we have failed to recognize.

On the surface, but on the surface only, Hardy is an unwieldly, ungainly poet; and it is true that one cannot substitute certain of his qualities for certain musical values that are characteristic of his great contemporary, W. B. Yeats. Yet he did possess a particular kind of mastery over a variety of lyrical forms. The reader is usually so intent upon what Hardy has to say that the ear does not respond to Hardy's lyrical virtuosity, and what he has to say often has the appearance of being cross-grained and grim. The consolations that he offers those who read him are not easily won. His is the kind of poetry that is best appreciated by readers who are past the age of twenty-five. In writing an apology for what he thought, or rather what he perceived, to be the nature of being, he quoted one of his own lines: "If way to the Better there be, it exacts a full look at the Worst"—a statement which gives Hardy complete relevance to the condition of being that we face today in the mid-twentieth century. He called his position one that demanded an "exploration of reality."

But for the purpose of this occasion and the nature of my subject, it is significant that his lyrics were essentially dramatic lyrics, that his *Satires of Circumstance* were for the most part dramatic monologues written by a philosophic poet. (And here I should say parenthetically that the primary distinction between the poet and the philosopher is one of means to an end. Not many philosophers have written excellent verse, for the speech of philosophic prose is not the same as that of poetry. Therein lies all the difference, a difference that has sometimes confused a few of the best critics.) In the writing of his *Satires of Circumstance* Hardy was concerned with the presentation of his beliefs in dramatic form, even to the extreme of melodrama. I am thinking of *The Newcomer's Wife,* the poem in which a naïve young man discovers that he has married a prostitute, and which closes with these lines:

> That night there was the splash of a fall
> Over the slimy harbour-wall:
> They searched, and at the deepest place
> Found him with crabs upon his face.

For some tastes this conclusion of the poem may be all too obvious. I happen to prefer other, and perhaps less well-known, examples of Hardy's dramatic art that does not seem to be a conscious dramatic art at all; and in the poem I am about to read, one finds an unexpectedly dramatic use of paradox:

> I look into my glass,
> And view my wasting skin,
> And say, "Would God it came to pass
> My heart had shrunk as thin!"
>
> For then, I, undistrest
> By hearts grown cold to me,

> Could lonely wait my endless rest
> With equanimity.
>
> But Time, to make me grieve,
> Part steals, lets part abide;
> And shakes this fragile frame at eve
> With throbbings of noontide.

And there is the poem *Heredity,* whose concealed art is of the same nature:

> I am the family face;
> Flesh perishes, I live on,
> Projecting trait and trace
> Through time to times anon,
> And leaping from place to place
> Over oblivion.
>
> The years-heired feature that can
> In curve and voice and eye
> Despise the human span
> Of durance—that is I;
> The eternal thing in man,
> That heeds no call to die.

Another short poem, *The Garden Seat,* which is lighter in movement than the others I have read, illustrates another aspect of Hardy's dramatic art:

> Its former green is blue and thin,
> And its once firm legs sink in and in;
> Soon it will break down unaware,
> Soon it will break down unaware.
>
> At night when reddest flowers are black
> Those who once sat thereon come back;
> Quite a row of them sitting there,
> Quite a row of them sitting there.
>
> With them the seat does not break down,
> Nor winter freeze them, nor floods drown,
> For they are as light as upper air,
> They are as light as upper air!

With *The Garden Seat* I come to what may seem a large gap between my two approaches to dramatic art in modern poetry. Yet I think the reach is not so far as it appears; the poem itself makes a step toward that genre in fiction that includes tales of mystery, the ghost story, stories of crimes and criminals, stories in which the action is metaphorical in meaning and transcends the more sensational devices of plot and incident. In some of these the mystery is never fully solved, nor is it intended to be. Strip Hamlet of his mysteries as Shakespeare has revealed them, delete the ghosts and witches of Macbeth's consciousness, and we have little left except two clients resting on an analyst's couch in an office not too far from the Lever Building on Park Avenue in the City of New York. Their transcendent being has been lost; more than that, their metaphorical relationship to human life is lost; they are in the process of being "cured"; their lives, which they will gladly, eagerly recite to us after the "cure" has taken place, are less revealing than they were before, and reflect all too vividly the footnotes in an analyst's casebook.

III

By this route I come to a particular element of dramatic art that has entered contemporary poetry by way of fiction. We speak of some poets as being poets' poets. But who are those who have become poets' novelists and writers of the short story? Herman Melville, Joseph Conrad, Henry James, Proust, Sir Arthur Conan Doyle, André Gide, St. Augustine (in his *Confessions*), Thomas Mann, and a singular Scotch lawyer, William Roughead, friend of James and Conrad, author of many books of essays concerning crime. Looking through the preceding list of authors, one might ask the question: Are poets willfully, capriciously, *morbidly* interested in crime? Not more than other people are; crime remains a staple, both up and down, on all levels of literature—and of dramatic poetry. To say that the fall of man is an engrossing subject is an understatement; it is a revelation of what the condition of being is.

But to return to those writers of fiction who are read by poets of the present mid-century; in each a metaphorical aspect of life is placed before the reader, an aspect that does not exclude the presence of evil. I need not enumerate all of their works; but the mysteries of good and of evil exist in *The Counterfeiters* as well as in *The Secret Sharer;* in *The Turn of the Screw* as well as in *Felix Kroll;* in *The Remembrance of Things Past* as well as in William Roughead's study of Deacon Brodie, who as he stood before the gallows said, "What is death, but a leap in the dark?" And Brodie was the living model of Robert Louis Stevenson's *Dr. Jekyll and Mr. Hyde.* There are few biographies that show more clearly and with greater dramatic stress the dual impulses toward good and evil than Roughead's recital of Brodie's career; a case record of schizophrenia is pale beside it. Roughead, like James and Conrad, was a moralist, and he intensified his Scotch Calvinism by the darkest strains of irony; he seldom preached; after his revelation he was content to rest his case. The best of moralists seldom descend to the writing of editorials; they are too deeply concerned with the action, the resemblance to human life itself.

Since poetry as we recognize it depends upon choice and economy in the use of words, it follows that dramatic action within a poem has the same laws; dramatic action is not extended to the length of a two- or three-hour play, but is compressed, and the action exerts its force through simile, paradox, wit, rhythm, rhyme—and all the resources of poetic art—but these are matters which have to do with the teaching of verse, the sometimes necessary shoptalk of the classrooms, rather than the essential and enduring elements of poetry. What I have just said does no more than indicate the way in which metaphor is transmuted from fiction into poetry.

The next question that arises is, Why is it that poets who have a highly evocative sense of dramatic art in poetry do not write successful plays? In our time only Eliot and Yeats have moderately succeeded, Yeats less so than Eliot, in translating their dramatic art in poetry from one art form into another. In both cases the effort was not one of days or weeks or months, but of a number of years. The answer is not as complex as it may seem: to sustain a metaphorical resemblance to life through the action of a play, to give it the character of the same reality that we demand in the reading of poetry, is a distinctly different art from that of poetry—as different as the writing of a novel. This fact need not prevent one from enjoying a good performance of Yeats's adaptation of Sophocles or *The Family Reunion* or *The Cocktail Party;* line for line they are better written than O'Neill's *Desire under the Elms,* yet O'Neill's play is better theater and does not fail in its analogy to life. If I have spoken of other mysteries, surely there is no mystery as to the reason why *Desire under the Elms* is a successful play.

IV

I still think it fair of you to ask me another question: Why is it that when I speak of a dramatic art in poetry I choose examples that ignore the joy of being, the sight of landscape and of the sky? These exist as surely as other aspects of reality; they complement the scenes that I have given you; they exist in many happy childhoods; they are also of the Garden of Eden—and for the most part I have insisted upon talking about the Serpent. It is because one has no clear view of the Garden without the Serpent—and so many of my well-intentioned countrymen have tried to drive him out of the world with questionable success. He is an extremely interesting and complex creature; in the Orient he is a dragon and is a source of goodness; in the West he is the sign of evil, closely associated with our Passion play, the fall of man, and after the fall, the resurrection. A little more than fifty years ago, we in America, or since we are a part of Europe, Western Europe, were fairly certain we had abolished the Serpent by the ingenuities of science; a few poets, who had no particular quarrel with science, were not so sure—and all of us are not so sure today.

Many poets today are willing to agree with Thomas Hardy that "pure literature" includes religion "in its essential and undogmatic sense, because poetry and religion touch each other . . . ."

Human action and the action of those forces that are both more and less than human are the essential dramatic elements in poetry; to perceive them at their extremes, the best and the worst, is to know in the original sense of the term, and untouched by latter-day associations of melodrama, the meaning of a "mystery" or "miracle" play.

As I come to the last paragraph of this lecture, I find that I have almost kept the promise which I made at its beginning. It is true that I have mentioned errors made by elder generations, errors that so far as I know extend back to the Garden of Eden. I shall not expect this generation or the next to correct them.

J. Donald Adams (born in New York City, September 1891) has been a newspaper writer for much of his life. Starting out on New Bedford, Providence, and Seattle (Washington) papers, he later became first a reporter then an editorial writer on several New York papers (1920–24). He was editor of the *New York Times Book Review* from 1925 to 1943 and since 1943 has been a contributing editor, conducting the weekly column "Speaking of Books." He is the author of *The Shape of Books to Come* (1944) and *Literary Frontiers* (1951), and is the editor of *The Treasure Chest: An Anthology of Contemplative Prose* (1946).

Louise Bogan (born in Livermore Falls, Maine, August 1897) is recognized as one of America's most distinguished woman poets. The honors she has received include the John Reed memorial prize of *Poetry: A Magazine of Verse* in 1930; the Helen Haire Levinson memorial prize of the same publication in 1937; Guggenheim Memorial Foundation fellowships in 1933 and 1937; Fellow in American Letters of the Library of Congress, 1944; and the Chair of Poetry of the Library of Congress, 1945–46. Miss Bogan has been the reviewer of poetry for the *New Yorker* since 1931, and has contributed poetry, fiction, and criticism to the *New Republic,* the *New Yorker,* the *Nation,* and *Poetry.* Her volumes of poetry include *Body of This Death* (1923), *Dark Summer* (1929), *The Sleeping Fury* (1937), and *Poems and New Poems* (1941).

Struthers Burt (born in Baltimore, October 1882), after a brief period as a reporter on the *Philadelphia Times* and as an instructor in English at Princeton, went west to Wyoming, where he has been ranching since 1908. He is the author of a number of works, both verse and prose; they include *Songs and Portraits* (1920), *The Interpreter's House* (1924), *The Other Side* (1928), *Festival* (1931), *Escape from America* (1936), *Along These Streets* (1942), and *Philadelphia: Holy Experiment* (1945).

Henry Seidel Canby (born in Wilmington, Delaware, September 1878) has been on the faculty of Yale University since 1900. In addition, he has held a number of editorial posts, such as that of assistant editor of the

Yale Review, from 1911 to 1920, and editor of the *Literary Review* (of the *New York Evening Post*), from 1920 to 1924. He was a founder of the *Saturday Review of Literature* in 1924 and served as editor from 1924 to 1936; he has been chairman of the board of editors since 1936. He has also, since 1926, been chairman of the board of judges of the Book-of-the-Month Club. Mr. Canby has written a novel, *Our House* (1919), short stories, and essays, but his chief contribution has been in biography (*Thoreau,* 1939; *Walt Whitman, an American,* 1943; *Turn West, Turn East: Mark Twain and Henry James,* 1951), and in literary criticism (*The Short Story in English,* 1909, and *Classic Americans,* 1931). He is a coeditor of several anthologies, including *A Literary History of the United States* (1948).

MARY M. COLUM, who was born in Ireland, is the wife of the Irish poet and critic, Padraic Colum. Both have lived in the United States since 1914. Mrs. Colum has been literary critic of *Forum and Century* magazine (1934–40) and has contributed to *Dial, Scribner's Magazine,* the *New Republic,* the *Saturday Review of Literature,* the *Yale Review,* and other literary publications. Her critical work has received wide recognition: in 1930 and again in 1938 she was awarded a Guggenheim fellowship in literary criticism; in 1934 Georgetown University conferred on her the John Ryder Randall gold medal for distinction in literature; and in 1941 she received a $500 prize for literary criticism from the American Institute of Arts and Letters. Mrs. Colum is the author of *From These Roots: The Ideas That Have Made Modern Literature* (1937) and *Life and the Dream* (1947).

NORMAN COUSINS (born in Union, New Jersey, June 1912) started out as an editorial writer for the *New York Post* (1934–35), became literary editor and managing editor of *Current History* (1935–40), and was executive editor of the *Saturday Review of Literature* (1940–42). He has been editor of the *Saturday Review* since 1942. Mr. Cousins is the author of *Modern Man Is Obsolete* (1945), among other books, and the editor of *Writing for Love or Money* (1949).

MAX EASTMAN (born in Canandaigua, New York, January 1883) is known as an editor, translator, and author. He edited the *Masses* from 1913 to 1917 and founded and edited the *Liberator* from 1918 to 1922. Translator of a number of Russian works, including several by Trotsky and one by Pushkin (*Gabriel,* 1929), Mr. Eastman is also the author of more than twenty volumes of biography, poetry, social and political analysis (particularly on Russia and communism), and literary criticism. Of the last, his best-known works are: *Enjoyment of Poetry* (1913; 23d enlarged edition, 1948), which is "a study of the psychology of literature" and is used as a textbook in many colleges; *The Literary Mind, Its Place in an Age of Science* (1931); and *Enjoyment of Laughter* (1936), "a study of the psychology of humor." His *Enjoyment of Living* was published in 1948.

WALTER PRICHARD EATON (born in Malden, Massachusetts, August 1878) has been a dramatic critic, teacher, author, and lecturer. Starting as assistant drama critic of the *New York Tribune* (1902–7) he became drama critic of the New York *Sun* (1907–8), drama critic of the *American Magazine* (1909–18), and finally professor of playwriting at Yale (1933–47). He is the author of many volumes of nature essays, juvenile fiction, poetry, short stories, and criticism. Among his works on the theatre are *The Actor's Heritage* (1924), *The Theatre Guild, the First Ten Years* (1929), and *The Drama in English* (1930). He also served as editor of the *Yale One-Act Plays* from 1930 to 1937.

ZONA GALE (born in Portage, Wisconsin, August 1874; died December 1938) worked on newspapers in Milwaukee and New York for several years before she devoted herself entirely to creative writing. The author of many novels, short stories, plays, and essays, Miss Gale is perhaps best known for her novels *Birth* (1918) and *Miss Lulu Bett* (1920). Her dramatization of *Miss Lulu Bett* won the Pulitzer prize in 1920.

HORACE GREGORY (born in Milwaukee, Wisconsin, April 1898), poet and critic, has been a lecturer at Sarah Lawrence College since 1934. He has received a number of awards, including the Lyric prize in 1928 and the Helen Haire Levinson prize in 1934, both from *Poetry: A Magazine of Verse,* the Russell Loines award for poetry from the American Institute of Arts and Letters, May 1942, and a Guggenheim fellowship in 1951. He is the translator of *The Poems of Catullus* (1931) and the author of several volumes of poetry, among them *Chelsea Rooming House* (1930), *No Retreat* (1933), *Poems, 1930–40* (1941), and *Selected Poems* (1951). His literary criticism includes *Pilgrim of the Apocalypse: A Critical Study of D. H. Lawrence* (1933), *The Shield of Achilles: Essays on Beliefs in Poetry* (1944), and *A History of American Poetry, 1900–1940* (in collaboration with Marya Zaturenska, 1946).

HARLAN HATCHER (born in Ironton, Ohio, September 1898), author and critic, has for some time had an administrative career in education quite aside from his writing. He taught English at The Ohio State University from 1922 to 1944, was dean of the College of Arts and Sciences from 1944 to 1948, and served as vice-president of the University from 1948 to 1951. Since 1951 he has been president of the University of Michigan. Mr. Hatcher is the author of several novels, of various histories and descriptions of Ohio and the Midwest, and of a number of works of literary criticism. Among his critical writings are *The Versification of Robert Browning* (1928) and *Creating the Modern American Novel* (1935); he is the editor of *Modern Continental, British, and American Dramas* (3 vols., 1941) and of *Modern Dramas, Shorter Edition* (1944).

HENRY HAZLITT (born in Philadelphia, November 1894), starting as a financial writer and editor on the *Wall Street Journal* and other New York papers during the years 1913–23, became, in succession, editorial writer for the *New York Herald* and the *Sun* (1923–25), literary editor on the *Sun* (1925–29), literary editor of the *Nation* (1930–33), editor of the *American Mercury* (1933–34), and a member of the editorial staff of the *New York Times* (1934–46). He has been an associate on *Newsweek* magazine since 1946. Mr. Hazlitt is the author of several studies on economics and politics, as well as of *Thinking as a Science* (1916) and *The Anatomy of Criticism* (1933). Among his recent works is a piece of fiction, *The Great Idea,* which appeared in 1951.

ROBERT MORSS LOVETT (born in Boston, December 1870) taught English at the University of Chicago from 1896 to 1936 and served on the editorial board of the *New Republic* from 1921 to 1940. He is well known for his critical studies, which include *A History of English Literature* (with W. V. Moody, 1902), *Edith Wharton* (1925), *Preface to Fiction* (1931), and *The History of the Novel in England* (with Helen S. Hughes, 1932). He has also written two novels, *Richard Gresham* (1904) and *A Winged Victory* (1907), as well as a play, *Cowards* (1914). His autobiography, *All Our Years,* appeared in 1948.

F. O. MATTHIESSEN (born in Pasadena, California, February 1902; died April 1950) taught English at Harvard from 1929 until his death, was a member of the executive committee of the Massachusetts Civil Liberties Union, and was prominent in other political and professional groups. He was the author of a number of outstanding works of literary criticism, including *The Achievement of T. S. Eliot* (1935; new and enlarged edition, 1947), *American Renaissance: Art and Expression in the Age of Emerson and Whitman* (1941), *Henry James, the Major Phase* (1944), *The James Family* (1947), and a posthumously published collection of essays and reviews, *The Responsibilities of the Critic* (1952). Mr. Matthiessen also edited an anthology of poems by Herman Melville and two collections of stories by Henry James. He was coeditor of *The Notebooks of Henry James* (1947).

CHRISTOPHER MORLEY (born in Haverford, Pennsylvania, May 1890), a prolific creative writer and critic, served for many years on the editorial staffs of various publications. His last such connection was with the *Saturday Review of Literature* (1924–40). He is the author of more than fifty works, including novels, poetry, short stories, plays, and essays. Among the best known are *Parnassus on Wheels* (1917), *The Haunted Book Shop* (1919), *Thunder on the Left* (1925), *The Trojan Horse* (1937), and *Kitty Foyle* (1939). *Letters of Askance* (1939) is a collection of essays. Recent works include *The Man Who Made Friends with Himself* (1949) and *The Ballad of New York, New York, and Other Poems, 1930–1950* (1950).

JOHN CROWE RANSOM (born in Pulaski, Tennessee, April 1888) taught English at Vanderbilt University from 1914 to 1937 and has been at Kenyon College since 1937. He was an editor and publisher of *Fugitive: A Journal of Poetry,* in Nashville, from 1922 to 1925 (this was the magazine that brought together and published the famous "Fugitive Group" of poets), and is now editor of the *Kenyon Review.* A distinguished poet, Mr. Ransom won the Bollingen award in poetry (Yale University Library) and the Russell Loines award in literature (National Academy of Arts and Letters), both in 1951. His volumes include *Poems about God* (1919), *Chills and Fever* (1924), *Grace after Meat* (1924), *Two Gentlemen in Bonds* (1927), and *Selected Poems* (1945). More recently, Mr. Ransom has edited *The Kenyon Critics* (1951).

CARL VAN DOREN (born in Hope, Illinois, September 1885; died July 1950) taught English at Columbia University from 1911 to 1930. He was literary editor of the *Nation* (1919–22) and of *Century* magazine (1922–25), editor of the Literary Guild (1926–34), chairman of the Readers Club (1941–44), and editor of the Living Library (from 1946 until his death). He also edited several anthologies, and was the managing editor of the *Cambridge History of American Literature* (1917–21). Mr. Van Doren wrote in various genres, including biography (his *Benjamin Franklin,* 1938, won the Pulitzer prize), autobiography (*Three Worlds,* 1936), and short stories (*Other Provinces,* 1925). His many works of literary criticism include *The American Novel* (1921; revised edition, 1940), *American and British Literature since 1890* (1925; revised edition, 1939), and *American Literature, an Introduction* (1933; reissued as *What Is American Literature?,* 1935).

MARK VAN DOREN (born in Hope, Illinois, June 1894), poet, writer, and critic, has taught English at Columbia University since 1920. He has written many volumes of poetry, including *Collected Poems, 1922–1938* (1939), which won the Pulitzer prize in 1940, *The Seven Sleepers and Other Poems* (1944), and *New Poems* (1948). Among his collections of short stories are *The Witch of Ramoth and Other Tales* (1950) and *Short Stories* (1950). His essays in literary criticism include *Henry David Thoreau, a Critical Study* (1916), *The Poetry of John Dryden* (1920, 1931, 1946), *Studies in Metaphysical Poetry* (with Theodore Spencer, 1939), *Shakespeare* (1939), *Nathaniel Hawthorne* (1949), and *Introduction to Poetry* (1951). Mr. Van Doren has also edited many anthologies, among them *The Oxford Book of American Prose* (1932), *The Portable Walt Whitman* (1945), and *The Best of Hawthorne* (1951).

ROBERT PENN WARREN (born in Guthrie, Kentucky, April 1905), poet and novelist, has been teaching English since 1930. He is now at the University of Minnesota. One of the original Vanderbilt University "Fugitive Group" of poets, Mr. Warren has received many awards, among them Guggenheim fellowships in writing (1939–40 and 1947–48), the Shelley prize for poetry (1942), the Chair of Poetry of the Library of Congress (1944–45), and a Pulitzer prize (1947) for his novel *All the King's Men* (1946). His works also include *Night Rider* (1939), *Selected Poems, 1923–1943* (1944), and *World Enough and Time* (1950). Mr. Warren was a founder, and editor (from 1935 to 1942), of the *Southern Review*. More recently, he has been coauthor (with Cleanth Brooks) of *Modern Rhetoric* (1949).

EDWARD WEEKS (born in Elizabeth, New Jersey, February 1898) has been connected with the *Atlantic Monthly* through most of his life, for he started out there as an associate editor in 1924 and has served as editor since 1938. He was also editor of the Atlantic Monthly Press from 1928 to 1937, and still exercises a supervisory hand. Mr. Weeks has written many essays, articles, and book reviews; he is the author of *This Trade of Writing* (1935).

INDEX OF AUTHORS

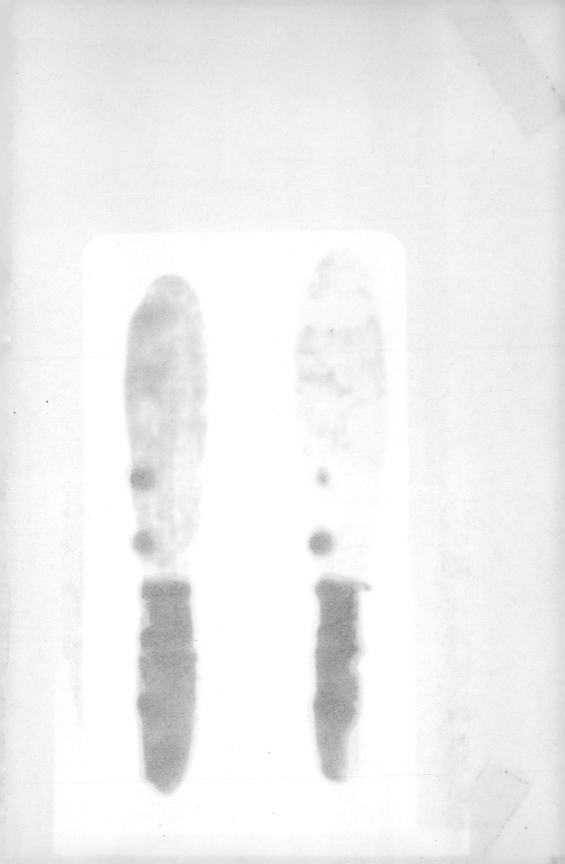

DATE DUE	

GAYLORD   PRINTED IN U.S.A.